A TIME TO SPEAK

To Ann
love from
Rob xx
16.9.98

D1322896

Also by Eric James:

Judge Not: A Selection of Sermons Preached in Gray's Inn Chapel, 1978–1988
Word Over All: Forty Sermons 1985–1991 (SPCK 1992)
The Voice Said, Cry: Forty Sermons 1990–1993 (SPCK 1994)

A TIME TO SPEAK

Forty Sermons

ERIC JAMES

First published 1997
SPCK
Holy Trinity Church
Marylebone Road
LONDON
NW1 4DU

Copyright © Eric James 1997

British Library Cataloguing in Publication Data

A catalogue record for this book is available from the British Library

ISBN 0-281-05042-2

Typeset by The Midlands Book Typesetting Company, Loughborough
Printed in Great Britain by The Cromwell Press, Melksham, Wiltshire

To
the Masters of the Bench
and other Members of Gray's Inn
whom I have been privileged to serve
as Preacher
1978 – 1997

CONTENTS

PREFACE

This is the fourth of my books of sermons; but I should warn the reader that I have a 'bin' containing several hundred more that are as yet not published!

It seemed to me appropriate to call this collection *A Time to Speak*, because, clearly, that's what a sermon is. But it's not a time to say just *anything*, as the sermon with that title I preached in Winchester Cathedral last September makes clear, and the sermon 'The Preacher of the Year Award'. There's 'a time to keep silence' too. Sometimes, if you keep silence, the stones will cry out – and sometimes they will if you speak!

Some parts of one sermon may sometimes be duplicated in another. It may be *A Time to Speak* what one has to say to more than one congregation.

Now that I am past my threescore years and ten, and in my forty-fifth year of ordained ministry, I should record my thankfulness for my vocation as a preacher – and in particular, for my years from January 1978, as Preacher to Gray's Inn; for, to use the text I used in Gray's Inn only last November, 'What hast thou which thou hast not received?'

I should like to acknowledge the help the staff of the SPCK have been to me in preparation of this volume, and thank Ms Jane Spurr and Mr Ronald Keating, successively secretaries of Christian Action.

Eric James

ACKNOWLEDGEMENTS

The author and publishers would like to thank the following for permission to reproduce the material listed in which they own the copyright.

Faber and Faber Ltd: excerpts from 'Choruses from The Rock' and 'Journey of the Magi' published in *Collected Poems 1909–1962* by T. S. Eliot; excerpt from 'For the Time Being' published in *Collected Poems* by W. H. Auden.

David Higham Associates Ltd: excerpts from Charles Williams, *The Descent of the Dove* (Longmans 1939); *He Came Down from Heaven* (Heinemann 1938); *The Passion of Christ* (Oxford University Press 1939); 'Apologue on the Parable of the Wedding Garment' in *Time and Tide* (Faber and Faber 1940).

John Murray (Publishers) Ltd: excerpt from 'Christmas' in *Collected Poems* by John Betjeman.

Penguin Books Ltd: excerpt from *Collected Poems and Selected Prose* by A. E. Housman, ed. C. Hicks.

The Peters, Fraser & Dunlop Group: excerpt from *Margin Released* by J. B. Priestley (Heinemann 1962).

In addition acknowledgements of sources are given as follows:

Chapter 1: John Donne, *Complete Poetry and Selected Prose*, ed. John Hayward (The Nonesuch Press 1946).
Chapter 5: John Knox, *Chapters in a Life of Paul* (SCM 1989).
Chapter 6: Hansard, June 1963.
Chapter 7: Harold C. Goddard, *The Meaning of Shakespeare* (University of Chicago Press 1951).
Chapter 8: P. Teilhard de Chardin, *Le Milieu Divin* (Collins 1960).
Chapter 12: *The Letters of A. E. Housman*, ed. Henry Maas (1971).
Chapter 14: Eberhard Bethge, *Dietrich Bonhoeffer* (Collins 1970). Dietrich Bonhoeffer, *Ethics* (SCM 1955); *Letters and Papers from Prison* (SCM 1970); *The Cost of Discipleship* (SCM 1959).
Chapter 15: P. Teilhard de Chardin, 'Le Pretre' (unpublished) and 'The

Mass on the World', published as part of *Hymm of the Universe* (Collins 1961).

Robert Speaight, *Teilhard de Chardin: A Biography* (Collins 1967).

Chapter 16: Edith Sitwell, 'Eurydice' in *Collected Poems* (Macmillan 1957).

Chapter 17: William Temple, *Inaugural Clarke Hall Lecture 'The Ethics of Penal Action'* 19 March 1934 (Norman House Publications, reprinted 1967).

Chapter 19: Sebastian Faulks, *Birdsong* (Vintage 1994).

Chapter 20: Grace Davie, *Religion in Britain Since 1945: Believing without Belonging* (Blackwell 1994).

Chapter 22: Nelson Mandela, *Long Walk to Freedom* (Little Brown 1994).

Chapter 25: Alan Bennett, *Writing Home* (Faber and Faber 1994).

Chapter 26: *The Letters and Friendship of Sir Cecil Spring-Rice: A Record*, ed. Stephen Gwynn (Constable 1925).

Chapter 30: Bulletin of the Runnymede Trust, Spring 1995.

Chapter 33: R. C. D. Jasper, *George Bell, Bishop of Chichester* (Oxford 1967).

Chapter 34: Dr Harry Guntrip, 'Psychology and Spirituality' in *Spirituality for Today*, ed. Eric James (SCM 1968).

The text of the Authorized Version of the Bible is the property of the Crown in perpetuity.

Extracts from *The New English Bible* are copyright 1961, 1970 Oxford and Cambridge University Presses.

Extracts from The Book of Common Prayer of 1662, the rights of which are vested in the Crown in perpetuity within the United Kingdom, are reproduced by permission of Cambridge University Press, Her Majesty's Printers.

Every effort has been made to trace the copyright holders of material quoted in this book. Information on any omissions should be sent to the publishers who will make full acknowledgement in any future editions.

1

THE WAY OF TRUTH

Beginning-of-term Service, King's College, London;
6 October 1993

'I have chosen the way of truth . . .'
Psalm 119. 30

I wonder whether, when you first entered the gateway of the College –
or when you returned to the College for another academic year – I
wonder whether those seven words were anywhere near the front of
your mind: 'I have chosen the way of truth'. I'd be surprised if they
were. Certainly when *I* first entered these portals, in 1946, my heart and
my mind were some way from such a sentiment.

I actually came here first to night school. Before I could start a degree
course – after seven war-time years out at work at a riverside wharf on
the Thames, from fourteen years of age to twenty-one – I had to
matriculate by evening classes here, in Latin, Maths, Geography, Roman
History, English, New Testament Greek, and one or two other subjects;
then, in 1947, I was allowed to begin my BD. I was by then twenty-two;
and I thought of that degree course rather as another series of subjects.
Now I had to attend lectures in Hebrew, Dogmatic Theology, Pastoral
Theology, Comparative Religion, New Testament, Old Testament,
Psychology, and so on. It's only looking back that I can see I had 'chosen
the way of truth'.

I don't mean that arrogantly. I've never thought that the Church of
England – or, indeed, any other Christian denomination – had the
monopoly on truth. I didn't think that theology was the only way of truth,
but I think I did choose to read theology because I knew that truth mat-
tered: truth not least in the sense of a meaning and a purpose to existence.

In the forty-seven years since I began here, I have had a rather
fortunate existence. Four years after ordination I went up to Cambridge
to be chaplain of Trinity College, and there, at dinner of an evening, I
would have to sit next to people like G. M. Trevelyan, the historian, and
Otto Frisch, who had worked on the atomic bomb at Los Alamos, and
Lord Adrian, the physiologist, who had worked on the electrical impulses
of the brain. Our director of music in the chapel was Raymond Lepp-
ard, who was already becoming a considerable conductor, and my boss,

1

Harry Williams, as Dean of Chapel, made it an exciting time because he had decided that alongside teaching academic theology he would try to ask himself how far and in what way a doctrine of the Creed or a saying of Christ had become part of himself; he had resolved that he would not preach about any aspect of Christian belief unless it had become 'part of my own-life-blood' – to quote his own phrase. From such people I learnt unforgettably that truth is a many-sided and many-splendoured thing, and that a university is not primarily a place for training for a career – in medicine, or law, or engineering, or theology, or whatever: primarily it's a place concerned with truth with a capital T.

I had, of course, begun to learn that here at King's – and I learnt it not least here in chapel. I don't necessarily mean in sermons, though they were often memorable. I remember, for instance, a sermon from the New Testament Professor R. V. G. Tasker, at a beginning-of-term service like this, on the *Narrow Way* of Truth. 'Enter by the narrow gate' was his text, 'for the gate is narrow and the way is hard that leads to life'.

It so happened that my seat here in chapel was usually against the south wall. I used purposely to sit near a memorial, which is still there. Just listen to what it says:

> In affectionate memory of Samuel Rabbeth MD
> Born August 19th 1858: Died October 20th 1884
> He entered the medical department of King's College in
>   October 1877.
> In 1882 he was appointed senior resident officer at the
>   Royal Free Hospital.
>   Where on October 10th 1884
> he contracted diphtheria by sucking a tracheotomy tube
> in the hope of saving the life of a child.
> The self-sacrifice of his death answered to the
>   unselfishness of his life.

I remember wondering about Samuel Rabbeth – probably, I thought, a Jew – twenty-four years old. What way of truth was he on, I wondered, that made him suck that tracheotomy tube, hoping to save the life of the child, but risking – and, indeed, sacrificing – his own life?

In chapel in summer, if the windows were open, I would sometimes forsake my seat by the wall for one where I could see out of the window; for in those days the *Discovery* was moored alongside the Embankment, and I could see its crow's nest through the open window. I knew that Edward Wilson, the physician, naturalist and explorer, who went with Scott to the Antarctic, used to climb up to that crow's nest to say his prayers; and it helped me in mine to remember that man who had lost his life, with Scott, on their ill-fated journey from the South Pole. From my days here I learnt that the way of truth was bound to be, to some extent, a way of exploration.

Some of you may know that forty years after I was here I was privileged to be the biographer of Bishop John Robinson – author of the 1963 best-seller *Honest to God*. I'd got to know John Robinson at Cambridge, and I went from Cambridge to a parish in Camberwell, south London, when he went to be Bishop of Woolwich. So I was close to him, and read *Honest to God* in manuscript – as I did his even better book, with the significant title *Exploration into God*. Both those books, though they emanated from the now despised Sixties – were written by someone very concerned with the way of Truth.

I think here I learnt most about the way of Truth from Eric Abbott, the then Dean of the College, who was later Dean of Westminster. He became a very close friend, and one day while I was here he said to me, 'Boy,' – yes, it was nearly fifty years ago, but he called people 'boy' long after their boyhood was past – 'Boy,' he said, 'you're a romantic, and you won't survive unless you have a very high doctrine of corruption – corruption', he said, 'in Church as well as State.' 'But', he added, 'your doctrine of glory must always be higher than your doctrine of corruption.' I did not doubt Eric Abbott had given me there important guidance for the way of Truth, but I have to say that at the time I had no idea what he was talking about. It was thirty-six years later, when I came up against the full force of corruption – in the Church – that suddenly I realized the meaning of what Eric Abbott had said: 'You've got to *anticipate* corruption – expect it: learn to cope with it. You'll meet it often on the way of Truth.'

And I realized that you probably have to wait for certain things to happen before you can understand certain facets of the way of Truth. It doesn't all happen at the beginning of the way. University years are not the whole of the way of Truth for most people: neither is book learning the whole story.

Although the corruption of the Church – which, of course, is not entirely unrelated to one's own corruption – has made me sometimes despair of the Church – and, indeed, sometimes despair – I have never really regretted that I am an ordained priest, because that calling has never allowed me to forget for one day that I have 'chosen the way of Truth', and am called to be an interpreter of the truth: a 'steward of the mysteries' of God's Truth. So the life, triumphant suffering, death and resurrection of Jesus Christ have been for me at the centre of that way of Truth. Does not the Gospel of St John record Christ saying of himself: 'I am the Way, the Truth and the Life'?

When I was a chaplain in Cambridge, I received a salutary warning. An eccentric don, a historian who was ordained – F. A. Simpson – asked me one morning 'Eric, what are you going to preach about at the beginning of term?' Without waiting for a reply he said: 'For God's sake don't just talk "tripe about truth".' He meant that there's a way of talking about truth which is too easy, too glib, too smooth, too lacking in challenge and demand.

At the moment I am privileged to be writing the biography of a great contemporary Christian, Bishop Trevor Huddleston. That has meant looking carefully at, for instance, the history of apartheid in South Africa. I was quite surprised recently to find that on 27 July 1909, Randall Davidson, later Archbishop of Canterbury, spoke in the House of Lords, as Bishop of Rochester, in favour of imposing restrictions and limitations on the rights of the black people of South Africa, because, he said, 'they correspond with those which we impose on our children, and the overwhelming majority of the South African population would for generations to come be quite unfit to share equal citizenship with whites'.

In the last week or so, I have been trying to get at the truth of the relations between Geoffrey Clayton, Archbishop of Cape Town, and Trevor Huddleston. They were both undoubtedly good men, but in South Africa in the Fifties they were virtually incompatible. And you learn that good men and women will sometimes come almost to blows along the 'way of Truth'. Hegel pointed out that the greatest crises in history are not those of right versus wrong but of right versus right. If Christ is indeed the Truth, then the conflict of truth with truth will often be fought out within his Body.

When I was here at King's, I only wrote one prize essay. It was on the poetry of John Donne. I knew well that before Donne became Dean of St Paul's he was Reader in Divinity to the Benchers of Lincoln's Inn. Little did I know that *I* would become in time Preacher to *Gray's* Inn – which I have been now for sixteen years. That has only served to increase my admiration for Donne.

In the third of his Satyres, Donne writes:

> On a huge hill,
> Cragged, and steep, Truth stands, and hee that will
> Reach her, about must, and about must goe.

I believe that your time at King's will be of most value to you if you see Truth standing 'on a huge hill, cragged and steep', and if you resolve and consecrate yourself to going about and about that hill, whatever subject you may have chosen to read. I invite you to say to yourself today, however young or old you may be and at whatever stage of your academic career: 'I have chosen the way of Truth.'

2

CHRIST IN GLORY

Coventry Cathedral; 17 October 1993

I wonder whether there is anywhere in the world where that Gospel for today is so powerfully illustrated – as it is read – as it is in this place: 'Father, glorify your Son that the Son may glorify you. For you have made him sovereign of all mankind.' As he said those words, John says, Jesus looked up to heaven. Here we look up to Sutherland's 70-foot figure of the Christ in Glory: 'sovereign of all mankind'. And I wonder what it means to you – to those who worship here regularly week by week, even day by day: and to those who come here this morning, maybe from afar, as relative strangers, as I myself do.

Before I press that question upon you, I want to share with you a bundle of memories. I can never come to Coventry without thankfully remembering Cuthbert Bardsley, who of course, as bishop, presided over the consecration of this cathedral, and whose ashes now lie buried behind the High Altar.

I first met Cuthbert almost fifty years ago when I was nineteen. It was 1944. I was working then on a riverside wharf on the Thames. But I was sitting on the organ stool of Southwark Cathedral, where I learnt the organ during my lunch hours, when Cuthbert came up the stairs, into the organ loft, and introduced himself. He had just been appointed Provost. I remember him saying: 'I have been praying for people who will help me to wake up this cathedral. I believe God may have sent *me* to *you* and *you* to *me*. Will you join me in prayer this evening in the Harvard Chapel?' At first I tried to dodge the invitation, but that was impossible with Cuthbert. He would not let one escape. And soon I found myself caught up in Cuthbert's vision for the cathedral and for the Church in the surrounding world.

'Glorify thy name' was a prayer that Cuthbert often uttered and gradually enabled people like me to utter. And it was not long before I began training for ordination – via evening classes at King's College, London. Cuthbert was my confessor and spiritual director for several years, and one of the greatest influences in my life.

The second memory I want to share with you is of eighteen years later. It was 25 May 1962. I had been ordained for ten years. I was vicar of St George's, Camberwell, in south London. My bishop, Mervyn

Stockwood, had invited me to travel with him in his car to the consecration of this cathedral. There wasn't room inside the cathedral for everyone, but the Bishop of Southwark, who was to be with the other bishops *inside* the cathedral, gave me a ticket which enabled me to watch the service of consecration on closed-circuit experimental colour television, set up in the bar of the Leofric Hotel. And I beheld the glory of the consecration of this place from that bar in the Leofric. I joined in the prayers. I first saw on colour television the Christ in Glory. Thirty-one years ago I prayed with that great congregation, at that moment of hope and joy – not only for Coventry, but for the whole Church of England: 'Glorify thy name' we prayed; glorify thy name in this place.

I had several friends here on the cathedral staff, and after a few weeks I returned here. My friend Simon Phipps – we had both been chaplains together at Trinity College, Cambridge – asked me to stay with him in his flat in Willenhall, and promised he would take me round the cathedral.

Simon – later Bishop of Lincoln – many of you will know was a cathedral canon and a Chaplain to Industry here, and we came here to Holy Communion, in the Chapel of Christ the Servant, early in the morning. I remember during the Communion seeing the whole panorama of industrial Coventry, as it then was, through the clear glass windows of that Chapel. 'Glorify thy name', one prayed almost involuntarily: 'Glorify thy name' *inside* this cathedral and *outside* it.

Over breakfast, I met with another friend, Canon Stephen Verney. Like Simon Phipps, Stephen has since been a bishop. The Christ in Glory gave *him* a vision for the parishes and people of this Diocese of Coventry, and a vision for the people and cities beyond Coventry.

After breakfast, Simon Phipps gave me a conducted tour of the cathedral. I have two main memories of that morning: first, the golden mosaic in the Chapel of Christ in Gethsemane glowing beyond the grill-like crown of thorns. It seemed to me a sermon, wrought in iron and mosaic, on 'Glorify thy Son'. But quite unforgettable was the Piper Baptistry window above the rough-hewn boulder from Bethlehem: there was glory in that glass of many colours: inviting each person baptized, and each godparent and parent, to glorify God in their body and soul.

My third memory is several years after that. It was in 1974 that Cuthbert Bardsley asked me to preach, on Shakespeare's birthday, at Stratford-upon-Avon. Each year, some of you will know, it is a great festival. I preached on the 'Royalty of Human Nature' in the mind and heart of Shakespeare. *King John* was the play for the Festival that year. He says: ''Tis not vestures which shall make men royal.'

'But what *does* make men "royal"?' I found myself asking both myself and the congregation. And what made *Christ* royal: 'Sovereign of all mankind'? As we look at Christ in Glory here and now, we can ask,

'What is it that makes me royal?' That Festival was, alas, the last time I spent a good deal of time with Cuthbert Bardsley. He presided over the Festival and was what I can only call a 'heavenly host'. Stratford-upon-Avon was to him a most important part of his diocese.

The last memory I want to share with you this morning is only a few months old. This June I returned to Stratford. Two good friends took me to see my favourite Shakespearean play, *King Lear*. It was the best performance I had ever seen, with Robert Stephens as Lear. I waited to hear my favourite lines; for instance, Lear invites all those who are with him to 'take upon's the mystery of things as if we were God's spies'. But *this* year there was a surprise in store for me. I thought I knew *Lear* backwards, but one phrase in it, of only four words, I had never noticed before. One of the characters suddenly says, 'Thy life's a miracle.' Only Shakespeare can be as profound, and as simple, as that. Since June, that phrase has been with me every day.

It is possible to look at Christ in the Gospels and, after each incident, to say 'Thy life's a miracle.' It's possible here and now to look at Sutherland's Christ in Glory and say 'Thy life's a miracle.' But to say that would be to say only part of what we need to say. Jesus prayed, 'Father, glorify thy Son', and then his life became a miracle. But we need to see that as the truth about *our* life: day by day. We need to say of each baby baptized under that glorious window: 'Thy life's a miracle.' Yes, but we need to say it, too, of every homeless person and of every outcast person of our society: of every lone parent, of every so-called 'foreigner' – to use Cabinet Minister Peter Lilley's sad – indeed, sick – word of a few days ago – and of every person on probation or in prison. You cannot be racist and say of another person: 'Thy life's a miracle.'

'Father, glorify your Son' – in this person and that – we need to say, and let the vision of Christ in Glory thereby transform our social and political life, our day-to-day world, our one, but so sorely divided, world: of which Christ, to the eye of faith is, nevertheless, sovereign.

I have of set purpose brought to the Gospel this morning a bundle of memories. Memories sometimes only make us look back. Certainly I have reason, because of my memories, to look back here in thankfulness. But those first words of the Gospel, 'Glorify your Son', make me, make us, look forward in faith, and look up. They provide us with a prayer for, for instance, each day of the coming week, for the people who come on our television screens, and the people with whom we live and work. 'Father, glorify your Son in us.'

3

HOUSING AND HOMELESSNESS

Service for the Day of Prayer on Housing and Homelessness,
Westminster Abbey; 7 November 1993

I can remember, as if it were yesterday, the day when housing, as a subject, came alive for me. It was over thirty years ago: the beginning of 1960; and I had just become an inner-city vicar – of St George's, Camberwell, the Trinity College Mission south of the Thames.

A woman called at my vicarage, and asked for her baby to be baptized. She gave as her address 'Newington Lodge', which was a huge hostel for the homeless on the borders of our parish. When I asked her who would be the godparents of her child, I remember she was nonplussed. 'I haven't got any friends,' she said. 'Well,' said I, swallowing hard at the remark, 'you and your husband can be godparents.' 'My husband's left me,' she replied. The likelihood of the child receiving a Christian upbringing was small. But I remembered the words of the Victorian theologian, F. D. Maurice, who was chaplain to Guy's Hospital and Professor at King's College London: 'Baptism is the proclamation by God that this child is a child of mine.' However, I knew that if I proclaimed that fact about this particular child all sorts of other things had to follow: not least, a party – which our congregation in fact provided, as they tried to say that that homeless, fatherless child was as valuable to God as any child in the world, and that 'of such is the kingdom of heaven'. But I knew that a verbal proclamation – and a party – was not enough; I had to do something about that child's housing.

I was thirty-five then, and a complete ignoramus where housing was concerned. But it wasn't only that *baptism* which forced me to do something about housing. Any couple in the parish I *married* were at that time unlikely to be able to get a home of their own. They invariably went to live with one or other of their in-laws in overcrowded accommodation. If I took the subject of marriage seriously, I had to do something about housing conditions that would threaten the survival of most marriages. But what *could* I do? What could I do *alone*? I could raise my *voice*, but it wouldn't carry very far.

I had just spent four years as the chaplain of a Cambridge College. I decided to ask four of my recent undergraduates to form a housing study group to study every aspect of the local problem – facts, figures, finance and the law – and then report. They reported very soon. There were, in 1960, 20,000 people, 4,653 families, on the Camberwell Housing List alone, and a national shortage of three-quarters of a million to a million houses.

That little study group I found very supportive. It was quite different from working at such a huge subject on one's own. We began to write letters and articles to the newspapers, national and local. To my surprise, on 14 November 1960, I had a letter from Henry Brooke, the then Housing Minister, ending: 'If you would appreciate a talk about it all, I wonder whether you would ring up my Private Secretary.' Housing Ministers tend not to stay very long at their task, and soon I was hearing from a new Housing Minister, Keith Joseph. He said something to our study group which I shall never forget: 'Please attack me as much as you can in public,' he said, 'it's the only way I shall get power in the Cabinet.'

So I learnt early on in my apprenticeship that housing is not simply about housing. It's about power and powerlessness. And then, of course, I learnt that housing involves another aspect of power – money: rents economic and rents exorbitant and rent rebates; money to build houses; government money and the money of banks and building societies. But I kept on my mantelpiece the name of that woman in Newington Lodge, the hostel for the homeless, and the name of her child: neither of whom had a penny to bless themselves. They were penniless and powerless.

Keith Joseph, to give him his due, helped us greatly to work out what the churches might do, and by 1962 I found myself chairing something called the Housing Sub-Committee of the London Churches Group of the London Council of Social Service, and on my wall I put a card with a quotation from William Blake:

> He who would do good to another must do it in
>   Minute particulars.
> General Good is the plea of the scoundrel,
>   hypocrite and flatterer . . .

If ever a poet spoke profound theology, Blake did.

Keith Joseph encouraged the churches, with their pastoral concern, to get involved in setting up housing societies, particularly for the elderly, whose vacated housing might release accommodation for the homeless. He also wanted the churches to run housing societies that would specially care for the homeless who might have other special needs: aged immigrants, for instance; and that year he made available £25 million for loans in connection with such schemes. Creating such societies taught people of local churches not least the minute particulars of housing such families as the little family in Newington Lodge I've already mentioned: the details of housing them, but also the pain and frustration of not succeeding in housing them.

The years went by; much high rise housing was built and, after some years, was of course derided. T. S. Eliot had asked sixty years ago: 'What life have you if you have not life together? There is no life that is not in community.' But in the Sixties and Seventies we built houses with scant regard for what makes for, and what undermines and destroys, community: a very theological subject, and not simply a theoretical theological subject.

Housing the homeless is more than a matter of bricks and mortar. Housing is not only about building and architecture, it's about the idea of neighbourhood and about building communities. Some housing estates *look* abandoned – and *feel* like it – to those who have been decanted into them. Berthold Brecht called high rises 'vertical receptacles'. Some estates breed violence and vandalism. If it is clear from your housing that no one respects you, it is difficult to have respect for yourself or for others.

I was in Manchester ten days ago, where the great estate in Hulme, which won all the architects' prizes when it was erected in the Sixties, has recently been razed to the ground, with explosions of thankfulness from everyone – except the rats.

Since the days I've described, much has happened: but much has not happened. The organization Shelter, for instance, has now been with us for twenty-six years – thank God; but the subject of homelessness has been with us longer – and the homeless. And the homeless will continue to be with us, let us be clear, unless an *additional 60,000 to 80,000* low-cost, affordable homes are made available *each year* to the year 2000.

The difference between now and 1967 is that anyone who really *wants* to *do* something about housing and homelessness can easily get informed on the subject.

The local churches of Lambeth where I now live – as an old-age pensioner who does a bit of moonlighting on the side – try to help the homeless in the Waterloo area. It was my turn a few nights ago to help with the 'Soup Run' from the Lambeth Mission in Lambeth Road. I learnt a lot that night. It was a very cold night, with a bitter wind sweeping across the concrete space of the so-called Bull Ring. Most of the homeless were fairly aged, and I couldn't see many of them ever holding down a job. The very aged were already tightly shut up for the night in their cardboard boxes and sacking, and not even the offer of a hot cup of tea and sandwiches could lure them out. But we soon got rid of what we had brought with us, including the very welcome jumble which was eagerly searched through for warm clothing.

But there was one young lad there whom I engaged in conversation. He was quite a bright lad. He had not succeeded in getting a job for a 'very' long time, but he told me he had been successful in getting a bed for that night, in a hostel at King's Cross. But he said he'd still got to get some of the money he needed for his night's stay. I thought that meant he was about to ask *me* for some money, when he suddenly said, 'Well, can't stop here all night talking to you, guv, gotta get on with me begging'! And he raced off to beg from a more promising possibility: a businessman with a rolled-up umbrella, who was just entering the north side of the Bull Ring, *en route* for the station. I'm glad to say my young friend lifted enough from that professional-looking man to complete what he needed for safe lodging that night.

I've been speaking about the theology of homelessness: that it starts with the belief that each person is a child of God; that care in 'minute particulars' must follow from that; that it concerns power and powerlessness and the use of money; that it's about building community as well as houses; and about personal and pastoral care of the homeless themselves. But what Christian virtues do we need to bring to this subject? Obviously compassion; but I would want to underline two other necessary virtues: two opposite virtues – patience and impatience.

One of the reasons I have chosen to talk of housing the homeless over a period of more than thirty years is to underline the need of patience and perseverance. In the world of homelessness, there are few quick results. But patience is not the same as docility. I have always admired the title of Canon Dick Sheppard's book *The Impatience of a Parson*. It is right to be impatient and angry when those in power, locally or nationally, get their spending priorities wrong from a Christian point of view, or scapegoat lone-parent families or immigrants. It is never right to be patient with wickedness – however exalted its source. And there has been a lot of it about lately.

I want to end almost where I began, but not quite. Recently, I had to do another baptism visit. It was to a judge's daughter and her husband who had just had twins; Caspar and Julius. I had already baptized their first child, Freddie, and I was glad to see young Freddie again. The twins were radiant. The family had just moved into a new house that could better accommodate the new arrivals. It was a lovely house, and the parents and the three children were a delight. I was glad when they said to me, 'Come and see our new house and the twins.' Any house which allows three children like that to thrive and flourish is a house of the Lord.

But on my way to the house, on the corner of their road, what looked like their parish church turned out to be a church recently converted into a block of flats. My thoughts were somewhat contradictory when I saw what had happened: momentary regret that the decline in church-going had rendered that particular church now surplus to requirements; but I was also reminded of the many committee meetings I had put in, in years past, on something called the *Pastoral Measure of 1968*, to enable just what has been done to that church to *be* done, so that more housing can be provided.

Theology sometimes starts – but, alas, often ends – with theory. I have found over the years that housing, more than almost any other subject, has forced me to think and to act theologically.

And, by the way, the church building where I was vicar in the Sixties – St George's, Camberwell, a Doric building built in 1824 to seat 1,750 people – will soon be reopened as a block of flats; and the small new church that opened in the Eighties, long after I'd left Camberwell, flourishes. If I hear that the old St George's building is now housing homeless people – perhaps lone-parent families, and those who have been so wickedly scapegoated recently – I shall rejoice.

'Unless the Lord builds the house,' said the Psalmist, 'its builders labour in vain.' Building houses can be a very godly activity, and *not* building them can be very demonic. But the Psalmist goes on: 'Unless the Lord keeps watch over the city, the watchman stands guard in vain.' Houses need to be seen in the context of their community – town, city, village – and the building of a community in which people know themselves to be valued and valuable. That, too, is as godly an activity as can be conceived. Unless the Lord keeps watch over the City – I mean 'the City': the Stock Exchange, the Bank of England and all who create wealth – the watchman stands guard in vain.

*   *   *

There my sermon ended when I *wrote* it, but a curious event yesterday evening makes me want to add just a sentence or two.

Last night I spent a very happy evening with a judge and his wife, celebrating his eightieth birthday.

I returned home by taxi: sober, but happy. My taxi driver, at my door, seeing my clerical collar, suddenly said to me: 'You're a reverend gentle-man?' 'Yes,' I said. 'Would you be willing to keep your fare', he asked, 'and give it to the homeless for me? It's £4.50. I've a wife and a young child and a home. I'm very lucky.' He had no idea I was preaching here tonight on homelessness. I was very touched.

To God be the Glory: Father, Son and Holy Spirit. Amen.

4

FRA ANGELICO AND THE EPIPHANY

Oxford Mission Epiphany Service,
St Michael Paternoster Royal, London; 6 January 1994

[The death of Fr Theodore Mathieson had occurred on the eve of the Epiphany. Canon James began his sermon thus]:

You will have been as saddened as I was to hear this morning of the death of Fr Theodore, though our hearts are also full of thankfulness for him. And what a day for the Superior of the Brotherhood of the Epiphany – the eve of the Epiphany – to be called home.

Obviously I had prepared my sermon before I heard the news, but I prepared it with Theodore much in mind, fearing what has now happened would have happened, and knowing that we should want to have a special requiem for him on another occasion. But before I begin my sermon, I'd just like to read a paragraph or two from my diary of 1972, in memory of and in heartfelt thanksgiving for Theodore:

Calcutta: 11 May 1972

As soon as I had settled in, the Superior, Peter Thorman, who has been out here since 1937, took me round the 'compound'. It was marvellous to see all that is going on.

What amazed me was to discover fifty violins and cellos in the Music Room of the School. Fr Douglass was a man with music in his soul. This side of his work has been carried on by Fr Theodore Mathieson, who, when he heard at lunch (hot curry!) that I played the piano, immediately arranged for one of the boys to come over with his cello. I shall never, never, forget this Bengali boy, Anup, playing 'Slumber on' from Bach's Cantata No. 82. He should have a great future as a cellist before him, if, somehow, the money for his training can be found. It was a great privilege to accompany him.

12 May 1972

This afternoon, Fr Theodore collected in the library two of the boys who play first violin, and two who play second. He and Anup played the cello and

13

I played the piano for the first two movements of Bach's D Minor Piano Concerto. I had never looked at the score in my life and had to sight-read it, but the thrill of the occasion provided a curious afflatus, and we got through with surprising success. The rest of the Brothers and the Sisters had gathered in the library at the sound, and a crowd had gathered the other side of the open windows, pressing themselves to the iron grille – old men, middle-aged, youths and boys – they come in to the field surrounding the Mission building every evening after work to play football or to stroll and gossip. When we ended, the little crowd outside clapped and smiled. This Bengali love of music breaks all barriers down. At least, it breaks some down, and I'm deeply grateful for that. What amazed me is that the lads who play this heavenly music are either at the Industrial School, or, like one of the first violins, a particularly brilliant fellow, just out at work, and living in the workers' hostel. He in fact looks after the machines at a tobacco factory. He only has a job because he had been trained *here*.

[The Sermon]

We meet here today, on this Feast of the Epiphany, because all of us are friends, in some way associates, of the Brotherhood and Sisterhood of the Epiphany. We're almost, but not quite, a 'Third Order' of the Oxford Mission to Calcutta. Many, if not most of us, will have been to Behala or Barisal. The buildings of the Mission, which so shaped the communities at Behala and Barisal, will have made their impression on us as well. The smells, the temperature, and the times, as we recall them with our inward eye, as experienced 'out there', will have had their effect on most of us; indeed, on our lives and, not least, on our prayers.

I begin there, but I don't want to stop there for very long. I want to take you back several centuries: 500 years and more. I want to take you back to Florence: to the years between about 1438 and 1452. Fra Angelico and his shop made over fifty paintings in tempera and fresco for the Dominican priory of San Marco in Florence in those years. He himself belonged to the Order of Preachers, to the Dominicans, particularly to that reformed branch of the Order known as the Observance.

I want to say that just as Fr Theodore Mathieson and his music-making come immediately to the mind of many of us when we think of the Oxford Mission in Calcutta, so when some people thought of Florence and the Dominicans they thought immediately in those days of the artist member of their community, Fra Angelico. And the architectural spaces of San Marco, and its paintings and frescos, shaped the lives both of the community and of its friends. Ties of family, friendship and locality knit together the community and its associates. It was not only the monks whom they knew, it was the church and its worship. Friends and families met the monks in the parlour. The monks needed both seclusion and meeting: room to study and to chat. Fra Angelico decorated the public parts of San Marco, and also the brothers' cells and the passages. His paintings were a kind of Dominican preaching, not in words but in paintings.

I said that some of us can remember particular times in, say, Calcutta. Maybe the years of the Second World War. When you think of Fra Angelico and his paintings, it helps, I think, to know a little of his times and his surrounding society, and indeed a little of Fra Angelico's own story. He was born in the late 1390s in a village to the north-east of Florence. He was baptized Guido di Piero. He became a monk in about 1418. From the time he took the Dominican habit he was known as Fra Giovanni da Fiesole. Within a decade of his death in 1455, he became 'Angelico' – the angelic painter. But it was only in 1984 that Pope John Paul II authorized his beatification.

While Fra Angelico did not *owe* his gifts to the Dominicans, the opportunity to *develop* them undoubtedly came through his community. Most of his greatest art was produced for Dominican churches and convents, and much of the rest of it may be traced to Dominican connections. His career was a success story. It took him from the obscurity of a journeyman illustrator in a scriptorium near Florence cathedral to the renown of an artist whose last major commissions were monumental fresco cycles in St Peter's and the Vatican Palace.

There is not time today to tell the whole story of how Angelico became a Dominican. I want the fact that we are here *today* to celebrate the Feast of the Epiphany to concentrate our minds on 6 January 1443: a very significant day both for Fra Angelico and for his community. Early on that morning, hours before dawn, the monks of San Marco would have risen to sing the night office of the Epiphany. On a major feast the office could go on for more than an hour. That hour, stolen from sleep, may not have produced the best singing of which the monks were capable. The church would have been unheated, and probably ice-cold, though the monks could struggle into the fleecy cosiness of their white woollen habits.

But that particular Epiphany morning neither the youngest novice nor the oldest cleric could have had much trouble staying awake. They knew the entire Papal Curia would accompany Pope Eugenius IV himself to San Marco that day, and that the Pope had agreed to spend the night there. The Signoria and first citizens of Florence were to be among the honoured guests. No doubt, during the office, a thousand housekeeping details slipped through the minds of the monks, for San Marco that day was to provide a lavish banquet following the ceremonies that evening. Certainly Fra Angelico would have had a restless night, for his new altarpiece was to be the chief element in the choir chapel to be consecrated that day. Fra Angelico, like one of the Wise Men, was laying one of his finest paintings at the feet of Christ.

And just as in, say, Calcutta, one remembers the busy streets almost at the same moment as one remembers the singing in chapel, so when I think of Fra Angelico on that Feast of the Epiphany in 1443, I find myself thinking of the people of the city of Florence. Just south of San Marco, on the Via Larga, Cosimo di Medici probably awoke in his own house rather later than the monks, and when he opened his eyes it would be with a sense of happy anticipation, and not a little justifiable pride; for the dedication of San Marco marked the end of a major stage in his political career and the beginning of another. The Epiphany celebrations of 1443 may, indeed, have been deliberately organized to make that fact clear to all. They were to include the famous pageant, whose climax was the Procession of the Magi, staged by the confraternity of youths, in which Cosimo had a special interest, and whose meeting rooms were at San Marco. The procession was to pass by Cosimo's house, on the way to the Piazza di San Marco at the northern end of the street.

While the procession assembled in the Piazza del Duomo, at the southern end of the Via Larga, the rumble of carts and the laughter and shouts of the people, the restless neighing and stomping of horses and lowing of oxen may also have reached Cosimo's ears. He was right at the centre of things. He had played a crucial role in establishing the Dominicans at San Marco, and Fra Angelico's altarpiece, to be consecrated that day, was the direct consequence of his patronage. The new Dominican altarpiece was a landmark in the history of art. It was a traditional Dominican altarpiece designed around the Dominican themes inherited from a long series of similar paintings for the Order's main altars in central Italy, and yet the learned brothers at San Marco probably believed they had never seen anything quite like their new San Marco altarpiece.

The painting is a large rectangle, almost square. At the bottom of the painting, in the centre, is a small crucifixion, in a standing rectangle, which makes the main painting seem much larger. That shows a wooded glade, at the edge of a tranquil sea, surrounded by gently sloping hills. In the foreground, the Madonna and child, flanked by angels and saints, hold court in a kind of pavilion of sumptuous hangings, and the squares of the carpet underline the perspective. The child sits, naked, on his mother's knee, with his right hand raised in blessing, his left holding an orb, and on the orb is a map of the world. St Dominic is, not surprisingly, among the saints: and the patrons of Cosimo and his family are also gathered there.

I want to say just a word more about how they kept the Feast of the Epiphany that day in Florence. I've said that a confraternity of men, the Companions of the Magi, produced a pageant which told the story of the Wise Men's journey from Herod's Palace in Jerusalem to the stable at Bethlehem. For this occasion, the centre of Florence became, symbolically, the whole of the Holy Land, with Bethlehem at San Marco. There was an elaborate procession, and the Three Kings were always attired as richly as possible. There were sometimes as many as 700 riders on horseback. In addition, there was a veritable Notting Hill carnival: floats, dumbshows and various kinds of music. Having reached the Piazza of San Marco, the procession terminated with other representations of the events surrounding the Epiphany. The Slaughter of the Innocents provided huge possibilities for any pageant producer of imagination. The Epiphany celebrations were so expensive that, by the 1440s, it became the custom to produce the pageant only once every five years. The year 1443 was one of those years, and it was no accident that the altarpiece of San Marco was dedicated on the Feast of the Epiphany that year.

You may wonder why I have told you this story today. There are several reasons, besides the fact that today is the Feast of the Epiphany. I've already hinted at some: the place that the *artist* has had in the Brotherhood of the Epiphany – the artist/musician, pre-eminently Fr Theodore. The way that community life has sustained the artist monk. The place that beauty has had in the worship of the community. I think, even now, of 'My love's an arbutus' being played by the orchestra at Mass in the chapel at Behala. The relation of friends and family to the members of the community. Yes; and the message of the gospel, for the surrounding world, being proclaimed not by word alone. But I've wanted to say above all that what they did that Feast of the Epiphany, in 1443, is what we are doing here and now. And that all the street processions in Florence that year and other years would be a nonsense and a mockery if there was nothing at the heart of them.

John Betjeman, who loved artists and their colours – from 'Crimson Lake to Hooker's Green' – has put the question, and the answer, unforgettably for our age:

> And is it true? And is it true,
>   This most tremendous tale of all,
> . . . .
>   A Baby in an ox's stall?
> The Maker of the stars and sea
> Become a Child on earth for me?
>
> And is it true? For if it is . . .
> No love that in a family dwells,
>   No carolling in frosty air . . .
>
> Can with this single Truth compare –
> That God was Man in Palestine

And lives today in Bread and Wine.

Yes; and was vividly alive to Fra Angelico and to his Brothers and to the people of Florence in 1443, as he has been in Calcutta and Barisal in these last years, through, not least, the Oxford Mission, and lives today in bread and wine this Feast of the Epiphany: here and now. And, in this Epiphany Eucharist, the living and departed of all ages are one.

5

THE CONVERSION OF ST PAUL

St Paul's, Knightsbridge; 23 January 1994

The German philosopher Martin Heidegger wrote, eighteen years ago, 'Questioning is the piety of thought.' That's about as tough a sentence as I've ever used at the beginning of a sermon, but, to my mind, it's a brilliant perception; and today I want to relate it to the conversion of St Paul – which you, here at St Paul's, will particularly want to celebrate next Tuesday; and I want you to relate it to yourselves: 'Questioning is the piety of thought.'

Paul is usually characterized by his clear convictions – indeed, by his dogmas and his dogmatism. Yet when you examine his writings, it's interesting how much *un*certainty there is in Paul. It was of course Paul who said – in that most famous of all Pauline passages, in his great hymn of love – 'Now we know *in part*'; and, earlier in that same epistle to the Corinthians, Paul wrote a remarkable sentence: 'If any man think that he knoweth *anything*, he knoweth nothing yet as he ought to know.' Questioning, I would maintain, is characteristic of Paul's thought.

A few weeks ago I went to the loo in a vicarage in Poplar, east London, and written on the wall were the words:

Miss Jones:
Please take a letter to the Thessalonians.
Signed: Paul

Now you may not think of Paul quite like that; but, if not, I wonder how you do think of him? Do you think of questioning as the piety of his thought?

Paul was, of course, a Jew by birth; a Roman by citizenship; named after the first king of Israel; born in that meeting place of cultures, Tarsus: a cosmopolitan, polyglot welter of emperor worship, stoics, cynics, fertility cults, mystery religions, and all the varieties of sexual experience you'd expect in such a seaport. It was in the harbour at Tarsus that Antony seduced Cleopatra.

Paul, as far as we know, remained unmarried all his life. We can only guess at the year of his birth. He was a grown man at the time of his conversion, and still a vigorously active man when Festus succeeded to the procuratorship of Judea; but that means he could have been born any time between 10 BC and AD 10.

In the Acts of the Apostles we're told of Paul's education at Jerusalem at the feet of the noted Jewish teacher Gamaliel; but, surprisingly, Paul never himself speaks of Gamaliel – though he boasts of his Judaism, and of his zeal for the religion of his fathers, several times in his letters. He was a Pharisee for the first half of his life.

Certainly, Paul knew a good deal about rabbinical theology and exegesis, but where precisely he was educated as a young lad we can't quite be sure. We know that this sensitive, emotional boy – who had it in him to produce one of the most beautiful passages in all literature: the love poem in Corinthians to which I've already referred – was brought up as a Jew. We can assume he came from a devout Jewish home, and received his elementary education at the synagogue school. Tarsus was a university town, but we have no evidence that Paul went to that university or to any other.

We know he acquired a vigorous, conversational, question-and-answer style: the so-called 'diatribe' which characterizes his letters. Paul was undoubtedly a man of active and alert mind, and of very considerable intellectual ability. He clearly had some contact with Greek philosophy, and, as I've said, some knowledge of rabbinical theology. We can't be certain of his way of life before he became an apostle; Jewish boys of every class normally learned some trade. Paul alludes several times to his working with his hands, and, according to Acts, he was a tent-maker – though the word could mean 'a weaver'. The presumption is he supported himself by his trade in later years.

What is clear is that Paul enters the stage of history at Damascus, as a determined persecutor of a new movement within Judaism that seemed to him, and to many like him, to threaten that whole distinctive way of life upon which the Jew depended for the survival of the nation.

But given the kind of mind Paul later revealed, standing up to the Christians must have meant questions for him, however much at first he was dogmatic about his answers: dogmatic to the point of persecuting those he opposed.

The specific grounds for Paul's persecuting the new movement are not made clear in either the Acts of the Apostles or the letters of Paul. It was the Church in the city and district of Damascus that he persecuted, but as to why he was there in the first place, Paul tells us nothing.

It could not have been earlier than AD 34 that the persecutor Paul became the apostle Paul. In Galatians, Paul says, two or three years after his conversion: 'I was still unknown by sight to the Christian congregations in Judaea; they had simply heard it said: "Our former persecutor is preaching the good news of the faith which once he tried to destroy"' (REB).

The Acts of the Apostles and the letters of Paul, our two main sources for the story of Paul's conversion, have a good many irreconcilable contradictions concerning the life of Paul.

After his conversion, Paul himself says he went off to Arabia: the country just to the east and south of Syria. The border was close to Damascus. We do not know where Paul went in Arabia or why. Arabia means, to us, deserts and the solitary life, and Paul himself says he 'did not confer with flesh and blood'. But there were cities in Arabia. We know that Paul spent some years in Arabia, but, after a brief visit to Jerusalem, went to Syria and Cilicia, and became what he was most proud to be: 'a minister of Christ Jesus to the Gentiles'.

The American scholar John Knox, who died recently, in his nineties, suggested, in his splendid study *Chapters in a Life of Paul*, an approximate schedule of dates for Paul's life:

Conversion and call to apostleship	AD 34
First visit to Jerusalem	AD 37
Arrival in Macedonia	AD 40
Arrival in Corinth	AD 43
Second Jerusalem visit	AD 51
Last visit to Corinth	AD 54
Last visit to Jerusalem	AD 54 or AD 55

But such a schedule hardly begins to hint at what we know about Paul. Paul himself draws our attention to that when, in 2 Corinthians, he compares himself with other missionaries, and claims he had served Christ:

> . . . in labours more abundant, in stripes above measure, in prisons more frequent, in death oft.
> Of the Jews five times received I forty stripes save one.
> Thrice was I beaten with rods, once was I stoned, thrice I suffered shipwreck, a night and a day I have been in the deep;
> In journeyings often, in perils of waters, in perils of robbers, in perils by mine own countrymen, in perils by the heathen, in perils in the city, in perils in the wilderness, in perils in the sea, in perils among false brethren;
> In weariness and painfulness, in watchings often, in hunger and thirst, in fastings often, in cold and nakedness.
> Beside those things that are without, that which cometh upon me daily, the care of all the churches.

(And Paul's 'care of all the churches' must have taken as much out of him as the care of the Diocese of London takes out of its Bishop just now!)

Paul was greatly loved and greatly hated. He was charming, resourceful, manipulative: a man of vision, confidence, fear and trembling. There was an element of jealous pride in him. Indignation came easily to him. So, too, did thanksgiving. He was a fighter. He was of strong emotional temperament: subject to moods of great elation and of deep despondency. He had something of the ecstatic about him. He lacked humour. He may have been an epileptic. His 'thorn in the flesh' *could* have been malaria; but we do not really have much of an idea what his ailment was, or how long he suffered it.

* * *

Tuesday is the Feast of the Conversion of St Paul; and I want to end what I have to say with closer attention to that event as he himself describes it.

The one thing that Paul says about this experience is that it made him a witness of the resurrection, and so, qualified him to be an apostle: one who saw the Lord, and was thus commissioned directly by him.

I have now, after more than forty years of ordained ministry, known a good many who have been what they have called 'converted'. Very often, when that conversion has been sudden, they have been at pains to describe and emphasize, at first, the difference between their past life and their new life; but, as time has gone on, they have been able to trace the questioning, the preparation, that had preceded their conversion: indeed, the connections between the self before conversion and the self afterwards. Sometimes, conversion is a breakdown that has led to a break through: however sudden that conversion may seem. Often, after the event, it is possible to connect the questions that were there before the conversion with the answers that have arrived seemingly out of the blue.

Piety is not the preserve only of the converted. It will be there in some form in most of us.

Paul was quite sure that the revelation of Christ came to him not only suddenly and miraculously, but without psychological preparation. But we are justified in distrusting the accuracy of Paul's own statement, although it seemed true to him at the time.

I believe that such a person as Paul could not have witnessed, for instance, such an incident as the stoning of Stephen, without inner questioning. His policy of persecuting the Church in Damascus would have provoked questions in him. The titanic battle between the men within him, he would have known subconsciously, could not go on. The inner questioning just had to be faced.

Whether now you do or do not call yourself 'converted', I believe that the questions that lie in your deep heart's core are 'the piety of your thought'; and, please God, they will lead you, and lead all of us, to answers to those questions, and thus to the discovery of our true selves: as, thanks be to God, did the conversion of his servant Paul.

We need to question; and we need to arrive at answers. T. S. Eliot wrote in *The Rock*: 'O my soul, be prepared for the coming of the Stranger, Be prepared for him who knows how to ask questions.'

6

MR PROFUMO AND THE PROPHET ELISHA

Gray's Inn Chapel; 6 February 1994

'. . . Elisha, the prophet that is in Israel, telleth the king of
Israel the words that thou speakest in thy bedchamber.'
2 Kings 6.12

The Old Testament lesson this morning recounts how the king of Syria
found that all his military plans against Israel were going astray. He
suspected treachery, but his staff told him that Elisha, the prophet, had
supernatural gifts, which enabled him to penetrate the secrets of the
human heart, and thus to reveal the king's plans to his own master in
Israel. Verse 12 of chapter 6 of the Second Book of Kings is one of the
great verses of Scripture: 'Elisha, the prophet that is in Israel, telleth the
king of Israel the words that thou speakest in thy bedchamber.' That
one verse epitomizes for all time the problem of security, public and
private, and hints at some of its attendant problems.

When, recently, documents concerning the Profumo affair were
released under the Thirty-year Rule, it was that *text* which came
immediately to my mind.

By strange chance, I was present in the crowded gallery of the House
of Commons, on 17 June 1963, when the debate was held on what is
called in Hansard: 'Security: Mr Profumo's Resignation'.

Early in June 1963 I had received a letter from an erstwhile
undergraduate of Trinity College, Cambridge – a Ugandan, Nkambo
Mugerwa, to whom I had been chaplain. He had recently become
Solicitor-General of Uganda, and had written to me asking if I could
possibly go to the House of Commons on Monday, 17 June to listen to
the debate on Commonwealth Affairs and report on it to him. I agreed
to do so. Alas, that debate was postponed, but my request for a ticket
was granted. So, by chance, I possessed a ticket for the gallery for the
Profumo debate – and tickets that day were like gold-dust.

I cycled to the House, I remember, from my parish in Camberwell,
and chained my cycle to the railings of Victoria Gardens. I made my
way to the gallery and heard half-an-hour's questions at the beginning

of the day. A Mrs Thatcher, Joint Parliamentary Secretary to the Ministry of Pensions and National Insurance, answered the first question, from a member of Gray's Inn, Dingle Foot.

The gallery soon became uncomfortably crowded. I was delighted when 'Rab' Butler's wife, Mollie, the mother of another undergraduate to whom I'd been chaplain, Christopher Courtauld, came and sat next to me in the front row of the gallery. Next to her was Lord Home, and next to him, Sir Robert Menzies, the Prime Minister of Australia.

At about half-past three, Harold Wilson, then Leader of the Opposition, rose to speak. He must have spoken for an hour. It was as brilliant a speech as I'd ever heard; and I remember thinking, when he ended, that it was unanswerable. There were, of course, phrases like 'disclosures which have shocked the conscience of the nation'. But there was also a body of evidence of a sordid underworld, and a barrage of penetrating questions. The speech was delivered to a silent house. My memory is that there was only one interruption to his speech, on a point of detail.

The overall atmosphere was one of high tragedy: the awareness of the personal and family tragedy of a colleague, who stood condemned: not least for lying to the House. Harold Wilson was concerned whether any other Ministers had connived at the action of the Secretary of State for War – which it was clear he thought they probably had – and whether national security had been imperilled. There was a notable absence of moralizing.

The debate was, of course, concerned not only with Mr Profumo. In the background there was Stephen Ward, portrait painter, pimp, and self-confessed Soviet intermediary. There was Christine Keeler. There was the Soviet naval attaché, Ivanov – who died only last month – and others: of the London underworld of vice, dope, blackmail and violence.

Harold Wilson was able to quote Lord Hailsham, the Lord President of the Council. In a recent television programme he had said: 'A Secretary of State cannot have a woman shared with a spy – if he *was* a spy – without giving rise to a security risk. The question is not whether there was a security *risk*, but whether there was an actual *breach* of security.'

Wilson continued:

> When we say that there was a security *risk* we mean that through a personal defect of character, or a perverted political or other loyalty, or through the possibility of intolerable pressure, or through cupidity or financial need, or through a personal or family relationship, an individual is more liable than his fellows to disclose information.

Harold Wilson was concerned with those responsible in the security services as well as with the responsibility of the Prime Minister himself. I will quote the final two paragraphs of Hansard's record of Harold Wilson's speech:

They are wrong at home and abroad who see this as a canker at the heart of our society. I believe that the heart of this nation is sound. What we are seeing is a diseased excrescence, a corrupted and poisoned appendix of a small and unrepresentative section of society that makes no contribution to what Britain is, still less to what Britain can be. There are, of course, lessons to be drawn for us all in terms of social policy, but perhaps most of all in terms of the *social philosophy and values and objectives of our society* – the replacement of materialism and the worship of the golden calf by values which exalt the spirit of service and the spirit of national dedication.

Drawing to his conclusion, Wilson said:

> I once heard the Archbishop of York say that we were in danger of creating a system of society where the verb 'to have' means so much more than the verb 'to be', and now we are seeing the pay-off for that system of society. But our friends abroad are wrong if they draw the hasty conclusion that this country is entering the era of corruption which has heralded the decline of the great civilisations of the past. The sickness of an unrepresentative sector of our society should not detract from the robust ability of our people as a whole to face the challenge of the future. And in preparing to face that challenge, let us frankly recognise that the inspiration and the leadership must come first here in this house.

With those two paragraphs you may be beginning to see why I have thought it appropriate to reflect on this thirty-year-old subject in chapel today. In fact, I believe that only now are we able to reflect calmly and dispassionately on the affair, and I believe that this incident, involving the security of the nation in many different ways, has a lot to teach us – just as that Old Testament incident concerning the security of Syria has its lessons.

But let me first recall the speech of the Prime Minister, Harold Macmillan, that fateful day in 1963. (We shall be commemorating the centenary of his birth on Thursday of this week.) In his opening sentences, the Prime Minister said that what had happened had inflicted a 'deep, bitter and lasting wound':

> I do not remember in the whole of my life, or even in the political history of the past, a case of a Minister of the Crown who has told a deliberate lie to his wife, to his legal advisers, to his ministerial colleagues, not once but over and over again, and who has repeated this lie to the House of Commons. There is the question of good faith; there is the question of justice; and there is the question of good judgment. I know that I have acted honourably. I believe that I have acted justly; and I hope the House will consider that I have acted with proper diligence and prudence.

The Prime Minister's speech, though very different in style, was as impressive as Harold Wilson's. But what I most remember was an incidental paragraph, which, nevertheless, put the debate in context and perspective. 'I confess', said the Prime Minister, 'that the last few days have not been very agreeable to me.' But the week of most strain he could ever remember was, he said, the previous October, the week of the Cuban crisis, when the missiles were building up in Cuba and the world seemed again on the brink of war. It was during this time that the Soviet naval attaché Ivanov made approaches to the British government about Cuba. 'Ivanov', he said, 'was using all the methods at his disposal.' And we began to see the full dimensions of the Profumo debate. 'What thou speakest in thy *bedchamber*' had suddenly huge and horrifying implications. When the Prime Minister sat down, Mollie Butler turned to me and said, 'He's done it again', meaning that she thought Harold Macmillan had once again managed to *survive* – rather, as 'Rab's' wife, to *her* disappointment.

But the Prime Minister was immediately followed by Jo Grimond, the then leader of the Liberal Party, who savaged Macmillan. He reminded the House that four senior Ministers, Iain Macleod, William Deedes, Martin Redmayne and Sir John Hobson, then Attorney General, had helped Mr Profumo to frame his statement in which he had denied charges of sexual impropriety.

Mr Grimond said:

> Whatever the Prime Minister may say, this tribunal of Ministers, sitting in the middle of the night to examine one of their colleagues, with a solicitor, came to the conclusion – in spite of the fact that they knew there was a letter in existence addressed to Miss Keeler and beginning 'Darling' – came to the conclusion that Mr Profumo should be *believed* and that the association was entirely *innocent*.
>
> Did they ask *where* this letter was? Did they make any effort to *get* it? I would also ask, for what purpose did they think Mr Profumo saw Miss Keeler? Did they think it was merely to make *conversation*?
>
> They may say that at that time they did not know about Miss Keeler. Did they make any effort to find out who she was? Perhaps they did know; if so, did they think this was an entirely innocent affair? These are people who are *in charge of this country*.

It was a speech about truth, trust, judgement, gullibility and responsibility.

An hour later, Nigel Birch made a hardly less damaging contribution: 'There has been a suggestion that the whole moral health of the nation is at stake and is concerned in this debate,' he said. 'I do not believe this is true. As far as the moral health of the nation can be affected by any human agency, it is affected', he said, 'by prophets and priests and not by politicians . . .'

Then, having denied any personal association with priests and prophets, Mr Birch made one of the sharpest shafts in all the debate.

'Mr Profumo's word was accepted,' he said. 'It was accepted from a *colleague*. Would that word have been accepted if Profumo had *not* been a colleague or even if he had been a *political opponent*?' Another reference to truth and trust.

Birch continued:

> Mr Profumo was not a man who was ever likely to tell the absolute truth in a tight corner, and at the time the Statement was made he was in a very tight corner indeed. There are people – and it is to the credit of our poor, suffering humanity that it is so – who will tell the whole truth about themselves *whatever* the consequences may be. Of such are saints and martyrs. But most of us are not like that. Most people in a tight corner either prevaricate – or, as in this case, lie.

After Nigel Birch came George Wigg, whose attack on Lord Hailsham was more severe than his attack on Mr Profumo. 'Let me say frankly,' he said, 'that if the moment ever comes when I see Lord Hailsham on one side of the road and John Profumo on the other, it is to John Profumo I shall go.'

Sir Richard Glyn made an important contribution:

> Any politician who has ever kept a mistress is liable to blackmail. It applies either during or after the liaison. . . . It could be argued that any politician who has ever at any time kept a mistress is too great a security risk to hold office, but that would have denied this country many prominent leaders.

Richard Crossman said: 'How often in private life we are faced with a situation in which we do not *want* to know the truth. We do not *want* to change our conviction that something unpleasant is not true, so we do not ask the questions, we do not collect the evidence . . .'

He continued:

> It would be a fatal thing if the tolerance rightly extended to the private Member, who has not heavy responsibility, got confused with laxity in situations which demand great severity. We cannot apply to Cabinet Ministers who deal with security matters, the easy-going tolerance that we apply to each other in private life as ordinary members.

Lord Lambton followed Mr Crossman. 'Miss Keeler', he said, 'was owned by a very great number of people for a short time' – and he named several of them one by one: including the newspapers which had bought her. Truth suddenly looked like a very vulnerable virgin.

Ben Parkin, the MP – significantly – for Paddington North – you might call it Christine Keeler's constituency – came next:

> It happens that many people in my constituency were able to tell me in advance a great deal of the information which is now common knowledge. I cannot yet understand how it is that on the subject of this incident an ordinary

back-bench MP could have thrust upon him from his own constituency information which we are now told was not available to the government.

At 8 o'clock, Sir Cyril Black tried to turn the House into a court of morals. I agreed with him heartily, nevertheless, when he said that Nigel Birch – in saying that moral standards were for priests and prophets, not politicians – was giving an example of the kind of thinking which had landed not only the House, in its present difficulties, but the nation. Cyril Black brought to my mind Macaulay's dictum: 'We know no spectacle so ridiculous as the British public in one of its periodical fits of morality.'

Marcus Lipton reminded the House that the affair had already involved a shooting, with intent to murder.

The last speaker in the debate was George Brown. He said that the Prime Minister seemed to be saying that if he could show that he did not *know* what had happened, or *how*, he was somehow absolved. 'Responsibility', he said, 'is not just a word.' There again was the subject of responsibility for truth.

In replying to the debate, Iain Macleod took up the words of the Prime Minister and reminded the Members of the House that they had the same triple duty that night in voting as the Prime Minister said he had: to act honourably, justly and prudently.

* * *

Some people may think this a very odd sermon. I would strenuously maintain it is right to reflect, in the calmness of our chapel, on an incident in the life of our nation which still has many lessons for us today.

Clearly, in 1963, a good many people enjoyed gossip as much as we do now, and enjoyed passing on rumours for months, but *did* nothing. Some were too easily willing to give a man the benefit of the doubt, not for his sake but for their own. The incident reminds us all, if we need reminding, of the power of sexual compulsion, and of the ease with which men and women, held in high esteem, can live double lives.

Because of the exceeding sinfulness and pervasiveness of sin, the question of human trust is clearly often complex. As Christians, we need to be realists rather than idealists. Trust of a colleague, as Nigel Birch said, is different from trust of someone who is not a colleague. But the incident reveals the power of cynicism to weaken resolve, and the power of party politics to set the good of the party above the national good.

No one to this very day knows what impelled Mr Profumo to confess. He may suddenly have felt the pressures of guilt. Human motivation is complex and, indeed, inscrutable.

The lies of MPs in 1963 were no worse then than they are now, but that does not diminish their extreme seriousness. And the lies of MPs are no greater than the lies of people of other professions. But so frequently now the question seems to arise: 'Has the House been misled?' 'Was this or that politician lying?' Concern for truth seems cheap these days; perhaps it always was. It is easy to idealize the past.

A few weeks after the Profumo debate, Stephen Ward committed suicide. Truth often involves matters of life and death, especially when treachery displaces and destroys trust.

William Deedes, who was a Minister in the Macmillan government, and one of the four senior Ministers who helped Mr Profumo frame the statement that denied his guilt, has recently written that he has 'long felt uneasiness about the way some of us handled this business in 1963 and contributed to the disaster . . . and made the truth extremely hard to tell'. He went on:

> Was it really sensible to convene a meeting of Ministers at 2 a.m. . . . and summon Jack Profumo from his home to this Star Chamber, instantly to answer 'Yes' or 'No' to charges . . . ?
>
> Because the news media had laid siege to his house, Profumo had taken a sleeping draught not long before being woken and summoned. He reached the House in a mildly bemused state . . .
>
> I have often wondered whether in these bizarre circumstances I would instantly have owned up to the truth, the whole truth and nothing but the truth. I doubt it.
>
> Later, we were accused of being hoodwinked, but I think the charge against us is graver than that. We created circumstances which made the truth extremely hard to tell. If it emerged in court that policemen had been guilty of such procedures, I think it likely that a judge would order the accused to be discharged.

But William Deedes has also written what a good many of us who are close to social work in east London have reason to know: that, for thirty years, Jack Profumo – at the instigation of Archdeacon, later Archbishop, George Appleton – has been first, chairman, and later, president, of Toynbee Hall, the settlement in the East End named after the social reformer Arnold Toynbee. He has given himself selflessly and unsparingly to that work. William Deedes has written: 'Jack Profumo is a reminder of an important part of the human story which many seem to have forgotten. Man may fail: and yet, by seeking his own redemption, may rise again.'

There is another person in whom *I* find inspiration. Valerie Hobson, Jack Profumo's wife, has set the world a valiant and shining example.

If my sermon this morning is in part reflection on a sorry tale, I hope you will see it also as the rather remarkable story of a *redemption* which also has something important to say to us all: something of realism but, above all, of hope. And I hope you may also have seen my sermon as a reflection on that verse of the 119th psalm we sang this morning: 'I have chosen the way of truth'.

7

MACBETH: A MORALITY PLAY

St Luke's, Chelsea; 6 March 1994

I shall never forget the first time I came to preach to you – or to some of you – at nearby Christ Church. It was certainly over twenty years ago, and I didn't really know much about the congregation. I decided to preach on *King Lear*. I remember that Robert Eddison read a lesson most beautifully; and after the service, the much-loved vicar, Francois Piachaud, said to me: 'I suppose you know who the old lady was – in black, sitting under the pulpit.' 'No,' I said. 'Well, she's Sybil Thorndike and she's coming to sherry.' As they say: 'I could have *died*.' Fancy preaching about *Lear* to Dame Sybil – and Robert Eddison. They were, in fact, both very kind. Dame Sybil asked me to write an oration for her that she had soon to deliver in Southwark Cathedral – where I was then a residentiary canon. Alas, it's nearly eighteen years now since Dame Sybil departed this life.

That's all by way of introduction to the fact that this evening – instead of treating that first experience as a warning; in a curious way it has emboldened me – I want to preach about *Macbeth*: about what *Macbeth* has to say to us in Lent. (Dame Sybil played Lady Macbeth at the Old Vic during the war – the First World War.)

Last year there was a fine production of *Macbeth* at the National Theatre; Alan Howard played Macbeth. This year, Sir Derek Jacobi plays the title role in the Royal Shakespeare's production at the Barbican, which I was glad to see recently – though, in fact, I preferred the National Theatre's production. This third Sunday in Lent, I want to preach about *Macbeth* as a profoundly human cautionary tale: a tale for all generations and for all seasons, but particularly for the season of Lent. *Macbeth* is, to my mind, a Christian morality play. If you like, it's Shakespeare in the pulpit.

When Macbeth enters the Court within the Castle, immediately after murdering Duncan, there's this significant fragment of dialogue:

Macbeth: I have done the deed—Didst thou not hear a noise?
Lady Macbeth: I heard the owl scream and the crickets cry.

Did not you speak?
Macbeth: When?
Lady Macbeth: Now.
Macbeth: As I descended?

Macbeth is, I believe, Shakespeare's Descent into Hell. As I say, it's a cautionary tale – on the grand scale. It's a morality play; and the moral order within it is deeply Christian. It has a transcendent stability. There are things which cannot be shaken: not even by the cataclysm which the play unfolds.

> Angels are bright still, though the brightest fall;
> Though all things foul would wear the brows of grace,
> Yet grace must still look so.

In this moral order there is good and evil; and man is a swinging-wicket between the two, possessed of an essential ambiguity.

The first scene is, literally, evil – enter, of course, three witches. 'Fair is foul, and foul is fair,' they say. The second scene – so far as Macbeth and Banquo are concerned – is all goodness. The news is of 'noble Macbeth' and 'brave Macbeth'. The third scene, upon the heath again, is one of ambiguity – once Macbeth and Banquo have entered: 'So foul and fair a day I have not seen.' But not merely ambiguity, for Banquo is aware at the outset of the insidiousness of iniquity:

> And oftentimes, to win us to our harm,
> The instruments of darkness tell us truths,
> Win us with honest trifles, to betray's
> In deepest consequence.

Macbeth, however, already seems less on his guard against iniquity: less aware of the necessity of choice, and of the danger of confusion; less aware how temptation can soon get out of hand, how the suggestion that is greeted with shame and conscious rejection and rational repulse is in no time accepted:

> This supernatural soliciting
> Cannot be ill, cannot be good.

At her first entrance, Lady Macbeth reveals that it is Macbeth's very poise between the good and ill which is her anxiety:

> Yet do I fear thy nature;
> It is too full o' the milk of human kindness
> To catch the nearest way; thou wouldst be great;
> Art not without ambition; but without
> The illness should attend it: what thou wouldst highly,
> That wouldst thou holily; wouldst not play false,
> And yet wouldst wrongly win.

Lady Macbeth herself knows no such ambiguity:

> Make thick my blood,
> Stop up the access and passage to remorse,
> That no compunctious visitings of nature
> Shake my fell purpose, nor keep peace between
> The effect and it!

And Duncan is no fool:

> The love that follows us sometimes is our trouble,
> Which still we thank as love.

The final scene of the first act is the 'hurly-burly', the 'battle' scene, with the conscience of Macbeth as the battleground. On the one hand, he is tempted to put out of mind the transcendent moral order – to 'jump the life to come'; on the other, he is plagued by Duncan's virtues. On the one hand there are Lady Macbeth's taunts that moral considerations are for cowards:

> Art thou afeared
> To be the same in thine own act and valour
> As thou art in desire?

On the other, is his knowledge that the courage that leads a man to defy reason and moral law is not courage at all, and he who dares do so is no longer a man in the true sense:

> Prithee, peace.
> I dare do all that may become a man;
> Who dares do more is none.

By the end of that first act the die is cast:

> I am settled, and bend up
> Each corporal agent to this terrible feat.

In this first act, Shakespeare has fixed our attention on a mind that is being drawn to do evil. It matters little what the particular evil is. Coleridge styles the witches as 'the shadowy obscure and fearfully anomalous of physical nature, the lawless of human nature'. Bradley accepts the suggestion that Shakespeare dwells upon phenomena which make it seem that man 'is in the power of secret forces lurking below, and independent of his consciousness and will'. Certainly Shakespeare employs a device which does justice to our human experience that we are 'compulsively' inclined to this action and that which both have to some degree our consent and give us to some degree the feeling that we are victims of forces greater than we can understand or control.

In the second act, Shakespeare again draws our attention from the crime itself and its execution to its perpetrator and its effects upon him. First, there is the imagined dagger – before he has done the deed. Secondly, the inability to speak – after he has done it. Thirdly, the imagined voices:

> Methought I heard a voice cry, 'Sleep no more!
> Macbeth doth murder sleep'.

Fourthly, the knocking within the Castle has a significance beyond the ordinary within the imagination:

> Whence is that knocking?

It is the porter who gives the answer. Like the grave-diggers in *Hamlet*, he transports us by imagination to Hell-gate, to the transcendent dimension of judgement. (The porter reminds us also that somewhere, outside the maelstrom engulfing the principals, there is another world that goes on unconcerned.)

It is the full dimensions of the deed which Shakespeare now seeks to portray, and does this by pointing up the analogy between the murder of Duncan and the crucifixion of Christ. In the first act the Sergeant had foreshadowed such an interpretation, saying of Banquo and Macbeth:

> They meant to bathe in reeking wounds,
> Or memorize another Golgotha.

Macbeth has now done both these things, and Shakespeare packs into the various reports of what has happened 'this sore night' all the details that St Matthew records following the death of Jesus:

> And behold the veil of the temple was rent in twain,
> from the top to the bottom; and the earth did quake,
> and the rocks rent; and the graves were opened; and
> many bodies of the saints which slept arose.

Macduff reports:

> Confusion now hath made his masterpiece!
> Most sacrilegious murder hath broke ope
> The Lord's anointed temple, and stole thence
> The life o' the building!

Lennox says:

> The earth
> Was feverous and did shake.

Macduff rouses Banquo, Donalblain and Malcolm, calling them to re-enact the same anticipation of Judgement Day that caused the saints in Jerusalem to leave their graves:

As from your graves rise up, and walk like sprites,
To countenance this horror!

Lady Macbeth, entering, completes Macduff's metaphor:

What's the business
That such a hideous trumpet calls to parley
The sleepers of the house?

Macbeth, by analogy, has crucified the Lord afresh, the Lord of Glory. His knowledge of the nature of his deed grows apace:

To know my deed, 'twere best not know myself.

He becomes, deeply and perceptively – but helplessly – aware of the nature of the immoral, and the consequences of commitment to it. The whole order of our world is endangered:

Had I but died an hour before this chance
I had liv'd a blessed time; for, from this instant,
There's nothing serious in mortality,
All is but toys; renown and grace is dead,
The wine of life is drawn, and the mere lees
Is left, this vault to brag of.

He realizes he has given 'mine eternal jewel' to the 'common enemy of man'. And even Lady Macbeth shows some recognition of what has happened:

Nought's had, all's spent,
Where our desire is got without content;
'Tis safer to be that which we destroy
Than by destruction dwell in doubtful joy.

Macduff completes the diagnosis:

Boundless intemperance
In nature is a tyranny: it hath been
Th' untimely emptying of the happy throne,
And fall of many kings.

In the last act it is the effect of the crimes upon Lady Macbeth on which our attention is first fixed. Her sleep, too, has been murdered – and in her sleep-walking she washes her hands. The Doctor says of her:

This disease is beyond my practice . . .
Unnatural deeds
Do breed unnatural troubles: infected minds
To their deaf pillows will discharge their secrets.
More needs she the divine than the physician—
God, God forgive us all . . .

Meanwhile, the descent of Macbeth – and his awareness of it – continues. Angus remarks:

> Now does he feel
> His secret murders sticking on his hands;
> . . . now does he feel his title
> Hang loose about him, like a giant's robe
> Upon a dwarfish thief.

To which, Menteith replies:

> Who, then, shall blame
> His pester'd senses to recoil and start,
> When all that is within him doth condemn
> Itself for being there?

The denouement, the final degradation, the inevitable end of Macbeth's commitment to a moral nihilism, is not an action of his, it is nihilism itself:

> To-morrow, and to-morrow, and to-morrow,
> Creeps in this petty pace from day to day,
> To the last syllable of recorded time;
> And all our yesterdays have lighted fools
> The way to dusty death. Out, out, brief candle!
> Life's but a walking shadow; a poor player,
> That struts and frets his hour upon the stage,
> And then is heard no more: it is a tale
> Told by an idiot, full of sound and fury,
> Signifying nothing.

Yet at the end, there remains the ambiguity. There are some depths to which he has still no wish to descend – though the Gadarene slope will take him most of the way. To Macduff, he says:

> Of all men else I have avoided thee:
> But get thee back; my soul is too much charg'd
> With blood of thine already.

And now the witches are recognized as 'juggling fiends': Macbeth's words for them in almost his last speech in the last act.

Never is Macbeth 'single'. He is always a man divided within himself whose kingdom therefore cannot stand. His 'single state' is shaken; therefore his whole body is darkness:

> I have supp'd full with horrors.
> Direness, familiar to my slaughterous thoughts,
> Cannot once start me.

Harold C. Goddard wrote: 'Tragedy has to do with men possessing the capacity to become gods, who, momentarily at least, become devils.' Earlier, in his essay on *Macbeth*, he wrote:

> Macbeth is, at bottom, any man of noble intentions who gives way to his appetites. And who at one time or another has not been that man? Who, looking back over his life, cannot perceive some moral catastrophe that he escaped by inches? Or did not escape. Macbeth reveals how close we who thought ourselves safe may be to the precipice. Few readers, however, feel any such kinship with Macbeth as they do with Hamlet. We do not expect to be tempted to murder; but we do know what it is to have a divided soul.

Yes. *Macbeth* is a cautionary tale: a profoundly Christian cautionary tale on the grand scale; a morality play for all generations and all seasons, but particularly for the season of Lent.

8

THE EASTER FAITH

The Savoy Chapel; Easter Sunday, 3 April 1994

Many people who come to church on Easter Day come because they have been bereaved of someone they love, and want to remember them; and maybe to some extent are still baffled by their bereavement. If you are such a person, it is you who I particularly had in mind when I prepared what I had to say this morning. But I also had in mind anyone who wants to confront again the question: 'What has the Christian to say today about death?'

The simple fact is that the God who is love, love revealed supremely on and by the cross, has created us for death: for a brief life, and for growth: growth towards death; and for death itself, and what lies beyond. So the whole of our life has the shadow of death cast upon it, in one way and another – if only in the form of that anxiety which is the hallmark of our knowledge of our mortality, of our consciousness of our mortality, or of our suppressed consciousness of it.

Charles Williams wrote, 'Death is an outrage'; which, of course, it is – very often. Jesus himself was crucified as a thirty-three-year-old young man. It's difficult ever to think of death as other than an outrage at that age. (And in India, let me remind you, fifteen in every hundred children still die before they're one.)

But when you think of the alternatives to death: staying alive for ever and ever; never ageing – which means never growing – something of the blessing of death begins to appear. And you at least begin to see what the God who is love was 'up to', so to speak, in creating us for death.

And start thinking of death and the God who is love, and you are soon on to the blessing – and curse – of Time: that raw material out of which the whole of our life, and not only *our* life, is made. Time is the raw material of all history; but it's a curious, and profound, mystery. We have various ways of 'clocking up' the seconds, minutes, hours, days, weeks, months and years; but we rarely reflect on the nature of Time. Einstein plumbed some of the depths of Time, but he left a lot of them unplumbed. And they're probably best left to the poets rather than the philosophers, mathematicians and scientists.

Shakespeare, in his Sonnet LXIV, wrote:

That Time will come and take my love away.
This thought is as a death, which cannot choose
But weep to have that which it fears to lose.

Shakespeare, of course, knew more about the curse and blessing of Time than any of us; or, rather, he could articulate that curse and blessing more penetratingly, and more beautifully, than any of us. But the simple fact remains that the God of love, that love supremely revealed on and by the cross, has created us for death, and – unlike other animals – to be conscious that our death lies not far off, and that so does the death of everyone we love.

A very good American book on bereavement counselling states, 'No one can help anyone else to die who has not faced their own death.' That sentence hit me so powerfully when I first read it that I shared it with a seminar of medical students I was addressing in Cambridge. They didn't like it at all. They wanted to be doctors, but not to help people to die; and at their age they certainly didn't want to face their *own* death. Doctoring, they said, was for preventing death, and helping people to escape it, not face it. 'Yes,' I said, 'but suppose you *fail* to heal? It does happen *sometimes*, you know,' I said with a wry smile. If you're a doctor to someone, could you conceive it your task to help that person to die? I told them that my American book was, in fact, by a doctor – in a hospice for the dying, for 'terminal care', as we now prefer to call it. But these rather good medical students got even more angry. They wanted to avoid that subject.

A few weeks later I was talking to Dame Cicely Saunders, the pioneer of the modern hospice movement and the founder of St Christopher's Hospice. I asked her what she thought of that American doctor's phrase. She replied:

> Well, I find it difficult to 'face my own death' – not because I don't want to, but because it's so abstract. I don't know whether I'm going to have a heart attack, or a car accident, or a tumour on the brain, or a stroke, or what. I think that I have to get used to death now: to recognize it in my own life, in my own body now. I've had to retire – I didn't want to. I say I'm perfectly all right, and I could go on for years. But *that* is refusing to face my own death. Death is what happens to me a bit every day. It's written on every relationship. In the world of things they call it 'built-in obsolescence'. And the question is whether we can see the love of God behind it, or whether we meet it only with bitterness, regret and hatred.

There's no greater witness to man's true size and stature than the history of his speculations concerning what will happen when he dies. But, in fact, we are lost for words. Words fail. We may use innumerable pictures to comfort ourselves: the Islands of the Blest, Where the Rainbow Ends, and so on.

The Jews did not believe in any real life after death until shortly before the coming of Christ. But they had their word-pictures too. The dead led a kind of shadowy existence; and then they began to believe in a resurrection, and the pictures began to get more and more complicated. Subdivisions of heaven for this sort of person and that, and subdivisions of hell for that sort of person and this.

And then came Jesus, and the green hill of Calvary, and his triumph over death. What did Jesus teach us about death? Well, I hope that this year, in this last week, Holy Week and Good Friday, you may have been able to refresh your conviction that Jesus revealed, supremely upon the cross, that in the heart of God is greater love than we can conceive.

But this is so great a truth that even Christians have rarely been able to grasp it. They have preferred to go on with their picture-making, their complications and their words. Even within the pages of the Bible the simple fact of God's continuing love gets blurred into all sorts of fantastic pictures of the end of the world, and of the divisions and subdivisions of heaven and hell. But by the Middle Ages there seemed no limits to man's ability to obscure the simple truth of God's love.

So let us, this Easter Day, take hold again of that simple truth: of God's unimaginable love, and that he has prepared for us 'such good things as pass our understanding'. Let us admit, frankly and fearlessly, that, concerning the details, our knowledge of what happens when we die is small. Words do fail. The human imagination, great as it is, completely fails. 'Now we know in part.' But there is no need for us to try and penetrate the Unknown, because of one thing: Jesus has told us all we need to know. He has told us by his life that God is love. And doesn't this say all we need to know?

One of the greatest English saints, Julian of Norwich, said almost the last word that has to be said when she wrote in her *Revelations of Divine Love*:

> Wouldst thou learn thy Lord's meaning in this thing? Learn it well: Love was his meaning. Who showed it thee? Love. What showed he thee? Love. Wherefore showed it he? For Love. Hold thou therein and thou shalt learn and know more in the same. But thou shalt never know nor learn therein other thing without end.

As far as I am concerned, you can throw away almost all the hymns on life after death, so long as you leave me with those three words: God is love. Of course, those three words are not simple words, but the life and death of Jesus tell us all we need to know of the love of God. Our imagining cannot add to that. And if that is the truth we have no need to worry. Our loved ones are in more loving hands than ours. We shall be in more loving hands than we have ever known: than we can ever imagine.

The cross tells us: God is love – love like the cross – and that he always will be.

I was very privileged to be allowed to write the life of Bishop John Robinson, who died of a pancreatic tumour in 1983. He asked me to sit next to him when he preached his last sermon in Trinity College Chapel, Cambridge, just before he died, in case he couldn't finish it. But he did: and this was the last paragraph of his last sermon, 'Learning from Cancer':

> The Christian takes his stand not on optimism but on hope. This is based not on rosy prognosis (from the human point of view, mine is bleak) but, as St Paul says, on suffering. For this, he says, trains us to endure, and endurance brings proof that we have stood the test, and this proof is the ground of hope – in the God who can bring resurrection out and through the other side of death. That is why he also says that though we carry death with us in our bodies (all of us), we never cease to be confident. Paul's prayer is that 'always the greatness of Christ will shine out clearly in my person, whether through my life or through my death. For to me life is Christ, and death gain; but what if my living on in the body may serve some good purpose? Which then am I to choose? I cannot tell. I am torn two ways: what I should like' – he says more confidently than most of us could – 'is to depart and be with Christ, that is better by far; but for your sake there is greater need for me to stay on in the body.' According to my chronology he lived nearly ten years after writing those words: others would say it was shorter. But how little does it matter. He had passed beyond time and its calculations. He had risen with Christ.

John Robinson asked that at his memorial service a passage from *Le Milieu Divin* by the great Jesuit priest, palaeontologist and philosopher, Teilhard de Chardin, should be read. It's this:

> It was a joy to me, O God, in the midst of the struggle, to feel that in developing myself I was increasing the hold that You have upon me; it was a joy to me, too, under the inward thrust of life or amid the favourable play of events, to abandon myself to Your Providence. Now that I have found the joy of utilising all forms of growth to make You, or to let You, grow in me, grant that I may willingly consent to this last phase of communion, in the course of which I shall possess You by diminishing in You.
>
> After having perceived You as He who is 'a greater myself', grant, when my hour comes, that I may recognise You under the species of each alien or hostile force that seems bent upon destroying or uprooting me. When the signs of age begin to mark my body (and still more when they touch my mind); when the ill that is to diminish me or carry me off strikes from without or is born within me; when the painful moment comes in which I suddenly awaken to the fact that I am ill or growing old; and above all at that last moment when I feel I am losing hold of myself and am absolutely passive within the hands of the great unknown forces that have formed me; in all those dark moments, O God, grant that I may understand that it is You

(provided only my faith is strong enough) who are painfully parting the fibres of my being in order to penetrate to the very marrow of my substance and bear me away within Yourself.

The more deeply and incurably the evil is encrusted in my flesh, the more it will be You that I am harbouring – You as a loving, active principle of purification and detachment. Vouchsafe, therefore, something more precious still than the grace for which all the faithful pray. It is not enough that I shall die while communicating. Teach me to treat my death as an act of communion.

So, this Easter Day, let us see whatever lies ahead of us, and those we love, within the compass of that unimaginable love of God, and let us say of them and of ourselves, with our Lord himself, 'Father, into thy hands I commend my spirit.' And let us say it with faith, with hope, with love, and with Easter joy.

9

THE COMEDY OF ERRORS

Gray's Inn Chapel; 15 May 1994

It's the clear duty of the Preacher to Gray's Inn to preach at least one sermon this year on *The Comedy of Errors*. Every member of the Inn itself is, of course, well aware that this year, this December, we shall commemorate the 400th anniversary of the first performance of *The Comedy*; and we shall commemorate it here, by performing it in hall, where, of course, it received its first performance.

If you're like me, it's often far too late to be given an introduction to a play when you get to where it's being performed, however intelligent, artistic and detailed an introduction may have been produced. I need to prepare for many plays a long while before the performance, not least for the plays of Shakespeare, and certainly for a play as complex as *The Comedy of Errors*. So this morning I shall give you as a sermon some random remarks that may provide a Preacher's preparation for that 400th anniversary.

It's important, I think, to remember at the outset that *The Comedy of Errors* may well never have happened here – or happened at that time – but for one tragic fact: there was a severe outbreak of plague between June 1592 and the autumn of 1593, with only a short intermission in mid-winter. The Camden Society publish a diary of the time of one Henry Machyn, a Merchant Taylor, who records how houses infected with plague were required to display on the outermost post of the house, a blue headless cross on white paper, with the words 'Lord, have mercy upon us' affixed beneath the cross. And each morning the clerk of the parish had to see that the cross had been neither removed nor defaced. The theatres of London were closed, and their companies of players went on tour.

It's not improbable that Shakespeare wrote *The Comedy* where and when he was laid off as an actor-author because of the plague. Players got used to acting anywhere they could erect some sort of stage. 'The play's the thing,' they said to themselves. 'The show must go on' – away from the plague. After such a time of tragedy there was a need of comedy, for cheering up and entertainment. Shakespeare never *simply* entertained, though: under the guise of comedy, indeed, of farce, he would make his audience face and reflect upon the issues of life and death – as he does in *The Comedy of Errors*.

I suspect that I have shared with you on more than one occasion the fact that Shakespeare came alive for *me* when I was a lad of fourteen, and worked on Bankside, Southwark – on the very site on which the new Globe Theatre is now being built. At the same time I learnt to play the organ at Southwark Cathedral, 500 yards along the river, which, when it was called the church of St Mary Overie, was the regular place of worship of Shakespeare. (If he had *not* worshipped regularly he would have been fined.) Often, as I sat in the cathedral, I would think of William Shakespeare worshipping there – not in that building, which is the result of several rebuildings since Shakespeare's time, but in the church that stood on that site; and, indeed, if I looked into the organ mirror, as I sat on the organ stool, I could see the tombstone of Edmund Shakespeare, and recollect that William Shakespeare had paid twenty shillings for the great bell of St Mary Overie to be tolled with a forenoon knell at his brother Edmund's funeral, during the great frost of 1607 when the Thames was frozen over.

I make mention of Southwark and St Mary Overie in speaking about *The Comedy of Errors*, because, if you go there today, you will see the tomb of the poet John Gower, the contemporary of Chaucer – as Shakespeare himself would often have done (though the tomb of Gower was then in the Chapel of St John – now the Harvard Chapel – where Gower founded a chantry). In Book VIII of Gower's *Confessio Amantis* the tale of Apollonius of Tyre is told, which is one of Shakespeare's sources for *The Comedy of Errors*.

I mention Southwark and St Mary Overie, and Shakespeare regularly attending divine service there, also because, whatever Shakespeare believed, it was clear he was steeped in Scripture. His extensive knowledge of the Bible, and the use of it in *The Comedy of Errors*, is obvious to anyone familiar with the text of it. They will note Shakespeare's particular use of the Acts of the Apostles and of the epistle to the Ephesians. He makes his story, which has Ephesus as the scene of its action, fit the Ephesus of the New Testament in ways which reflect the biblical description.

Most scholars are agreed that *The Comedy of Errors* was one of Shakespeare's earliest plays, but it is undoubtedly a masterpiece of its own kind. That kind is the sort of farce which on the surface is all about a mix-up; a mix-up of two virtually identical pairs of twins. But a mix-up is never far from a mystery, and Shakespeare uses this particular mix-up to point towards the mystery of things.

It's a play, as it says in its title, about errors; about blunders. And every human being knows something about errors and blunders.

It's a play about confusion, which is also very human; and about confusion being straightened out.

It's a play about misunderstanding.

It's a play which provides the pleasure of being 'in the know' when others are ignorant. Manufacturing a misunderstanding – or two – and letting the audience in on them, and waiting for the results, is what theatre is often about. So it's about theatrical ingenuity. But ingenuity is never enough for Shakespeare. To him, that's just one of the tricks of the theatrical trade.

The C of E – that's to say, *The Comedy of Errors* – is a play about identity. It's about other people's identity and therefore raises questions about our own. And that's a very theological thing to do.

It's about looking alike, yet in fact being uniquely different.

It's about coincidences – what Carl Gustav Jung called 'synchronicity' – which, in the play, you can write off as, literally, farcical; but it speaks of those strange occurrences in life which remind us that there's a mysterious strangeness to the whole of life, and an inescapable element of transcendence.

It's a play about dreaming dreams: which, of course, comes in many a play of Shakespeare.

It's about illusion and reality: about illusion and delusion.

It's about transformation. If you like, it's about conversion. It's about regeneration.

It's about the way we are members one of another, and, for instance, through marriage become one body with another.

It's about the testing of love: that love must sometimes be tested to discover the reality of love.

It's about that grief and bereavement there always is when you lose someone you love.

There's an important speech of Luciana which would not be enthusiastically received by feminists today, but it's not only typical of Shakespeare's understanding of human nature and society; it reflects what he accepted as the role of the male and of the husband as it is portrayed in the Bible, and particularly by St Paul:

Why, headstrong liberty is lash'd with woe.
There's nothing situate under heaven's eye
But hath his bound, in earth, in sea, in sky.
The beasts, the fishes, and the winged fowls
Are their males' subjects, and at their controls.
Man, more divine, the master of all these,
Lord of the wide world and wild wat'ry seas,
Indu'd with intellectual sense and souls,
Of more pre-eminence than fish and fowls,

Are masters to their females, and their lords;
Then let your will attend on their accords.

There's a phrase of only six words, near the end of the play, which I regard as six of the most wonderful words in all Shakespeare. They are uttered by Aemilia, the Lady Abbess, who, once she enters, begins to bring order out of chaos. Her final words are simply: 'After so long grief, such nativity.'

Aemilia, in fact, invites the company to go with her to what she calls a 'gossips' feast' – that's to say, a godparents' feast: to a baptism at which each of the main characters is symbolically to be rebaptized, and will discover – or, rather, rediscover – his identity: who he really is.

That great phrase – 'After so long grief, such nativity' – spells out the wonder of the occasion. After being separated from your true identity, how wonderful it is to discover it. We'd talk today of a 'rebirth'. Psychoanalysts, and people who go to them, know much about it. But, of course, sometimes it's a profoundly religious happening.

Those six words – 'After so long grief, such nativity' – are so full of meaning. What they must have meant when, for instance, the plague – like AIDS – had carried off so many friends and relatives. 'After so long grief, such nativity' sums up for me an experience which I have only otherwise found comparably expressed in a poem of George Herbert's – who, coincidentally, was born within months of the first performance of *The Comedy of Errors*.

So, to end, let me read that poem of Herbert's – which he called 'The Flower' – to interpret that so significant phrase of Shakespeare's:

How fresh, O Lord, how sweet and clean
Are thy returns! even as the flowers in spring,
   To which, besides their own demean,
The late-past frosts tributes of pleasure bring,
     Grief melts away
     Like snow in May,
As if there were no such cold thing.

Who would have thought my shrivel'd heart
Could have recovered greenness? It was gone
   Quite underground; as flowers depart
To see their mother-root, when they have blown;
     Where they together
     All the hard weather,
Dead to the world, keep house unknown.

These are thy wonders, Lord of power,
Killing and quickening, bringing down to hell
   And up to heaven in an hour;
Making a chiming of a passing bell.

We say amiss,
This or that is.
Thy word is all, if we could spell.

O that I once past changing were,
Fast in thy Paradise, where no flower can wither!
Many a spring I shoot up fair,
Offering at heaven, growing and groaning thither:
Nor doth my flower
Want a spring shower,
My sins and I joining together.

But while I grow in a straight line,
Still upwards bent, as if heaven were mine own,
Thy anger comes and I decline:
What frost to that? what pole is not the zone,
Where all things burn,
When thou dost turn,
And the least frown of thine is shown?

And now in age I bud again,
After so many deaths I live and write;
I once more smell the dew and rain,
And relish versing: O my only light,
It cannot be
That I am he
On whom thy tempests fall at night.

These are thy wonders, Lord of love,
To make us see we are but flowers that glide;
Which when we once can find and prove,
Thou hast a garden for us, where to bide.
Who would be more,
Swelling through store,
Forfeit their Paradise by their pride.

I would maintain there is much of the gospel in that poem, and in *The Comedy of Errors*.

After so long grief, such nativity.

10

THE SEASON OF GIFTS

Gray's Inn Chapel; Whitsunday, 22 May 1994

'Unto every one of us is given grace . . .'
Ephesians 4.7

Whitsun – Pentecost – is the season of gifts: the gifts of the Spirit. And I want, this Whitsunday, simply to reflect on those gifts.

I shall remember *one* Whitsunday all my life. It was 21 May 1972, and I was in Delhi, staying at the Cambridge Mission to Delhi, the Brotherhood of the Ascension. In the evening, Fr Amos Rajamoney, a young Indian brother, took me out of Delhi, 8 miles across the Jamuna river, to a village which was entirely composed of people suffering from leprosy: about three hundred of them. Amos and I first walked round the little houses of the villagers to greet them. They were of all ages, and the leprosy had attacked them in different places. Some had stubs for arms; others, no fingers; others, a stub of a leg, or no legs, or no toes; some were affected in their eyes, with not much left for eyes at all, so some were blind; some had the leprosy on their flesh. Some hopped; some dragged themselves along the ground. The leprosy was in most cases no longer active.

We held a Communion Service in their minute church. It was full to overflowing. The sweat was pouring off me in pints, and I was very touched when one of the lepers passed his fan to me – for he was sweating just as much as I was. Fr Amos celebrated the Communion. I spoke to the people, and Amos translated. I couldn't say much, except that we were all brothers, and that though they spoke Tamil, and I, English, the language of God's love in us on that Whitsun evening made us understand one another, and was a bond between us. I had the hope that somehow one's smile, and the look in one's eyes, might convey to people the greetings in one's heart, telling them, unknown to each other as we were, and meeting by a strange chance, that they were not just strangers, but recognized, and loved as valuable, and that we belonged to one another in some odd way. Certainly they responded marvellously: the little boys and girls, the teenagers, the grown-up men and women. It was a huge privilege to be with them, and to be allowed to say to them what one was trying to say, whilst at the same time feeling it was a huge impertinence, too. How could I meaningfully say that I valued them? And yet that's what that Holy Communion was all about.

And their history alone made me long to say something to them. They were all from the Madras area in the south of India. Until a short while before, they had earned some kind of existence begging on the streets of Delhi. Then begging was banned in Delhi, and their livelihood was taken away. Fr Ian Weathrall, the Superior of the Brotherhood, had discovered them, through a funeral of one of their number which they had asked him to take, living then on the banks of the Jamuna. The Delhi authorities eventually transported them to the village I was visiting, and provided some kind of basic grant-aid on which they could just about survive. But their leprosy meant they were either cut off from, or by, their relatives. Often the Hindu community at large thinks the leper is someone who, for reasons best known to the gods, is rejected by them. Alternatively, leprosy is assumed to be tertiary syphilis. All of this was good reason to try and say in any language available: 'You are very valuable.' I was deeply thankful for the very great privilege of that Whitsunday. It was an unforgettable Holy Communion. As we got into the car, the people stood and waved and smiled. Amos and I could only grip each other's hands.

My account of that colony, that village of lepers, could end there. But seven years later, in December 1979, I went back to that little community. Let me read you just a few paragraphs from my journal for 15 December that year:

This morning, I went with Fr Amos Rajamoney across the Jamuna river to Anandagam, to a colony I first visited on Whitsunday 1972. My visit today revealed a transformation – not, of course, in the people's bodies: still some had no fingers, or stubs of fingers and legs; still some were blind, and so on. But now, what is called the 'Community Development' work of the Brotherhood, helping people to help themselves, has had remarkable results. This time, the people took me proudly round their chicken farm and their buffalo dairy, to look at their vegetable garden, their handloom, and their candle-making. They gave me a candle and a piece of cloth they had made, and a copy of what they called their 'charter'. This time, there was real self-respect. Whereas before I couldn't bring myself to photograph them, this time they were glad to be photographed with their chickens, handlooms and candles, no matter what they looked like. I have never seen such healing in a community. Of course, they will continue to need much help. The doctor who has come to them once a week for twenty years has just died, and at the moment they can't find a replacement; but again, astonishingly, I was present while one of the members of the colony, very severely affected by leprosy himself, gave injections and administered drugs which the former doctor had prescribed. They gave me their printed Appeal when I left, not in a begging way, but as people who had been helped to take a responsible hand in their own affairs.

49

'Unto every one of us is given grace . . .' I've begun what I have to say on that text with the colony outside Delhi, because so often I find people divide the world into the gifted and the ungifted; and that won't really do. Education should surely start with the presumption that every one of us is gifted. Of course, there are different gifts – as St Paul says; and different gifts are of different value in different situations. And there are different ways of suffocating, strangling and stifling gifts: different social situations of family and locality, for instance. And there are different ways of releasing gifts. To release gifts in others often requires a kind of sacrificial patience, enthusiasm and love.

To speak personally for a moment: I myself was brought up in a family of four of whom I was the youngest. My brother was brilliant academically. He got 'firsts' all along the line, and my parents, though brought up in Camden Town, accepted uncritically society's way of judging by academic achievement. I remember, as if it were yesterday, our local vicar coming to visit our home at my father's request, in 1939, when I was fourteen and the war had just broken out. I overheard the vicar say to my father: 'Mr James, I shouldn't worry. I think I would take Eric away from school and send him out to work. He's the *dunce* of the family.'

So that's what happened; and it didn't really occur to me then that I might, in fact, be 'gifted'. Indeed, it was pretty plain to me then that I was not. But God is the God of surprises, and the gift that he gave me was work for seven years at a riverside wharf on the Thames; and it was the most wonderful gift – or, rather, a series of gifts, for it gave me an education about the nature of society which was unique, and, I believe, has stood me in good stead over the years. And, in due course, those to whom it had been given to be pastors and teachers to me helped me to get to night school, and at night school at King's College, London, I began to realize that I might have some academic gifts.

'A bore is a person who when you ask him how he is, he tells you.' I do not want to be a bore, so I shall say no more about myself. The point of what I *have* said is to underline that gifts are not achievements or possessions; they are *gifts*. And when you thank God for your gifts, when you make up your own *Te Deum* of thankfulness, the last thing you are saying is 'What a good boy am I'; you are trying to say as realistically as possible that God is the giver of all gifts: all your gifts. When we recognize gifts as gifts, there's no harm in our sitting down and reflecting upon them. A sober and objective assessment of our gifts from time to time is one of the most important things we can do. But when we do that, as well as making our own *Te Deum* for our gifts, it's often right to ask what we ought to be doing with them – or, indeed, might have done with them.

Then there arises another series of questions: How do I care for my gifts? How do I use them? What would make for their growth and increase? And these are not questions only for the young. Each age we reach produces a new series of questions for us. One of the most important questions is: 'What shall I do with my gifts in retirement?' It worries me that so many people who have got near the top of their profession seem to collapse, in various ways, on retirement: when some of their gifts – of wisdom, for instance – are still in full flower.

But if gifts are thought of primarily as *achievements*, then at the end of a period of achievement it's all too possible to see one's self as having been suddenly flung on life's slag heap. Gifts are given, but they are also taken away; and how we handle our diminishments is a major question. To know how to handle our diminishing is, I believe, as important as to know how to handle our growth.

It's easy to conceive of our gifts simply as a series of skills; and undoubtedly these days education involves expanding our skills. I happen to be computer illiterate, and on most subjects technically inept. My school teachers said I was lacking in co-ordination, and they were largely right; but I've never quite understood how you can be co-ordinated when it comes to playing the piano and the organ (which I have done from an early age), but *un*coordinated in a wide range of other activities which school seemed to count as supremely important.

But there are major areas of gifts which are very different from skills. For instance: concern for truth. It astonishes and dismays me that in the Church there seems so little concern for truth. There's concern for producing people who can serve up the right answers in credal form; but in Cambridge, for instance, as a chaplain, I got used to mixing each day with people who were passionate in their pursuit of truth. They may have been philosophers, scientists, economists, historians – even some *lawyers* were concerned for truth! And so, too, were *some* theologians!

I have never thought that conformity was a great gift in itself – nor, of course, is *non*-conformity for its own sake. But the text 'Ye shall know the truth and the truth shall make you free' has always been important to me. The gift of truth and the gift of freedom, of liberty, have often seemed to me to go together.

Mere conformity so often destroys: destroys the gift of distinguishing the true from the false, and, indeed, good from evil. The pursuit of truth I have found literally life-giving. Mere conformity is death-dealing. It ministers to hypocrisy and pretence – pretence that the top surface is the real you – whereas the pursuit of truth involves relentlessly pursuing who you really are, and who you have it in you yet to be.

'Unto every one of us is given grace . . .' It's not given like a tracer bullet coming from nowhere; it's given primarily in relationships. So we also have to ask what we have done and are doing to help *others* realize *their* gifts.

I would have to put near the top of my *Te Deum* for gifts, the gift of friendship. I just don't know where I'd be without friends, and grace comes in such different ways from different friendships. Friends have opened my eyes to the world of art: have helped me to *use* my eyes. I thank God for those who have helped me to appreciate music and poetry – and love itself.

Under the heading of 'gifts', many people seem to include only very positive experiences. As a Christian, that's bound to worry me, because Jesus, in Gethsemane, said: 'The cup which my Father hath *given* me shall I not drink it?' But it was a cup of suffering and sacrifice. Again, speaking personally, I'd have to say that nearly twenty-five years ago, at a time when I was 'going through it', when I hit a very painful patch of life – that time I *now* regard as the best thing that ever happened to me. It was, of course, when Christ was betrayed that he did the best deed of his life. He took the thorns of that experience and twisted them into a crown of glory. The gift to do that is, I think, perhaps the greatest gift of all, the greatest grace of all.

This last week I've been reading a most remarkable book. It's called *Pain: The Gift Nobody Wants*. It's by a surgeon, Paul Brand, who has in fact specialized in looking after leprosy patients in India, and diabetics. They have one thing in common: that their nerves have ceased to register pain, in, for instance, arms and legs. Without pain, sufferers cease to take vital precautions to protect their bodies from further injury. Paul Brand does not minimize pain, but he asks his readers to contemplate what life would be like without it. Pain, he says – as a man of great experience as an orthopaedic surgeon – is the gift for which we should give continual thanks. Pain alerts us, gives us signals as to where the heart of the problem may lie.

'Unto every one of us is given grace . . .' Of course, there are times when chronic pain is a total curse. But those of you who know something of the care that is given now in, for instance, many a hospice, know that patients can now be promised an end free of pain, in which nevertheless they remain lucid. Sometimes to be freed of *debilitating* pain is a huge gift.

'Unto every one of us is given grace . . .': grace that calls from each one of us a *Te Deum*, a different *Te Deum* as we go from stage to stage in our own lives. And, as each of us comes to write our own personal *Te Deum*, we shall often find ourselves plumbing new heights and depths of our own existence and experience.

11

THE HASLEMERE
DECLARATION

St Margaret of Antioch, Fernhurst; 29 May 1994

Whenever I come to Fernhurst, I almost always come first to Haslemere
– as many people do; and very often when I come to Haslemere, a
phrase comes into my mind: *The Haslemere Declaration*.

There's only one difficulty: I couldn't for the life of me remember this
week what *The Haslemere Declaration* actually was! I knew that when it
was issued, twenty or thirty years ago, it was thought to be very
important, not least by those who made the *Declaration* – who, I
remember, called themselves 'The Haslemere *Group*'. But when, this
week, I tried to find out what *The Haslemere Declaration* was – from all
sorts of places, including the *Haslemere Herald* and the Haslemere
Museum and the offices in London of the *Encyclopaedia Britannica* – I
drew, at first, almost a complete blank.

'But', you may ask, 'why did you *want* to know about *The Haslemere
Declaration*?' And, 'How's it relevant to a sermon?' And the answer is
really: for several reasons.

First, my *recollection* was that *The Haslemere Declaration* had a great
deal to do with peace, economics and ecology; and the way that any
memory of that *Declaration* has vanished – not only from *my* memory,
but, seemingly, from Haslemere's – might be significant. Put simply, we
have probably all had, or thought we had, more important things to
occupy our mind. We all have our priorities.

But secondly, I am reminded that this Sunday is Trinity Sunday; and
soon we shall be saying together the Nicene Creed, which you could call
the Nicaea *Declaration*. Yet it's possible that though we shall *recite* that
Declaration, and begin with those very strong words – 'We believe in . . .'
– really we've got more important things to occupy our minds, and
really that Creed, that Declaration, is something which hardly engages
our mind and memory at any level of deep conviction. Yes, we all have
our priorities.

And that leads me to my third reason for bothering about *The Haslemere Declaration*. A great deal of time and energy is being spent at the
moment on the question of Europe: of Europe and ourselves – which

we shall vote upon, or not vote upon, on 9 June. Clearly there are issues of economics, ecology and peace involved in that vote – as I *think* there were in *The Haslemere Declaration*. But am I too cynical in thinking that many people, perhaps *most* people, barely below the surface believe they have more important things to occupy their hearts and minds? – rightly or wrongly.

And I'm asking myself: if the Christian people of Haslemere of all denominations – and I include Fernhurst in Haslemere – were asked to frame a Declaration *now* on 'Christians and Europe', what shape would you give it? Is there any passionate conviction on the subject on which most people are in fact going to vote in only eleven days' time?

Shaping such a Declaration might in fact be something particularly worth doing on Trinity Sunday, because what the Council of Nicaea was at pains to declare was the truth of the incarnation of Jesus: that was what the Nicaean Declaration was about. And those who wrote that Declaration knew perfectly well that the incarnation – or the 'humanization', as they sometimes called it, of the Word of God – wasn't a matter of somebody who lived in heaven suddenly moving to live somewhere else – that is, on earth. Nor did they think the Word of God had come down from the sky to the human level. They wanted to say that God, who might have seemed far off, became unbearably close, in a baby who, in time, became a marginalized man, a society outcast and a suffering man, and, for a while, a dead man; and that what goes on in this world of power and weakness, marginalization, suffering and death is always part of the concern of God, and, indeed, of the life of God. So Nicaea and Haslemere – and Europe, and society's outcasts – are curiously closely connected.

Christians believe in a God who literally 'planted his tent' among us – to use words which convey what the Hebrew word means – so that the whole of human history is part of the concern of God. That phrase 'the whole of human history' is the kind of generalization which remains comfortingly distant. But if I say that the bit of human history we are making at the moment, in and through the European elections, is part of the concern of the God who was incarnate in Jesus, then that might make us sit up and take notice; and might furnish us with at least the beginnings of a *new* Haslemere Declaration.

That Declaration might well begin with a statement about God, creation and history, and might go on to a statement about the significance of the incarnation of Jesus. It might have a biblical section, and might go on further to say something about how Europe, in its past, has been greatly affected by Christian history, so that the Christian contribution to Europe is no new thing.

Now is not, of course, the time to set out each section in detail. The biblical section might include something on what Christianity inherited from Judaism: the vision of Isaiah, for instance, of a time when all nations would come together and feast at the same table. It might go on to Jesus' condemnation of petty nationalism, both when he talked to the Samaritan woman at the well, in the heat of the day, and when he told the story of the Good Samaritan. It might include Paul's revolutionary assertion: 'There can be neither Jew nor Greek, there can be neither slave nor freeman, there can be neither male nor female – for you are all one in Christ Jesus.' Indeed, it might include Paul's vision of a Macedonian – from Europe – saying to him: 'Come over to Macedonia – to Europe – and help us.'

There could be an ecumenical section, with quotes from, for instance, the social teaching of some of the Popes. I'm particularly thinking of Pope Pius XII, nearly fifty years ago, in 1947, writing that we should throw ourselves 'joyfully and with faith' into the new Europe, and work away at the fundamental issues of justice, peace, co-operation and personal responsibility.

I think I'd want to find room somewhere in the new Declaration for some old words from a very well-known figure, who said in 1951: 'Sovereignty is not inviolable. It may resolutely be diminished for the sake of all the men' – we were still sexist in 1951 – 'for the sake of all the men in all the lands, finding their way home together.' That was what someone called Sir Winston Churchill said.

But, of course, since then we've learnt a lot about that 'way home together', to a united Europe. And our Christian Declaration might comment on that journey 'home together' in the last fifty years: a journey towards, for instance, equality under European law. We are, of course, still a very long way from what many of us would want to call home:

> There are 52 million people, out of 340 million in the European Union, living in poverty.
> Some 17 million are unemployed.
> Nearly half of these are long-term unemployed.
> Nearly a third are young people who've never had a job.
> Over 2½ million people in the European Union are in fact homeless – a curious description of people on the way home together. Some even beg on the streets of Europe's cities: including, of course, London.

If a Haslemere Declaration today didn't look far further afield for experience than Haslemere itself, that Declaration would be fatally flawed from the beginning.

I'm aware, coming here from Kennington in south London, how amazingly different areas of England now are. If you had gone to my parish church, St Anselm's, Kennington, this morning, most of the congregation would be black. Drawn originally by the promise of employment at a time of national labour shortages, ethnic minority groups came mainly to the larger cities of Europe. So, for instance, 40 per cent of

France's ethnic minority population lives in the Paris metropolitan region, with most of the rest in Lyons or Marseilles. In such situations, ethnic minority groups are more likely to be trapped in unemployment, or unskilled jobs, and in the worst housing – or no housing. In Britain, the average unemployment rate for black people in the late 1980s was 32 per cent, compared with 13 per cent for whites.

The last two years have seen a devastating rise in the electoral success of avowedly racist parties in Europe and incidents of racial violence. During the first three months of 1992, the number of attacks on foreigners in Germany increased by 400 per cent over the same period in the previous year; and of those 600 attacks, more than half were perpetrated by people under the age of twenty. There have been countless assaults on young Asian men in the East End of London throughout 1993.

Christians have a particular duty not *only* to make verbal declarations – spoken, or written, or printed. They have to *work* at the actual situations. I am rather proud of what the Churches did together in Docklands and the Isle of Dogs at the beginning of this month, to escort voters of different races and religions to the polls, so that the avowedly racist candidates were defeated – though ominously, their voting supporters increased. It's not too late for Christians still to be an important influence on Europe: not as simply 'Fortress Europe', but as a major part of the whole wide world.

I said at the beginning of what I've had to say that earlier this week I couldn't for the life of me remember what *The Haslemere Declaration* was, and when I tried to find out, I drew, at first, almost a complete blank. So I got on with writing my sermon. But as time went on, I learnt a little more. Someone at the Foreign Office in fact produced for me a newspaper cutting from 1972, and that led me to a charity in Oxford called 'Third World First'. And, almost in the nick of time on Thursday, they said they would send me a copy of *The Haslemere Declaration*. Alas, it hasn't yet arrived! But perhaps that's for the best. Perhaps had it arrived, we would all have wanted to concentrate on that bit of history. Its absence actually makes me concentrate on the *present* and think that the Church in Haslemere *now*, in this year of grace 1994, should work at and produce a Haslemere Declaration for *today*, on Christians and Europe. Because if you're going to vote, you'll need to be clear whether you have 'Anything to Declare' – and, if so, what.

12

THE MUCH WENLOCK FESTIVAL

Holy Trinity, Much Wenlock; 12 June 1994

I was delighted, and greatly honoured, to be asked to preach to you at your Festival. There are many good reasons for holding such a Festival as has brought us together today; and one of the best is simply friendship.

I am so very glad to have reason to see again my good friend, Roy Davies, your rector, whom I have known for well over thirty years. He encouraged me to bring here today, from the United States, another friend of mine, Dr Ralph Deppen, a former Archdeacon of Chicago, who, like me, has never before set foot in Much Wenlock.

There are, as I say, many good reasons for holding such a Festival as yours, and for visiting a Festival with such a varied programme. I only arrived last evening, which happened to be one of the loveliest of the year. There was only time for a late walk across the fields to the Priory grounds, and then to stand and stare. It may sound trite, but there are few lines more true than W. H. Davies's couplet:

What is this life if, full of care,
We have no time to stand and stare?

Whatever else such a Festival as yours is for – and no doubt it has made some of you very busy – it is a 'time to stand and stare'. Last evening I felt very privileged simply to stand and stare, within the Priory ruins, at the marvellous exhibition of 'banners and boulders'; and to think back over the thousand years of the Priory's history – and, indeed, later to reflect on the town's history. In the fading light of a June evening, it was a moving and magical experience.

I have, in fact, wanted to come here for forty years; and I will in due course explain the reason why. But when I casually said the other day, to a learned geologist friend of mine, that I was coming to Much Wenlock, he almost went into a trance of envy and ecstasy, and uttered words the like of which I'd never heard before. 'Oh that particular scarp!' he said, and then fell silent – but not for long. 'That wooded scarp!' he exclaimed, 'that runs for so many miles unbroken! That long straight line of Wenlock Edge! That outcrop of richly fossiliferous limestone of Silurian age! Oh, how I envy you seeing for the first time Corve Dale, Hope Dale and Ape Dale! And', he added, 'the red tiles that come from the red marl, and the old red sandstone! And do try and see', he said, 'Brown Clee, Titterstone Clee, Norton Camp and View Edge.' I confess I was beginning to feel exhausted by the very thought.

Yes, there are many different reasons for our gathering here today.

When I was a chaplain in Cambridge, now nearly forty years ago, I had my rooms where the great poet of these 'coloured counties', A. E. Housman, had had his rooms, twenty years before, in the shadowy enclosure of Whewell's Court in Trinity College; and the maquette of the seated bronze figure of a Grecian youth, which still adorns the centre of Whewell's Court, graces my own sitting-room in Kennington, south London, at this very moment. I knew well-aged Classical scholars who remembered and reminisced of Housman, so I have longed to see the Shropshire of which he so wonderfully wrote.

Housman was, in fact, no 'Shropshire Lad' himself; he was a Bromsgrove boy. On 14 April 1934 he wrote to the book-collector Houston Martin:

> I am Worcestershire by birth: Shropshire was our western horizon, which made me feel romantic about it. I do not know the county well, except in parts, and some of my topographical details are wrong and imaginary. The Wrekin is wooded, and Wenlock Edge along the western side, but the Clees and most of the other hills are grass or heather. In the southern half of the county, to which I have confined myself, the hills are generally long ridges running from north to south, with valleys broad or narrow between . . .

But Housman's readers have rarely read his poems as a geographical guide book; he mapped *the country of the heart*, and thus he touched and moved his readers:

> With rue my heart is laden
> For golden friends I had.

And:

> Into my heart an air that kills
> From yon far country blows:
> What are those blue remembered hills
> What spires, what farms are those?
>
> This is the land of lost content,
> I see it shining plain,
> The happy highways where I went
> And cannot come again.

Housman is, above all, the poet of 'the land of lost content'. I think, however, it needs to be said here and now – here in your church, and now at your Festival – that lovely as Housman's poems are, and much as they may have moved most of us – for all of us know something of the 'land of lost content' – his vision, in the end, falls sadly short of the Christian vision, and of *that* vision I believe we all of us have need. In the world of his imagination, Housman looked back only in nostalgia and forward only with wistfulness. He had no *faith* in the future; for him it held no promise of joy.

I was present in the Chapel of Trinity College, Cambridge, at the funeral of one of the friends of Housman I have already mentioned – Andrew Sydenham Farrar Gow. We sang at that funeral the bleak hymn that Housman himself had written for his own funeral; and that wintry February day, as we sang that hymn, we were given little of hope or of vision, only a promise of further loss:

O Thou that from thy mansion,
   Through time and place to roam,
Dost send abroad thy children,
   And then dost call them home,

That men and tribes and nations
   And all thy hand hath made
May shelter them from sunshine
   In thine eternal shade:

We now to peace and darkness
   And earth and thee restore
Thy creature that thou madest
   And wilt cast forth no more.

There could hardly be a bleaker future than that. I contrast it with, for instance, St Paul's words to the Christians in Rome:

I am persuaded, that neither death, nor life, nor angels, nor principalities, nor powers, nor things present, nor things to come, nor height, nor depth, nor any other creature, shall be able to separate us from the love of God, which is in Christ Jesus our Lord.

Housman's words were set to music by great British composers: not least George Butterworth, Ralph Vaughan Williams and John Ireland. None of their music was quite so chilling as Housman's words.

George Butterworth's orchestral rhapsody of 1912, *A Shropshire Lad*, is a *rhapsody*; though he himself was soon to lose his life in the slaughter of the Somme. John Ireland was attracted by Celtic legend and history as well as English folk-song. Such songs as 'Is my team ploughing?', from *A Shropshire Lad*, enter into the spirit of Housman, but, mercifully, never quite match the bitterness of his words. Ireland's setting of Samuel Crossman's 'My song is love unknown', and his anthem 'Greater love hath no man than this', speak more characteristically of his faith. And Vaughan Williams' vision, although he was a self-confessed agnostic, had always something of *Pilgrim's Progress* about it – which was, of course, later, in 1951, to be the subject of his visionary opera.

Vaughan Williams sat at table with us, in Trinity, shortly before he died in 1958: such a different man from Housman – who had sat at that same table for so many years. Always in Vaughan Williams there is, as I say, a warmth and nobility of vision. Not for nothing had he, in 1906, edited the music of the English Hymnal, and composed for it that tune, redolent of faith, *Sine Nomine*, for 'For All the Saints', three years before he wrote *his* Housman song cycle *On Wenlock Edge*, which Gervase Elwes first performed.

As I say, in Vaughan Williams there is always something of Bunyan's courageous faith – in, for instance, his setting in 1909 of Walt Whitman's 'Toward the Unknown Region':

> Darest thou now, O Soul
> Walk out with me toward the Unknown Region

and, a year later, in his 'Fantasia on a Theme of Thomas Tallis'.

Dare I suggest we most of us are come to this Festival, 'summoned by bells' this morning, to this act of worship, here in Holy Trinity where the Cluniac monks once worshipped, to be renewed in vision; to 'lift up our eyes unto the hills' – perhaps through the beauty of the country that surrounds us; perhaps also through what Rose Macaulay called *The Pleasure of Ruins*; perhaps simply through being again for a while with 'golden friends'.

We are right sometimes consciously to withdraw awhile from the battle of life, to seek some transfiguring time before we return again to the fray: as the disciples of Jesus withdrew with him, one day – as your Lady Chapel window records – and ascending, apart, their local Wenlock Edge – Mount Hermon or Mount Tabor – he was transfigured. A Festival like this can provide such a transfiguring time.

But, even while we're here, I think it's right for us to bear in mind those in our society for whom such withdrawal is simply not possible.

There is an increasing custom in our society of blaming the victim, scapegoating those who are already marginalized and excluded; identifying them as the problem; responsible for holding back society from a more prosperous future. But in Christian Scripture and history, those outside the mainstream of society have often been called by God to be the source and promise of its salvation.

The renewal of our vision comes in many and different ways. In homeless people the Christian Church tries to recognize and minister to the person of the suffering Christ, outside the boundaries of what is most often considered a so-called 'normal' life for the mass of the population. Perhaps that's why those who work with the homeless so often come to feel it is *they* who are being ministered to. The homeless strip us of all illusions about ourselves and about society. They earth us in reality and minister *to* us.

Yes, the renewal of our vision comes in many and various ways. And we are right to take time out for such a Festival as this, so long as we do not totally turn our backs on the world in need. But, of course, in the end, it is a vision *beyond* this world that all of us ultimately need. Housman's vision ended in darkness in 'thine eternal shade'. I believe that faith – and thankfulness for what we have received and experienced in this life – can do better than that.

Parry, who gave us his incomparable setting of Blake's 'Jerusalem', also set to sublime music the vision of Henry Vaughan – the Silurist, which it is apt to quote, I think, in the setting of the Silurian limestone of Wenlock, and is as apt to end what I have to say to you this morning:

My soul, there is a country
  Far beyond the stars,
Where stands a wingèd sentry
  All skilful in the wars:

There above noise, and danger,
  Sweet Peace sits crowned with smiles,
And One born in a manger
  Commands the beauteous files.

He is thy gracious friend,
  And – O my soul, awake! –
Did in pure love descend,
  To die here for thy sake.

If thou canst get but thither,
  There grows the flower of peace,
The Rose that cannot wither,
  Thy fortress and thy ease.

Leave then thy foolish ranges,
  For none can thee secure
But one, who never changes,
  Thy God, thy life, thy cure.

13

THE MEANING OF MONARCHY

Gray's Inn Chapel; 10 July 1994

In Gray's Inn we have particular reason for sharing the general concern for the future of His Royal Highness the Prince of Wales. He is, of course, a Master of the Bench. His portrait by June Mendoza graces our Small Pension room. Most of us will remember one or more of his visits to the Inn. Some of us will particularly remember when the Prince, to celebrate his engagement to Lady Diana Spencer, read us a charming poem written by his ancestor, Frederick, Prince of Wales, to celebrate a similar occasion.

We are concerned for the future of the Prince for a score of reasons: not least because we are concerned for the future of our country and for its governance. Most of us who meet here have a concern for the relations between Church and State, and therefore for the relations between Church and Monarch, and thus with him who, as things stand, is destined to be our future monarch. The Archbishop of Canterbury has, earlier today, shared his thoughts on the subject on the BBC's *Sunday* programme.

Age – or what is now, alas, referred to often as 'the ageing process' – provides one, I find, with a certain perspective on such a matter. I was ten years old when on 6 May 1935, King George V celebrated his Silver Jubilee, and, along with all other school children, I was given a mug to mark the occasion.

I remember well the solemnity of the Lying-in-State and the funeral of the King in January 1936, so soon after the celebration of the Silver Jubilee. But hardly had the new king, Edward, left his father's death-bed before he ordered the clocks at Sandringham to be put back, so as to tell the proper time. There was clearly not only a new king, but a new age. And before that year was out, there was all the anxiety of the abdication of Edward VIII. By then I was in my first year at Dagenham County High School; and in the midst of that solidly Labour constituency I caught the general anxiety for the throne: an anxiety which was exacerbated, I remember, by the pontifications of a certain Dr Blunt, Bishop of Bradford.

No monarch ever succeeded to the throne more reluctantly than George VI. But again, looking back, I now realize that, as a twelve-year-old, my heart went out to a king and his queen who were so unprepared for office, who so disliked publicity and the limelight, and who had not sought in any way their new dignity, but had it thrust upon them, not least by their simple willingness to serve their country.

I can remember how heartfelt were our prayers when we prayed for the King's Majesty in the little church near my home of St Chad, Chadwell Heath: 'So replenish him . . . endue him . . . grant him . . .' And when too we prayed for the Royal Family: 'Our gracious Queen Elizabeth, the Princess Elizabeth . . . Endue them . . . enrich them . . . prosper them . . .' The faltering voice and stammering tongue of the King on the radio were, paradoxically, his strength, and the sure sign of his courage.

In school – in, as I say, left-wing Dagenham – we were taught to sing at the Coronation, not Parry's 'Jerusalem' but his less well-known but as beautiful 'England', which was Parry's setting of an edited version of John of Gaunt's speech in *Richard II*:

> This royal throne of kings, this scepter'd isle,
> This earth of Majesty, this seat of Mars,
> This other Eden, demi-paradise,
> This fortress built by Nature for herself
> Against infection and the hand of war,
> This happy breed of men, this little world,
> This precious stone set in a silver sea,
> Which serves it in the office of a wall,
> Or as a moat defensive to a house,
> Against the envy of less happier lands,
> This blessed plot, this earth, this realm, this England . . .

It was the first speech of Shakespeare that I ever learnt by heart.

Little did we know, that Coronation Year, how soon we should so sorely need the sea, the Channel, as a defensive moat, and how well King George VI and Queen Elizabeth would serve us at that time. And how little did I know that soon I would be at work at a wharf on Shakespeare's Bankside, on the very site on which the Globe Theatre is now rising again; that I would spend much of my ministry in and around Southwark and its cathedral, and that, as a result, for fifty years I would have reason to meditate on what Shakespeare had to say about royalty in play upon play.

Shakespeare lived in an age of revolution, not unlike our own. The world was a tempest, a pitiless storm of violent and rapid social change; and the royalty of human nature could not simply be assumed. Among the thorns and dangers of this world, a man, however royal, could lose his way.

The king himself, the crown of humanity, the figure of God's majesty, his captain, steward, deputy elect, could be deposed, or killed, or lose his wits, or have his eyes put out. Kings could, like men, prove to be little kings, sneaping kings; the crown a wretched, cankered, blistered, hollow thing; the majesty of kings, all counterfeit; their royalty banished or confounded.

The crown had constantly to be defended – but not by mere assertion or assumption. No man's authority in Shakespeare's time could rest secure upon his status or his ancestry. A bastard might prove to be more kingly than the king. And a man-on-the-make, coming up from the country, like Will Shakespeare himself, might rise from nothing – or, like Shakespeare, from next to nothing: from the house of a small farmer-leather-merchant-butcher-glovemaker, who had lost all his money and his status; such a man in no time could arrive at Court. The 'Outsider' could comparatively soon be 'In'.

'God Save the King!' is as often as not in Shakespeare a heart-felt prayer from one who knew that kings, like commoners, are in need of saving; for they too 'live with bread, feel want, taste grief, need friends'. A king, so quickly made, could be unmade as quickly. A king may be a king, but have no kingdom. Even kings 'break faith upon Commoditie'. And he who now is king may now be clay. Kings – like King John – can be unkingly: ''Tis not vestures which shall make men royal.'

Yes, but if that's the truth, what does make kings of men? What does make human nature 'royal'? Shakespeare was above all concerned with this question of authority. It was not simply the Divine Right that hedged a king that concerned him, but the divine right of Everyman, whose royalty is all of a piece with kings. 'There is a divinity which shapes our ends . . .'

In an age of change, the more violent the speed of change, the more acute the crisis of authority. Shakespeare's age was an age that was strangely like our own. A society not yet outgrown, its standards come down from another age, assuming a co-operative, reasonable decency in men – God to be worshipped, parents to be honoured, others to be used by us as we ourselves would be by them; that Old Society existed, cheek by jowl, with another – the brash beginnings of another age: the age of science, enquiry and discovery; the age of industry and bureaucracy; the age of mining, prospecting, merchant venturing and exploring; the age of empire and competition – and the careerist on the make. The Old Society desired to disregard the New. The Old Economy despised the New. The New Man in government thought not of what is morally right and wrong, but of what is socially expedient, and found that love and pity may sometimes be a governmental handicap. The New Man was a master of men all right – full of psychological insights, and hypocrisy; and successful – within limits. It was a society fit for a king – for a self-made king.

Shakespeare surveyed his time; looked at the children of his age of change lovingly, pityingly, penetratingly. He saw to the heart of them; and at their heart was the problem of authority. With the new knowledge, what shall we believe? With the new power, what shall we do? What shall we permit? What place shall we give to tradition and custom? What is the authority of the past – and of the contemporary? Amongst the 'tug and scamble of England now, what is the life, the right and truth?'

King John is, of course, about authority: how can the illegitimate be legitimized? So is *King Lear*. King Lear lays aside his authority, and his crown, lays aside the authority of a monarch and a father; and we watch what happens. At the beginning there is a king with his court and his ministers. Later, there are just four beggars, wandering about in a wilderness, exposed to raging winds and rain. At first, Lear has a retinue of a hundred men, then fifty, then only one man. Everything that distinguishes a man is lost: his crown, his titles, his social position, even his name. Now, Lear is just a man.

When authority goes, the questions multiply – What shall we do? What shall we say? What shall we think? – and there is always inevitably what we have come to call a 'crisis of identity'. The question presses itself: 'Who am I?'

Because *Lear* is about the Crisis of Authority it is also therefore centrally about the Crisis of Identity. Everyone goes around asking everyone else: 'Who am I?' 'Who are you?' You may remember what Lear says to his Fool: 'Dost thou call me fool, boy?' To which the Fool replies: 'All thy other titles thou hast given away; that thou wast born with.' And later: 'Doth any here know me? Why, this is not Lear: Doth Lear walk thus, speak thus? . . . Who is it that can tell me who I am?' And, once more, the same question.

When the banished Kent returns in disguise to the king, Lear asks: 'How now! What art thou?' 'A man, sir,' Kent replies. Later, Lear, suffering and tormented, says, 'In the last night's storm I such a fellow saw which made me think a man a worm.'

But how shall we solve this problem of identity, this problem of authority? This problem of man: crown of creation or worm? Shakespeare knew that you do not solve it by not facing the questions, or by oversimplifying them. He also knew that the new knowledge could be hardly less misleading than the old. What is needed above all is insight, vision – not simply knowledge.

King Lear – because it is a play about the problem of authority, the problem of identity, the problem of the royalty of man – because it is all these, *King Lear* is a play about vision: about the need for vision.

Everything in it turns upon seeing. It is a play about blindness and vision: those great New Testament words.

Gloucester has his eyes plucked out, on the orders of the king's unfaithful daughter, Goneril, because he is faithful to the king. 'Pluck out his eyes,' she cries. 'Out of my sight,' cries Lear, banishing Kent. And Kent replies: 'See better, Lear; and let me still remain the true blank of thine eye.' From this moment on, the story of Lear is indeed a royal progress: it is the story of Lear's slow and painful acquisition of that better vision.

In the last scene of the play, when the loyal Kent, his disguises at last thrown off, stands in the presence of the dying king, a misty figure to a dimming eyesight, Lear murmurs 'Who are you? Mine eyes are not of the best. I'll tell you straight, this is a dull sight. Are you not Kent?' 'The same, your servant, Kent,' Kent replies. The king's physical eyesight has faded, but he has learned to 'see better'. He can now see a man; and, what is more, he can recognize him under any name.

It would not be appropriate this morning to enumerate all the allusions in *Lear* to 'eyes' and 'vision', for that would be to review a large part of the play. But there is to me one particularly moving passage.

Gloucester, blinded, thinks only of suicide, and seeks a guide to the cliff over which he has made up his mind to leap to death. He enters, led by an old man who has befriended him. It is one of his own tenants who, by plain intention on the part of Shakespeare, is of almost exactly Lear's age. The blinded Gloucester begs his guide to leave him, lest the guide injure himself with those in authority, for helping him. 'You cannot see your way,' the old man protests. 'I have no way, and therefore want no eyes,' Gloucester replies. 'I stumbled when I saw.'

Shakespeare widens and deepens our understanding of human vision:
'Dost thou know me?' the blinded Gloucester asks of Lear.
'I remember thine eyes well enough,' Lear replies.
'Were all the letters suns, I could not see,' says Gloucester.
'O, ho, you are there with me,' cries Lear, recognizing their common plight.
'No eyes in your head, nor no money in your purse. Your eyes are in a heavy case, your purse is light; yet you see how the world goes.'
'I see it feelingly,' replies Gloucester. He has had to substitute touch for vision, but he has also learned, through suffering, that he whose senses, however perfect, are not backed by human sympathy, perceives nothing.

The authority of vision: of what you see; of what you see by feeling; of what you see by experiencing and suffering: that there is no more royal feature of human nature than vision. That, I think, is what *King Lear* is about.

But what we watch Lear experience is conversion: from a tyrannical father into the likeness of a child; from an inherited, imperious, monarchical authority into the authority of love, patience, kindness, gentleness, goodness. He it is who says to Gloucester, in revulsion against the very thing that he himself had been:

'Thou hast seen a farmer's dog bark at a beggar?'

'Ay, sir.'

'And the creature run from the cur?'

'There thou mightest behold the great image of authority: A dog's obeyed in office.'

At the outset, Lear is an old man, liable to neurotic rage: that neurosis which comes from a combination of things – old age and absolute power; the deprivation of companionship involved in being a king; the absence of equal interchange; the impossibility of any education of the will or feelings among court flatterers or subservient hypocrites. He resolves to give away his crown to be more of a man. The cure is self-prescribed – always a dangerous thing – and Lear out of office is as testily obsessed with dignity and authority as he was when he was on the throne.

But conversion takes place. In the first act, we see Lear with crown and robes and all the other marks of authority and accoutrements of office, exercising – as in the banishment of Kent – an extreme form of absolute power. In the fourth act we see him, after his buffeting by night and tempest, crowned and robed with common flowers and wayside weeds, his arrogant authority exchanged for an emerging humility; his egotism for the sympathy and wisdom of an incoherent mind; his court for the loneliness and society of beggars and the blind. But he discovers his true identity.

'The trick of that voice I do well remember,' says the blinded Gloucester, hearing the tragedy in lieu of seeing it. 'Is't not the king?' 'Ay, every inch a king!' replies Lear. But it is now that he is every inch a king – the crown of creation – now he has taken the first steps towards self-conquest; now that he has questioned his own infallibility; now that he has recognized the sufferings of others. From this it is but a step to mercy; for increasingly he sees that madness lies in dwelling on his own wrongs; salvation, in thinking of the sufferings of others.

There is nothing more moving in all of Shakespeare than Lear's prayer that is the result of his conversion. It sounds like an Elizabethan 'Shelter' advertisement:

> Poor naked wretches, wheresoe'er you are
> That bide the pelting of this pitiless storm,
> How shall your houseless heads, and unfed sides,
> Your loop'd and window'd raggedness defend you
> From seasons such as these? O I have ta'en
> Too little care of this: take physic, pomp,
> Expose thyself to feel that wretches feel,

That thou mayst shake the superflux to them,
And show the heavens more just.

The royal daughters, Goneril and Regan, needed to be converted but never were. Lear asks: 'Is there any cause in nature that makes these hard hearts?'

Cordelia – did she never need to be converted? Was she royally born, 'full of grace': the crown of creation? Shakespeare has created her in a way that combines most marvellously passion and order, innocence and maturity, defencelessness and strength. Of her it is said: 'It seemed she was a queen over her passion, who, most rebel like, sought to be king o'er her.'

And Edmund, the outsider, like the Bastard Philip (and there are bound to be outsiders in any crisis of authority) – Edmund cries, like every outsider today: 'Why should I stand in the plague of custom?' Was he then, as rebel, opening or closing himself to grace: to that royalty which is the birthright of every man?

I do not think Shakespeare would have given a rounded answer to these questions. But if you pressed him on what he was doing in all this, in all his wrestling with what is real authority, with what is regal authority, with what makes man the crown of creation – in *King Lear*, *King John*, and in so many of his plays about 'this royal throne of kings' – if you pressed him on what he was trying to say about the royalty of man, I would not be surprised were he to seize a book from his shelves, a new translation of which had become popular since the time of his birth: I would not be surprised if he were to turn to his Genevan Bible, and to the thirteenth chapter of St John's Gospel:

Before the feast of Easter,
when Jesus knew that his houre was come,
that he should departe out of this worlde unto the Father,
forasmuche as he loved his which were in the worlde,
unto the ende he loved them.
And when supper was ended
(after that the devil had put into the hart of Iudas
    Iscariot, Simon's sonne, to betray him)
Jesus, knowing that the Father had given all thynges into
his handes, and that he was come from God,
and went to God:
He riseth from supper,
and layeth aside his upper garments,
and took a towel, and girde himself.
After that, he poured water into a basyn,
and began to washe his disciples' feet,
and to wype them with the towel wherewith he was gird . . .
So, after he had washed their feet and received his
    garments,

and was set down again, he said unto them:
Wot ye what I have done to you?
Ye call me Master, and Lord,
and ye say well: for so am I.
If I then your Lord and Master, have washed your fete,
Ye ought to washe one another's fete.
For I have given you an ensample, that ye should do as I
    have done to you.

I would not be surprised if Shakespeare were to turn to this passage in his Genevan Bible, because it seems to me that the concept of conversion to humility, to love, tenderness, patience, forgiveness, to the full expression of man's royal nature, is taken from the Gospel itself – in which also, of course, the whole concept of 'seeing', of having our eyes opened, our blindness healed, is set before us by our Lord. This passage is the very pattern of him who laid his glory by, and thereby achieved a more glorious authority. There are passages in *Lear* which one could in fact almost add to the Gospels.

The king asks Kent: 'What wouldst thou?'
'Service.'
'Whom wouldst thou serve?'
'You.'
'Dost thou follow me, fellow?'
'No sir; but you have that in your
    countenance which I would fain call
    master.'
'What's that?'
'Authority.'

If to be a royal chaplain is to be invited to give counsel to Her Majesty The Queen and to all the Royal Family, I would respectfully counsel them to ponder a great deal at this time the meaning of monarchy: the meaning of kingly rule and the meaning of the royalty of human nature in Shakespeare and in the Gospels. But I would want to urge that not only upon our Royal Family, not only upon the heir to the throne, but upon us all; for at this crucial time, I believe we all need to ponder again the meaning of monarchy in order to discuss the meaning of our humanity.

14

VON STAUFFENBURG
AND BONHOEFFER

Royal Foundation of St Katharine; 23 July 1994

What sort of sermon should I preach to you on this celebratory day of the Royal Foundation of St Katharine of Alexandria?

I'm sure you all know that Armitage Robinson, Dean of Westminster and of Wells, and Bishop John Robinson's uncle, on just such an occasion as this delivered a paper, published, of course, in the *Journal of Theological Studies* for 1925, entitled 'The Passion of St Catharine and the Romance of Barlaam and Joasaph'. Well, I'm just not up to *that* kind of thing!

But this week I've been down to Chichester for a conference called 'Faith in Resistance 1933–45', and for a very moving service to commemorate the deaths of Count von Stauffenburg, who was killed when he attempted to murder Adolf Hitler, and Dietrich Bonhoeffer, and others like them, who lost their lives in resisting Hitler.

And since Saint Katharine was, according to tradition, a *martyr*, and since a *Royal* Foundation raises the whole question of the curse and blessing of establishment, I thought I would preach about the meaning and message of a *modern* martyr, like Dietrich Bonhoeffer, for the Royal Foundation of St Katharine today, and for those of us who are privileged to count ourselves friends of the Royal Foundation.

When I was in Chichester Cathedral on Wednesday, I reflected that I was only there because fifty years ago that day a very brave man had attempted to kill a murderer: to murder a murderer.

An attempt to murder someone, albeit Adolf Hitler, may seem an odd beginning for a celebratory sermon, but amongst the conspirators eventually eliminated was the theologian Dietrich Bonhoeffer – although when the attempt on Hitler's life was made, he was already in prison in Tegel, Berlin. Bonhoeffer gave a *theology* to that attempt to kill Hitler. He said it was the duty of a pastor not only to comfort the *victims* of a man who drove like a maniac in a busy street, but to try to stop him.

Bonhoeffer was born in Breslau in 1906. His father was an agnostic Professor of Psychiatry and Neurology. Home, his upper-middle-class home, meant a great deal to Bonhoeffer: father, mother, brothers and sisters. (Dietrich's brother, Klaus, was shot by the SS only a fortnight after Dietrich.) They were a close family, centred a good deal on amateur music-making of a very high quality. It was primarily within the family that Bonhoeffer's first seventeen years were spent.

The next four years are mainly a record of study: Tübingen, Rome, Berlin. But it was this young German Protestant's visit to *Rome* that gave him a longing for the Church to be united. As a Protestant student of eighteen, he spent Good Friday and Easter in Rome, and there's no doubt that his first book, his doctoral thesis, completed when he was just twenty-one, was the direct outcome of that time in Rome. He called it 'An Enquiry into the Sociology of the Church'. It was an investigation into what the word 'community' really means, and really should mean, when related to the *Church* today in the *world* today. From that first book, *Sanctorum Communio*, comes one of Bonhoeffer's most challenging phrases: 'The Church is Christ existing as community'. Had you thought here, I wonder, that you are 'Christ, existing as community'?

In 1928, Bonhoeffer went to Barcelona as a pastor to the German congregation there. In 1929, he was back in Berlin. In 1930, he went to the United States for a year, to study, and he saw for himself the grim social facts of unemployment in the Depression. He became friends with a black fellow student at Union Theological Seminary, Frank Fisher, who introduced him to the realities of life in Harlem. Bonhoeffer became a regular worker in the Sunday School of one of the Baptist churches in Harlem, and in the various clubs attached to the church, and so gained entry to people's homes, learning just what it meant to be black, then and there.

In 1931, Bonhoeffer went back to Germany, until 1933. There, the brilliant young intellectual became a local pastor. He earthed himself in things like a youth club, and confirmation classes: in the minute particulars of caring for ordinary individuals of a locality, one by one. The craft of preaching meant a lot to him, but his sermons were always closely related to the world: to the concrete situation, and to the hard economic facts of the Depression which surrounded him.

His book, *Creation and Fall*, was published then; but he was already working on another, which wasn't published until several years later: *The Cost of Discipleship*. In it, he tried to work out what should be his attitude to the Nazis, who by then were coming to power, and to his fellow German Christians, many of whom were already compromising and collaborating with the Nazis. I think it's worth pausing there and asking ourselves a question – one which we cannot answer. Had *we* been in the Germany of the Thirties, where would we have found ourselves: with the majority of the Christians of the nation, supporting Hitler, or with the small Confessional Church which risked martyrdom;

indeed, produced a crop of martyrs like von Stauffenburg and Dietrich and Klaus Bonhoeffer?

It was in 1933 that the author of *The Cost of Discipleship* paid his first visit to England: to a youth conference of the Ecumenical Movement, in Cambridge. And friendships were fashioned there which were to support and sustain him till his dying day.

He came to England for two years: to south London, as minister to the German congregation at Sydenham. He had a flat, with a grand piano, on the second floor of a Victorian house in Forest Hill. It was then that the great and courageous Bishop of Chichester, George Bell, became his guide, philosopher and friend: that bishop who was later to make the support of Christians in Nazi Germany, and refugees from Germany, his special and unremitting responsibility.

Bonhoeffer's decision to return to Germany wasn't easy. For five years he had dreamed of going to India. He had been turning to pacifism as the Christian way of coping with the problem of war, and the example of Gandhi and of Hindu spirituality had come to mean much to him. Bishop Bell wrote to Gandhi on Bonhoeffer's behalf, and at the end of 1935 Bonhoeffer received a warm letter of invitation from Gandhi inviting him to come and stay with him.

But the pressures to return to Germany became too urgent, and Bonhoeffer accepted the post of principal of a new theological college, at Finkenwalde, which had been formed by the Confessional Church: the Church in Germany which had decided there could be no compromise or collaboration with Hitler. It was a remarkable college, with a close-knit fellowship and a life founded pre-eminently upon the Sermon on the Mount. Bonhoeffer described the life of that Community at Finkenwalde in a way which has something to say to us all, in a little book called *Life Together*.

One evening a week at Finkenwalde was devoted to the discussion of topical questions. The new law in Germany relating to compulsory military service came into force on 1 May 1935. Hitler proclaimed Germany's resurgence as a military power. The ordinands listened excitedly to his speech on the radio, wondering when their turn would come to put on military uniform. Most of them looked forward to it. There was only a handful of conscientious objectors, even in the Confessional Church, at that time. And of the 150 students under Bonhoeffer during his time as principal of that seminary, more than eighty were, in fact, eventually killed in action in the Second World War.

But the days of Bonhoeffer as a pacifist were numbered. He had a brother-in-law, Hans von Dohnanyi, who was in a position to know the full truth of the Nazis' deeds: in the end, of course, the slaughter of millions of Jews, and enemies of the state, in concentration camps. Bonhoeffer and Dohnanyi were very close friends and shared much agonized thinking together. Bonhoeffer had to decide what was his Christian duty. If he really was to take opposition to Hitler seriously, it meant opposition by getting into a position of power: military power, from which at some time there might emanate a successful military plot.

The decision wasn't simple; indeed, at one stage he was tempted to evade it by fleeing to England. In March 1939, he came to London with the possibility of staying, and went on to America. But in June he wrote:

> I have made a mistake in coming to America. I must live through this difficult period of our national history with the Christian people of Germany. I will have no right to participate in the reconstruction of Christian life in Germany after the war if I do not share the trials of this time with my people. Christians in Germany will face the terrible alternative of either willing the defeat of their nation in order that Christian civilisation may survive, or willing the victory of their nation and thereby destroying our civilisation. I know which of these alternatives I must choose; but I cannot make that choice in security.

Bonhoeffer's involvement in the conspiracy against Hitler meant first a weight of dangerous and detailed secret knowledge which fomented searching questions in his conscience. Step-by-step involvement in conspiracy required the abandonment of much that Christian life seemingly demands. He could not but be involved in expert *lying*, built up into layer upon layer of closely woven deception, and, ultimately, the willingness to *murder*. Bonhoeffer never for a moment regarded these evils as anything other than what they were – evil; but he regarded them as necessary.

In 1938, he was involved in the military revolt which General von Beck was attempting to raise. He was involved with the group which in 1943 attempted to assassinate Hitler when he visited the Headquarters of the Central Army Group on the Russian Front at Smolensk, and only a week later, a second attempt at another army group centre. And, as I've said, he was involved in the preliminary planning of the attempt on Hitler's life by Count von Stauffenburg – which actually took place *after* Bonhoeffer and Hans von Dohnanyi had been arrested.

Some people in this country – I am Preacher to an Inn of Court – sometimes assume that the law is virtually above reproach. Bonhoeffer had to think out what his behaviour should be when the law is virtually the established disorder.

In May 1942, Bonhoeffer made an extremely dangerous secret visit to Sweden to meet, for the last time, the Bishop of Chichester – not least, to inform the British government of the nature and strength of the resistance movement within Germany. Neither Churchill nor Eden were interested. They were totally committed to the policy of Unconditional Surrender.

Bonhoeffer was arrested on 6 April 1943, and sent first to Tegel Prison, in Berlin, then to the Gestapo Cellars in Prinz-Albert-Strasse, then to Buchenwald, then, in the last week of his life, to Flossenburg. His last message, which he gave to a British fellow prisoner on the morning of his execution, 9 April 1945, was a message to the Bishop of Chichester: 'Tell him that for me, this is the end, but also the beginning.'

It's almost the quintessence of irony that Bonhoeffer, the conspirator, during these last three years was writing his greatest book, simply called *Ethics*. It remained unfinished when they killed him. The ambiguities, the contradictions, the tensions, the compromises, the realities of his life as a conspirator were the very material of his theology and his commitment: his commitment to Jesus Christ.

Let me just read you a paragraph or two from Bonhoeffer's writings against the background of the brief sketch of his life that I have given you. First, a passage from that last unfinished book, *Ethics*:

> In a world where success is the measure and justification of all things, the figure of Him who was sentenced and crucified remains a stranger and is at best the object of pity. The world will allow itself to be subdued only by success.
>
> The figure of the Crucified invalidates all thought which takes success for its standard.

Many of you will know that a number of Bonhoeffer's remarkable theological and devotional writings, in the form of letters, were smuggled out of prison and have been published as *Letters and Papers from Prison*. One phrase of Bonhoeffer's from those letters, more than any other, sums up his life and thought: 'I should like to speak of God not on the boundaries but at the centre . . .'

The day *after* Hitler had his lucky escape from the attempt on his life by Count Stauffenburg, Bonhoeffer wrote in one of his letters to Eberhard Bethge, his pupil, friend and, later, his biographer:

> I am still discovering right up to this moment, that it is only by living completely in this world that one learns to have faith. By this worldliness I mean living unreservedly in life's duties, problems, successes and failures, experiences and perplexities. In so doing we throw ourselves completely into the arms of God, taking seriously not our own sufferings, but those of God in the world – watching with Christ in Gethsemane. That, I think, is faith; and that is how one becomes a man and a Christian.

Only three weeks after Bonhoeffer was executed, Hitler committed suicide, and within a few days the war was over and the Third Reich was at an end. The wheel had been wrenched from the hands of the maniac.

On such a delicate thread of time, and decision, and choice, human life hangs – and falls. But no one can ever tell the results, the harvest, the resurrection that follows upon that kind of life, any more than anyone could tell the results and effects of *Jesus*' life on the first Good Friday, when it all *looked* like failure.

Sometimes people say to me, 'I wish you didn't mix politics so much with your religion.' I often want to reply: 'I'm afraid I was brought up in the days of the rise of Adolf Hitler. That taught me once and for all that politics and religion must never be separated. Dietrich Bonhoeffer and Claus von Stauffenburg were my teachers.'

And I must also say that, to my mind, one of the strongest arguments for belief in God is the heroic moral courage and faith of people like von Stauffenburg and Bonhoeffer. Where else does such faith and courage *come from*? There is no greater faith than this, that we lay down our lives for our friends.

But we lay down our life not only in *death*, but also, as Bonhoeffer did, in, for instance, working for unity with his Roman Catholic friends, with his friends of different races, like Frank Fisher, with those with whom he lived in *community* and in *Life Together*, with those he had to *confront* because of their *politics*: local and national. George Bell, Bishop of Chichester, wrote in his foreword to Bonhoeffer's *The Cost of Discipleship*:

> 'When Christ calls a man,' says Dietrich Bonhoeffer, 'he bids him come and die.' There are different kinds of dying, it is true; but the essence of discipleship is contained in those words . . . Dietrich himself was a martyr many times before he died. He was one of the first as well as one of the bravest witnesses against idolatry. He understood what he chose, when he chose resistance . . .

In the message of this modern martyr there is, I believe, a clear challenge to all of us who are associated with the Royal Foundation of Katharine, saint and martyr, of Alexandria.

15

TEILHARD DE CHARDIN

St Clement and All Saints, Hastings; 18 September 1994

I'm delighted to come here today, at the invitation of my good friend, Charles Richardson, your rector, to preach to you about someone who lived in Hastings for only a few years, but who has a street named after him, and indeed became one of the most notable Christians of our time.

Pierre Teilhard de Chardin was born on 1 May 1881, the son of an Auvergne landowner. He was educated at a Jesuit school, and took his first vows as a Jesuit in 1901. 'At last I'm a Jesuit,' he wrote to his parents. 'If only you knew the joy I feel, now that I have at last given myself completely and for ever to the Society, particularly at a time when it is being persecuted.' The three years from 1905 to 1908 he spent as a Reader in Chemistry and Physics at the Jesuit Secondary College in Cairo.

The French Jesuits had three houses in England, all within easy reach of one another. One of them was at Ore Place, on the summit of the hill above this town. While he was there, he wrote home, describing Hastings as the 'Cannes de l'Angleterre'; but he was soon saying that Eastbourne was more elegant than Hastings, and we find him visiting Winchelsea and Wadhurst, Bodiam and Battle, Rye, Folkestone, Hythe, Selsey and Chichester. But his favourite haunt was Ashburnham Park.

He was attracted to the flora as well as the fauna of Sussex, and struck up a friendship with the curator of the Hastings Museum. He was made a deacon on 26 March 1911, and wrote: 'When you make your vows, you have rather the impression of offering yourself; when you receive the grace of ordination, you should feel above all else that someone is taking hold of you.'

Teilhard was ordained priest on 24 August 1911. Bishop Amigo of Southwark ordained him, in the Chapel at Ore Place; he said his first Mass the next morning. He was four years at Ore Place. He went exploring from one quarry to another in Sussex, and the makings of the great geologist and palaeontologist that he became were already apparent.

When the First World War broke out, he was soon at the heart of the Battle of the Somme. There's a record of a Mass celebrated by Teilhard in a rat-infested shelter, so low that he was obliged to officiate while kneeling.

By that time, Teilhard the philosopher was also beginning to make his appearance. In 1918, he became a Professor of Geology in Paris. In 1923, he undertook geological expeditions in China; but increasingly the conclusions he drew from his research did not conform with Jesuit orthodoxy. In 1944, Teilhard learnt that the censors at Rome forbade the publication of his great work *The Phenomenon of Man*; and all his major writings had to go unpublished until after his death in 1955.

I simply want now to read you some passages from the writings of this great Christian. In 1918, in a meditation on the priesthood, he wrote:

As far as I can, *because I am a priest*, I would henceforth be the first to become aware of all that the world loves, pursues, suffers. I would be the first to seek, to sympathize, to toil; the first in self-fulfilment, the first in self-denial. For the sake of the world I would be more widely human in my sympathies and more nobly terrestrial in my ambitions than any of the world's servants.

The second passage comes from another meditation, which he called *The Mass on the World*, and is likely to rank among the spiritual classics of the twentieth century. He wrote it on the Feast of the Transfiguration, 6 August 1923, when he was in China:

Since once again, Lord – though this time not in the forests of the Aisne but in the steppes of Asia – I have neither bread, nor wine, nor altar. I will raise myself beyond these symbols, up to the pure majesty of the real itself; I, your priest, will make the whole earth my altar and on it will offer you all the labours and sufferings of the world.

Over there, on the horizon, the sun has just touched with light the outermost fringe of the eastern sky. Once again, beneath this moving sheet of fire, the living surface of the earth wakes and trembles, and once again begins its fearful travail. I will place on my paten, O God, the harvest to be won by this renewal of labour. Into my chalice I shall pour all the sap which is to be pressed out this day from the earth's fruits . . .

One by one, Lord, I see and I love all those whom you have given me to sustain and charm my life. One by one also I number all those who make up that other beloved family which has gradually surrounded me, its unity fashioned out of the most disparate elements, with affinities of the heart, of scientific research and of thought. And again, one by one – more vaguely it is true, yet all-inclusively – I call before me the whole vast anonymous army of living humanity; those who surround me and support me though I do not know them; those who come, and those who go; above all, those who in office, laboratory and factory, through their vision of truth or despite their error, truly believe in the progress of earthly reality and who today will take up again their impassioned pursuit of the light . . .

All the things in the world to which this day will bring increase; all those that will diminish; all those too that will die: all of them, Lord, I try to gather into my arms, so as to hold them out to you in offering. This is the material of my sacrifice; the only material you desire . . .

Receive, O Lord, this all-embracing host which your whole creation, moved by your magnetism, offers you at the dawn of a new day.

The third passage comes from an essay in which, in 1926, Teilhard tried to write down the spiritual convictions by which he had been living and preaching for many years. He called it *Le Milieu Divin*. This particular passage is for me one of the profoundest spiritual perceptions I know:

It was a joy to me, O God, in the midst of the struggle, to feel that in developing myself I was increasing the hold that you have upon me; it was a joy to me, too, under the inward thrust of life or amid the favourable play of events, to abandon myself to your Providence. Now that I have found the joy of utilizing all forms of growth to make you, or to let you, grow in me, grant that I may willingly consent to this last phase of communion, in the course of which I shall possess you by diminishing in you.

After having perceived you as he who is 'a greater myself', grant, *when my hour comes*, that I may recognize you under the species of each alien or hostile force that seems bent upon destroying or uprooting me. When the signs of age begin to mark my body (and still more when they touch my mind); when the ill that is to diminish me or carry me off strikes from without or is born within me; when the painful moment comes in which I suddenly awaken to the fact that I am ill or growing old; and above all at that last moment when I feel I am losing hold of myself and am absolutely passive within the hands of the great unknown forces that have formed me; in all those dark moments, O God, grant that I may understand that it is you (provided only my faith is strong enough) who are painfully parting the fibres of my being in order to penetrate to the very marrow of my substance and bear me away within yourself.

The more deeply and incurably the evil is encrusted in my flesh, the more it will be you that I am harbouring – you as a loving, active principle of purification and detachment. . . . Vouchsafe, therefore, something more precious still than the grace for which all the faithful pray. It is not enough that I shall die while communicating. Teach me *to treat my death as an act of communion*.

That passage was written thirty years before Teilhard died, in 1955. But a few days before he died he jotted into his notebook some casual notes, which were half prayers and half resolutions, addressed to the 'Lord of my childhood and Lord of my ending':

1. Because trials and age come from him
2. Because trials and age lead to him
3. Because trials and age will only touch me as
   measured out by him.

Accept death as it comes to me in Christ.

The difficulty in old age is to fit one's interior life to a life without a *future* for oneself. (One has one's face to the wall.)

If a crowd of immediate interests vanish (career, sympathy, influence) some higher interest must take the place of them all.

Find a place, and an *elevating* place for the approaching end, and for the decline of life (within the limits of God's will).

'To be ready' has never seemed to me to signify anything else than 'to be stretching forward'.

At the end, Teilhard was living a lonely life in New York: his works still under the ban of his Church. He said to a friend how much he would like to die on the day of the resurrection; and on Easter Sunday 1955, having made his confession on Easter Saturday, he said Mass, and then went on to High Mass at St Patrick's Cathedral. He walked through Central Park, attended a concert, and called in for tea with a woman who looked after him a good deal. He was about to sip his tea when he suddenly fell full length upon the floor. He had died – just as he had wished – on Easter Day.

Only a handful of people were present at his funeral. The ground was too frozen for him to be buried at the time, and when his body was finally buried, alongside his brothers of the Society of Jesus, no one was present. But it wasn't long before his writings began to be published, and it wasn't long after that that a vast audience of people, who appreciated him for what and who he was, began to gather all round the world.

For Teilhard de Chardin: Thanks be to God; and may we, each one of us, in our own way, follow his example.

16

HARVEST THANKSGIVING

All Saints, Milton Ernest; 25 September 1994

It's particularly lovely to be asked to preach at your Harvest Thanksgiving. You see, your vicar, Christopher Gonin, was my curate thirty and more years ago; and coming to see where he is vicar now is, of course, something of a 'harvest' in itself; but I have known and loved this parish of Milton Ernest ever since I became Canon Missioner to the Diocese of St Albans in 1972.

When I was ordained – forty-three years ago in four days' time – I received a telegram from Bishop Stephen Verney's mother, who was blind. It simply said: 'Harvest Home. Alleluia'. It's a phrase which has kept on coming back to me at different times in my ministry and I want to make it the theme of what I have to say to you this evening; but I want to couple it with a second, not dissimilar, phrase. Edith Sitwell, in a poem called 'Eurydice', wrote:

> Love is not changed by Death,
> And nothing is lost and all in the end is harvest

I've come straight to you from conducting a baptism, in the chapel of Gray's Inn, where I'm what's called the 'Preacher'. I can never baptize a baby without experiencing several emotions. As I hold the baby in my arms, and look at him or her, I am always filled with wonder. Anyone who doesn't experience wonder when they look at a baby must be soulless. But I also have a sense of relief – so much can *still* go wrong before birth: miscarriages are not infrequent, and birth itself is still a time of anxiety. So baptism is a time of relief and thanksgiving. Put it another way: at baptism I'm always tempted to say, 'Harvest Home. Alleluia'.

Last month I had to go to the Indian Ocean. I wouldn't expect many people in England to know much about Madagascar. I didn't. Until 1960, it was a French colony, but I learnt there that since 1960 the population has doubled to 12 million, and in twenty-five years' time it will have doubled again. Half of the population is under fifteen.

Of course, Madagascar is typical of many places in what we nowadays call the 'Third World'. Should you say 'Harvest Home' every time a child is born in Madagascar? Most people there are not rich – indeed, it's one of the poorest countries in the world. Should you be as glad when a child is born in Madagascar as when one is born in Milton Ernest? It's surely hard on a Madagascan mother or father not to be. But, clearly, the recent conference in Cairo on population control, with its arguments on contraception and abortion, was very relevant to Madagascar – and to us. Madagascar is still mainly an agricultural country – more even than this part of Bedfordshire. Rice is the most important commodity in Madagascar's economy. In the deep south of the country in recent years, about 40,000 people perished through famine. The paddy fields look simply marvellous where and when the harvest is good, but poverty is almost a way of life for people in parts of the country. 'Harvest Home' can always be a kind of 'I'm all right, Jack' sort of cry – 'We've got *our* Harvest in. That's all that concerns me.'

There's a verse or two in one of the lesser-known Old Testament prophets which I think we all need to ponder at Harvest Festival. The prophet Habakkuk wrote:

> Although the fig tree shall not blossom, neither shall fruit be in the vines; the labour of the olive shall fail, and the fields shall yield no meat; the flock shall be cut off from the fold; and there shall be no herd in the stalls: yet I will rejoice in the Lord, I will joy in the God of my salvation. (Habakkuk 3.17).

Habakkuk reminds us that if you only thank God for harvest when things are going well, you'll be in trouble. Your faith will be a kind of 'cupboard love'. If you only thank God when the cupboard is full, you will be bowled over when it's empty. We all need to discover a faith for when the cupboard is bare.

There is a verse in what we call the *Benedicite*, which is very relevant – we used to sing it at Mattins – and provides food for thought at Harvest Thanksgiving. The writer simply exclaims: 'O ye light *and darkness*, bless ye the Lord.'

I've told you that the person who sent me my ordination telegram – 'Harvest Home. Alleluia' – was blind, but she had learnt to say, 'O ye light *and darkness*, bless ye the Lord.' She *had* to.

William Blake, the great English poet, wrote:

> Joy and woe are woven fine,
> A clothing for the soul divine;
> Under every grief and pine
> Runs a joy with silken twine . . .
>
> It is right it should be so;
> Man was made for joy and woe;
> And when this we rightly know
> Through the world we safely go . . .

There's a harvest of pain as well as of joy in this life – for everyone. I talked, when I began, about baptism and harvest. I have on my mind at the moment Charlotte, whom I baptized five years ago and who now has leukaemia.

You may have wondered why I went to Madagascar. Well, several years ago, Bishop Trevor Huddleston asked me whether I would write his biography, which he didn't want published until after his death. I agreed to do it, and I've had to go to various places where his life has taken him: South Africa, Tanzania, where he was a bishop, the Indian Ocean, where he was archbishop – including Madagascar. But I had to begin with his birth – not many miles from here – in Bedford. When you write someone's life, it's not unlike surveying a harvest field.

Trevor Huddleston is eighty-one now, and very frail. The harvest of his life is nearly all gathered. He's diabetic, and, for that reason, when he broke a knee-cap recently it has not healed as it should. In many ways, when South Africa was freed from the scourge of apartheid it was the conclusion of his life. Nelson Mandela said: 'No Englishman has done more in his life for the black people of South Africa.' Part of him would like to dictate to God *when* he leaves this life. But we are not really in charge of that sort of decision, no matter how powerful we are! 'Harvest Home' is in God's hands and God's time, not ours. But I encourage you this evening to think of your biography, and the harvest of *your* life.

'"Harvest Home" is in God's hands,' I just said. But is it?

When I was Canon Missioner in this Diocese of St Albans, there was a young chaplain at the Abbey at St Albans, Andrew Daynes. I so well remember one Easter when he and his wife were expecting the birth of a child. When their daughter, Rachel, was born, she alas, had Down's Syndrome. Andrew and his wife have a very special relationship with that daughter of theirs. They also had a son, Jo. When I left St Albans in 1983, Jo was still a curly-haired sunny lad. Last year was his final year at school, and he went away for his year out to Zimbabwe; but while he was there he was killed in a car crash. 'Harvest Home. Alleluia.'

Andrew came to see me a few days ago. What could I say to him? Words failed. He brought with him a book of reflections he has written on Jo's death. He has called it *Jo's Book*. I much hope it can be published. It will be such a help to others. It's a book which is part of the harvest of *Jo's* life – and death – *and* of Andrew's and his wife's.

I couldn't say much to Andrew; but I did say:

> Love is not changed by Death
> And nothing is lost and all in the end is harvest

And I also quoted something Ben Jonson wrote, 400 years ago, about the different sorts of harvest of trees and flowers:

It is not growing like a tree
In bulk, doth make man better be;
Or standing long an oak, three hundred year,
To fall a log at last, dry, bald, and sere:
A lily of a day
Is fairer far in May
Although it fall and die that night,
It was the plant and flower of light.
In small proportions we just beauty see,
And in short measures life may perfect be.

We say in the Holy Communion: 'The same night Jesus wás betrayed, he took bread, and gave thanks.' It was when the harvest was the experience of betrayal that Jesus gave thanks. It was then that he made his 'Harvest Thanksgiving'. At the worst time he did the best deed. He took the material of betrayal and made it the means of our redemption. He didn't let betrayal embitter him. He gave thanks – harvest thanks. He gathered up the fragments of his life, and nothing was lost. All in the end was harvest – even betrayal. 'I, if I be lifted up,' he said, 'will draw all men unto me.'

This particular harvest I must leave one more thought with you: Haiti and harvest.

Florida is a place of great wealth: not least, of holiday homes for rich people. Haiti is an island that, so to speak, floats less than 300 miles off Florida. Of its people – nearly 7 million – only one in five can read and write; only four out of ten have clean drinking water. One in five children never reach five years of age. Most of those who live in the capital exist in absolute poverty. Some 40,000 live on the streets, lacking any shelter. 'Harvest Home' in Florida and 'Harvest Home' in Haiti are so near and yet so far. They are worlds apart. Christians at Harvest Thanksgiving cannot be content to leave things like that. Just as joy and woe are part of life's harvest, so too are justice and injustice. When we come as thankful people to harvest, we are challenged to bring joy to others and to do what we can to bring justice to them.

Some people think Harvest Thanksgiving is simply a time for rejoicing. I have always found it also a very challenging and demanding festival – just because 'All in the end is harvest'.

17

WILLIAM TEMPLE AND JUSTICE

The Celebration of Justice Service, St Mary the Virgin, Nottingham; 16 October 1994

People so often begin speeches with phrases like 'I count it a privilege to be asked to address you', that the phrase has lost almost all its power; but when faced with such a congregation of people as you are today, most of you living busy lives, and lives that involve you continuously in some of the most painful aspects of the life of our nation, no other phrase than 'I count it a great privilege' will do. And the reality of your lives lays upon me a huge obligation not simply to mouth sweet nothings and platitudes. I therefore thought long before I decided on my subject.

I first visited Nottingham in 1940, but I've been coming here regularly ever since: more recently staying in inner-city Nottingham, in Meadows, with a priest who's a friend, on my visits to the prison at Sherwood, to see another friend of mine who was an undergraduate when I was a chaplain in Cambridge in the 1950s. He has been in prison for murder for thirteen years. His appeal, which I sat through earlier this year in London, failed; but his case has now been lodged with the European Commission on Human Rights.

If my work as Preacher to Gray's Inn were not to have put me in touch with aspects of your work, those visits to my friend in Sherwood Prison are amongst the things that have; so too has my close association with the Archbishop's Commission on Urban Priority Areas.

So what shall be the subject of our thoughts together this afternoon? It so happens that in a very few days we shall be keeping the fiftieth anniversary of the death of one of the greatest men of our day and one of the greatest thinkers and teachers who ever filled the Archbishopric of Canterbury. William Temple was Archbishop of Canterbury for no more than two and a half years, yet his influence on the British people in the field of social justice, on the whole Christian Church, but particularly on ecumenical relations, was of a kind to which it would be difficult to find a parallel. So I have concluded we would be well occupied if, in memory of Temple, we were simply to reflect together about some of the things he had to say concerning justice in our society.

Many of you will know that, surprisingly, Temple was known to all and sundry as 'The People's Archbishop': surprisingly, for he was born to the purple, in the Bishop's Palace at Exeter. William's father, too, became Archbishop of Canterbury. William went to public school, to Rugby, and to Balliol College, Oxford. He was a Fellow of Queen's College, Oxford, and Lecturer there in Philosophy. However, then, did he manage to bridge the huge gap between his upbringing and the appellation 'The People's Archbishop'?

I have no doubt myself that two involvements of Temple were the ultimate instruments of the education and, indeed, emancipation of Temple: the agents of the change in him from don to 'People's Archbishop'.

The first, he himself described. While he was still at Balliol, he began to learn about the deprived and distressed parts of Oxford through Balliol Boys' Club. He also took part in the activities of the Rugby School Club at King's Cross, and in the life of three university settlements in London: Toynbee Hall in Whitechapel; Oxford House in Bethnal Green, and the Oxford Medical Mission in Bermondsey. He wrote: 'At my lodgings there was a tin bed, rather rickety, and I lay on it with anxiety, for I always "carried weight" with every assembly. There was a tin wash basin, and a chair with three legs.'

I do not myself underestimate the need of many people, if ultimately they are to do something about justice in our society, to experience as deeply as they can, as part of their continuing education, how the other half lives.

May I say, in parenthesis, that Viscount Runciman, recently Chairman of the Royal Commission on Justice, was someone to whom I was also chaplain at Cambridge, and at the end of his time there, after Eton and the Grenadier Guards, when he asked what I thought he should do next, I unhesitatingly said: 'Spend some time in the East End of London.' He did; and I am not surprised that for over twenty years since he has been Treasurer of the Child Poverty Action Group: working away at justice in and for our society.

Similarly, William Temple, after his experiences in university settlements, became closely associated with the Workers' Educational Association, of which he was president from 1908 to 1924. For several years he *thought* about the principles of liberty and justice, but his friendship with people like R. H. Tawney and Albert Mansbridge gave him the clear conviction that if you want a truly emancipated society, and a truly just society, none can be excluded from the development of their powers: education must not be for 'dons' delight' alone; it needs to expand everyone's capacities and to release everyone's gifts.

A just society would not simply involve the law and the courts. They might, in due course, have to deal with people, not least because their gifts had not been employed: because they had been virtually excluded from participation in their society. Education, for Temple, became primarily something *co-operative* that elicited the gifts of all. It was a campaign against waste: the waste of human gifts and human lives.

It was Tawney who wrote:

> The We and They complex, which is so marked even among the most virtu-ous members of the privileged classes, might have clung to Temple as a habit, even though he knew it to be damnable in principle. It could not survive co-operation with colleagues whose educational interests he shared, and whose experience of life was quite different from his own.

It was undoubtedly the Workers' Educational Association which – whatever it did to the workers – wrought the emancipation of Temple. And, may I say, I'm glad to discover what good work the Workers' Educational Association is still doing, in collaboration with the University of Nottingham. Temple became a passionate believer in educating everyone in *belonging*: in social order – and that to him was education for justice and for a just society.

Everyone of us needs to be earthed; and Temple's earthing took place not least when Lloyd George, in 1922, appointed him to the Bishopric of Manchester. Housing, health, poverty and wealth, education, moral welfare and politics became inescapable and immediate concerns for William, Bishop of Manchester – who was, of course, the bishop to Strangeways Gaol.

Two years after his appointment to Manchester, a national confer-ence centred to a striking degree on Temple, both in its inception and its achievements. It was called 'Copec': the Conference on Christian Politics, Economics and Citizenship. It made Temple one of the lead-ers, if not *the* leader, of thought on social justice and the life of the nation.

In 1928, Temple was translated to York. How he found time to prepare all the addresses he was then asked to give, God alone knows. I note, for instance, that in July 1930 he appeared before a Select Committee of the House of Commons to give evidence before it on capital punish-ment. The chairman asked: 'What would you reply to the argument that the life *taken by* the murderer was sacred, and that the sanctity of life was still further emphasized by the community *taking* the life of the murderer?' Temple replied:

> The effect of the State so respecting life as to *refuse* to take it would undoubt-edly be greater than the effect of its so condemning murder as to take the life of the murderer. The reaction of the individual to the behaviour of the community-as-a-whole is so largely imitative, rather than argumentative, that

the effect of the State taking life tends to lower the general conception of the sanctity of life.

That same year, Temple was preaching the John Howard Anniversary Sermon in St Martin-in-the-Fields.

On 19 March 1934, in the hall of Gray's Inn, Temple delivered the Inaugural Clarke Hall Lecture on 'The Ethics of Penal Action'. It is magisterial in its combination of intellectual power, eloquence and simplicity. I have time now only to quote its concluding paragraphs:

No character is fully formed till death, and there is always place for remedial and reformative treatment. But the more established the character is, the more completely may the man who has committed a crime be treated as merely criminal. Where, through immaturity of age or through lack of opportunity to develop some side of nature, the character is unstable, it is good to think more of what the man may become than of what he is. For in such a case the potentialities are actually greater than the actualities; and to treat the character as what it may be is to treat it as what in actuality it is; for it *is* chiefly potentiality. Sympathy and justice are here coincident.

It was, I think, the perception of this truth that made so vital and so effective Clarke Hall's work for young folk. He was not a sentimentalist, treating them as something other than they were. He was the true realist, who saw in them what they had it in them to become – the potentiality which was the greater part of their actual being. And in this he was profoundly Christian. According to Christianity every man truly is that which God's eternal knowledge apprehends, and this includes the effects upon him of all work of grace. We are not what we appear, but what we are becoming; and if that is what we truly are, no penal system is fully just which treats us as anything else. For this reason also it is true that though Retribution is the most fundamental element in penal action, and deterrence for practical reasons the most indispensable, yet the Reformative element is not only the most valuable in the sympathy which it exhibits and in the effects which it produces, but is also that which alone confers upon the other two the full quality of Justice. It is here that the whole system of Probation fits into the scheme; and so far as the argument of this lecture has a moral, it is a plea that the work of Probation Officers and that whole aspect of judicial procedure with which the name of Sir William Clarke Hall is so conspicuously associated, should not be regarded as a dispensable though estimable adjunct to the administration of Justice, but as an essential part of it without which it cannot be altogether just.

During the Second World War, the question 'What was to be done at the end of it?' began to be asked with urgency. Men in the Services, some of whom had not forgotten the promises of 'homes for heroes' of twenty years before, needed to be assured there would be no repetition of the aftermath of the First World War. Temple was again the convenor and chairman of a conference of great importance. The Malvern Conference of 1940 attracted some of the finest minds of Church and Society:

T. S. Eliot, Dorothy Sayers, Donald MacKinnon. Temple's writings that immediately preceded the Conference, and that were published immediately after it, are significant not least for their titles: *The Hope of a New World* (1940), *Citizen and Churchman* (1941), *Christianity and the Social Order* (1942)

On 23 April 1942, Temple was enthroned Archbishop of Canterbury. 'Where there is no vision, the people perish.' I can myself testify that Temple, in that hour, gave many of us a new vision of the just society. Temple, thou shouldst be living at *this* hour! England hath need of thee.

It was one day in October 1944 that I arrived to begin the day at my riverside wharf office, where I was then working, on Bankside, on the South Bank of the Thames, opposite St Paul's. There was already a queue of horses and carts waiting for deliveries from the wharf. I switched on the eight o'clock news – as I did first thing every day – to get the latest news of the war. The first item of that news – 26 October 1944 – was the sudden death of the Archbishop. I had to dry my eyes before I could face my wharf foreman. I knew Temple's death was a calamity not only for the Church, but for our land.

The last public engagement of William Temple in London had been to stand among the ruins of the bombed City, outside the Mansion House, opposite St Stephen's, Walbrook, to preach at a lunch-hour service.

I have no doubt that I learned from Temple in those days that it was possible even for an archbishop to be, and to remain, a prophet whom no one could silence. In those days the pundits of Threadneedle and Throgmorton Streets presumed that they alone knew the mysteries of the City of London, but Temple – theologian, leader, philosopher, pastor and prophet – was not afraid to take them on.

When the war was over, I forsook the world of the wharf, and in 1946 went to King's College, in the Strand, to train for ordination. In 1951, I was ordained in St Paul's Cathedral, where I had often heard Temple preach. It still clearly bore its battle wounds and scars: the choir and the sanctuary were perforce closed to the public; but I was proud to be ordained in St Paul's. It was William Temple above all who had taught me to take justice in our society seriously.

Christians are not people who look back simply in anger, nostalgia, or, indeed, bereavement. They look to him who is able to make us *all* prophets new inspired.

The memory of William Temple should surely today rekindle in us that flame of love which makes us long for justice; and which can renew and refresh in us our resolve to earth that justice in our world and our land today.

18

IN MEMORIAM:
RICHARD DU CANN

Gray's Inn Chapel; 6 November 1994

November is the month of memory. It began with All Saints' Day, last Tuesday, followed, next day, by All Souls' Day. So it's highly appropriate that this morning, the first Sunday of term, we should remember all those of the Inn whom we love but see no longer, and especially Richard Du Cann, who departed this life on 4 August, after the end of term.

Richard was clear that he did not want a memorial service, and his wish has been respected; but we are very glad to welcome Marley, Richard's wife, and Christian, his son, to the Chapel this morning.

I believe *we* need to remember Richard here: to reflect here thankfully on the significance of having had such a person as Richard amongst us: such a person of such skills and gifts; and to reflect on the significance of his *absence* as well as his presence.

It may seem strange for a preacher to say so – and from a pulpit – that I find that belief in God does not come easily to me, any more than it did to Richard, or does to many of us; and I find I need to reflect on the facts of life – again and again – not least on suffering and death; and to reflect particularly on those who people the world around me: in order to fashion and refashion such faith as I possess.

One thing is without doubt: 'Richard Du Cann was one of the foremost *Advocates* of his generation.' When such a statement occurs in, say, a *Times* obituary, we are apt to read it, assent to it, be thankful for it, but not quite know what to do with it: where we go from there. That is *something* of what we mean by bereavement.

But here in chapel I think we may presume to ask, reverently, some more questions. Of what significance are the gifts of someone like Richard Du Cann? Did they just happen? Did they *arise* from nowhere and *lead* nowhere? Such questions are, of course, of importance to each one of us, for they relate to others besides Richard; indeed, they relate to ourselves.

Let me put it this way: the obituary of Richard in the *Independent* quoted Judge Parry's 'Seven Lamps of Advocacy', and said that Richard Du Cann possessed them all: honesty, courage, industry, wit, judgement, eloquence, fellowship. Well, let us press the question: Where do such gifts emanate?

To my mind, faith in God begins with faith in ourselves – or, rather, faith *related* to ourselves: faith that we are more than merely complex machines – machines that are *self*-made – that have just arisen *ex nihilo*.

I was privileged in 1987 to sit at the feet of Richard at a Gray's Inn weekend in Cumberland Lodge. His lecture was so persuasive that early the next week – albeit very much a layman – I found myself eagerly buying a copy of his book *The Art of Advocacy*.

I particularly noticed that he quoted Lord Birkett as adding one more lamp to the 'Seven Lamps of Advocacy'. 'Without presence', Birkett said, 'there is nothing.' Presence. The word is not easy to define, but it is undeniably something personal: highly personal – intensely, uniquely personal. I believe in the utter uniqueness of every person, but I wonder if any profession does more to establish that than the profession of advocacy?

That Saturday morning at Cumberland Lodge, I still remember the presence, the unique presence, of Richard Du Cann. But am I right in thinking that there is a uniqueness to presence-related-to-advocacy? As a layman – I purposely use the phrase again – as a layman who has been an observer in court many times, I have observed not only the advocate in *presence*: I have observed in the advocate a unique combination, a paradoxical combination, of both involvement and detachment. However involved an advocate needs to be, he also needs to maintain an essential detachment if his judgement is to be true: and there the profession of advocacy teaches us all something about true humanity itself. As persons we all need to be both deeply involved and detached, and have that extraordinary capacity.

Perhaps as someone who has read theology now for nearly fifty years, I should say that I have often reflected on what I will call the *theology* of presence. In the New Testament it records that on one occasion people 'fell backwards to the ground' at the presence of Jesus. Presence and personal authority go together. When Jesus entered the synagogue of his home town it says that 'every eye was fastened upon him'. There was presence, there was involvement, but in Jesus there was detachment too.

I remember that morning at Cumberland Lodge Richard Du Cann saying that 'the examination and teaching of advocacy by Quintillian is still far and away the finest that has ever been written on that subject'. And in *The Art of Advocacy*, Richard quotes Quintillian as saying, 'Advocacy is the highest gift of Providence to man.' That is, of course, a bold claim. Some, no doubt, would say it is exaggeration – or, at least, hyperbole. But Richard does not query or qualify it. He quotes it with approval. And I think this morning we need to reflect on that assertion.

Richard wrote that the right of a man to be represented in the courts has been recognized since at least the year 1200. I have little doubt that in other lands and civilizations the advocate has an even more ancient ancestry. It is essentially, surely, the role of the intercessor: the man of impetrative skill.

Am I wrong, I wonder, in thinking that what has happened over the years is that one aspect, a very important aspect, of that personal care we take for one another has been professionalized? There is a sense in which advocacy is one of the 'caring professions'.

Now I've no doubt that some of you, as you think of some of the displays of advocacy you recollect over the years, or know of, may give a smile. 'Caring?' you may say to yourself: '*Carson* caring?' Well, whatever their weapons, *surgeons* are undeniably members of a caring profession.

But again I want to ask: Where does the capacity for caring, and for this aspect of caring, emanate? 'Advocacy is the highest gift of Providence to man.' Thus Quintillian. But it could be St James: 'Every good gift and every perfect gift is from above and cometh down from the Father.'

I've always loved that verse of Charles Kingsley:

> From thee all skill and science flow,
>   All pity, care and love,
> All calm and courage, faith and hope,
>   O pour them from above.

I remember recounting in this pulpit, several years ago now, how I was due to make an after-dinner speech to the Richmond Magistrates and was stuck for a story. Master Mars-Jones and Lord Edmund-Davies came to my rescue with a rattling good story concerning Caleb Evan Davies, who'd been up before some magistrates in one of the Welsh valleys, conducting his own defence. At the end of the proceedings, the Chairman of the Bench informed him that they had concluded that there was a very serious charge to answer and that they were committing Caleb Evan Davies to a higher court. 'And may I advise you', said the Chairman, 'to get all the help the law affords: solicitor, advocate, the lot!' 'Never!' exclaimed Caleb Evan Davies. 'The Lord Jesus Christ is my only Advocate.' 'None better!' said the Chairman. 'None better! But we think you need somebody *local.*'

It's a good story, but it would be easy simply to dismiss it as such. I think it underlines a rather important truth: that in the 'locality' of this world the divine justice has to be revealed *locally*: in down-to-earth situations and down-to-earth ways. By 'honesty, courage, industry, wit, judgement, eloquence, fellowship and presence'. By, indeed, *advocacy*.

And those 'Lamps of Advocacy', I would maintain, though their light *shines* in this world, are not fired and fuelled simply from *this* world. Of course, 'Now we know in part'. And how painfully true that is to those who are bereaved. But what we know and see in the here and now lights the way to another world than this.

In concentrating on the gifts of Richard Du Cann as an *advocate*, there is just one danger – even after what I've said about the very personal gifts of an advocate such as 'presence'. It is possible to think of an advocate – even one of the finest of advocates – as *nothing but* an advocate. But if an advocate is a person, he is also, as a person, husband and father, and subject to suffering and mortality – as, alas, we know all too well Richard was.

But it won't quite do to attribute, say, the 'Lamps of Advocacy' to providence but make no comment as to where that suffering, which was Richard's, and his mortality came from.

And I would be failing in my duty in this place if I did not say that one of the titles of Christ himself which I most treasure is simply that word 'Advocate'. 'We have an Advocate with the Father, Jesus Christ the Righteous,' wrote St John. To believe that makes, of course, huge demands on faith; it means that the loving Providence which gives us our gifts – and gave Richard his – did not stop there, but is to be seen not least in that human suffering Jesus shared and that mortality which he shared with us. So that when we leave this world we are received into the hands of a loving compassionate Providence who is our Beginning and our End and *our Advocate*, who ever lives to intercede for us.

It is, surely, not unreasonable and not surprising that any gifts any of us human beings may have as an *advocate* do but reflect something in the very nature of him who gave those gifts their origin.

19

REMEMBRANCE DAY 1994

Gray's Inn Chapel; 13 November 1994

For most of us who meet here this morning, coming to make our annual act of Remembrance is something we *want* to do. We are, in a sense, glad to be here. Being here is a duty we recognize, and would not want to neglect. For many, however, Remembrance Day has lost its meaning – or much of it. Maybe, by reason of their years and their youth, it never had one.

It is with no sense of self-righteousness that *we* are here. As I say, we want to be here. We are here to discharge a debt – or to do something towards discharging it, a debt that can never wholly be paid.

Each year, nevertheless, we recognize our memory fails a little and our memories fade a little. And yet, each year, some anniversary seems to fall which renews and refreshes our memory. This year there was in June the celebration of fifty years since the Allied invasion of Normandy; and, more recently, there has been the commemoration of fifty years since Arnhem. And I know that with us this morning there are those who participated in one or both of those events, and their memories of them are all too vivid.

But, of course, we are here primarily to remember those who did not return from such events: those who might have been the light and lamp of our generation, which now halts and stumbles along its uncertain way. Alas, they were removed from our earth and our company, and we from them.

As I say, there are, each year, particular events which keep their memory green: this year, Arromanche and Arnhem. But besides the particulars of Remembrance, I think I am right to say that Remembrance Day always involves a *general* commemoration, which is nothing less than the commemoration of the glory and the shame of man.

In the wars we commemorate this day, there was indescribable horror and the depths of man's inhumanity to man, and – at the same time – the revelation, in courage, bravery and endurance, of the heights of our humanity.

The art and literature associated with war portrays both the particular events of war and the more general glory and shame. This year, I have come across two pieces of writing that arise from the wars that we commemorate today, which have both meant much to me.

It is, this year, the centenary of the birth of J. B. Priestley. Some of us will remember with gratitude his rich Yorkshire voice and the genius of his 'Postscripts' after the nine o'clock news on the Sunday evenings of the dark days of 1940, when he spoke both to and for the nation.

But it was only returning to Priestley's writings, because of the centenary of his birth, that revealed him to me as one of the great literary men of the First World War. And it seemed not inappropriate that I should read to you today some paragraphs from those Great War reminiscences and reflections entitled *Margin Released*. Priestley wrote:

It was not long before our own B Company, with a nominal fighting strength of 270, had been reduced to a grim and weary seventy. Two hundred men had gone, somehow and somewhere, with nothing to show for it.

Spring came suddenly, and between the pounded and bloody chalk of the front lines and the mining area in the rear, there would be glimpses, good enough for Pissarro and Sisley, of fields bright with poppies and lanes beginning to smell of honeysuckle. When we were given a few days' rest, we went back to a mining village that had an enormous slag-heap. Far away, behind the ridge they held, the Germans had a great naval gun that had the range of this village. The shell it fired was of such a monstrous calibre that you could easily hear it coming, like an aerial express. We would be hanging about, smoking and talking, enjoying the sunshine and the quiet, when suddenly we would hear this monster coming. There was only one safe place, behind the slag-heap, and everybody would run for it pell-mell. *Shirrr-brirrr-bump*! There it went, and we would come from behind the slag-heap and see the smoke clearing and another six houses gone. Fortunately that gun did no night-work, and we did not really mind it during the day. Up in the line, what we did mind, what soon began to get us down, were the *Minenwerfers*, the big trench-mortars; and at Souchez we always appeared to have the *Minenwerfer* specialists against us. Often we asked for their attention; not us, the ordinary infantry who had to stay in the front line, but the Brigade, the Division, the Corps, the Army. What happened all too often was that our specialists would rush their Stokes guns up into the support trenches, blast away for a quarter of an hour, and then hurry off with their infernal things to where their transport was waiting. Pampered and heartless fellows – this is how we regarded them – lunatic experts who had to interfere, off they went to some back area, to roofs and beds and *estaminets*, beer and wine, chips and eggs; while we poor devils, left behind in holes in the ground, now had to face the anger of the Boches they had been strafing. The *Minenwerfer* teams got to work on us. Up and then down came those monstrous canisters of high explosive, making hell's own din when they landed, blasting or burying us. If there was any infantryman who was not afraid of these things, who was not made uneasy by any rumours they would shortly be arriving, I never met him. Perhaps because they were such short-range affairs, perhaps because if you were on the alert, looking and listening hard, you could just dodge them, perhaps because they made such a hellish row, they frightened us more than bullets, bombs, shells of all calibres. And in and around Souchez we crouched below a nest of them.

So one day it had to happen. It was June now, hot again, thirsty weather, a lot of chalk dust about, and we were in the front line on a beautiful morning. The platoon rations had just come up. I sent Private O'Neill down the communication trench to bring up some water – and sixteen years went by before we saw each other again. I helped a young soldier, who had only just joined us out there, to take the rations into a dugout, not a deep dugout but a small one hollowed out of the parapet. In this dugout I began sorting out the bread, meat, tea, sugar, tinned milk, and so on, to give each section its proper share, a tricky little job. I had done it many times before, hardly ever to anybody's complete satisfaction; but on this morning I suspect that it saved my life. After the explosion when everything had caved in, nobody was certain I was there, but several fellows knew the platoon rations were in there somewhere: that stuff would have to be dug out. There I was then, deciding on each section's share, when I heard a rushing sound, and I knew what it meant and knew, though everything had gone into slow motion, I had no hope of getting away before the thing arrived. Just as on earlier and later occasions when I have thought all was up, the first shrinking in terror was followed, as I went into the new slow time, by a sense of detachment. I believe from what I learnt long afterwards that the *Minenwerfer* landed slap in the trench, two or three yards away. All I knew at the time was that the world blew up.

I do not remember how and by what route I travelled from the front line at Souchez to the military hospital at North Evington, a suburb of Leicester. Any man who was ever around, not as close as I was but, let us say, about three times the distance, when a big German trench-mortar went off, will agree that I was lucky to be carted away in one piece.

I think you'll agree that is a most remarkable reminiscence of the First World War.

The second piece of writing is also about the First World War. I shall not quote at length from it, but I must tell you that I have read no other novel to equal it in the last ten years and more. It's called *Birdsong*, and it's written by Sebastian Faulks, who's in his early forties, and who was for a time the literary editor of the *Independent*. His book is, as I say, about the First World War, though he was born more than thirty years after the Armistice. So if some ignore Remembrance Day by reason of their age, that is not true of all. And I mention this particular book because it seems to me to bring a new dimension to the word 'remembrance'.

Faulks is calling to mind something he never experienced at first hand, yet his writing about the Great War is so terrifyingly real that no writing has ever made me more feel I had myself experienced the horrors of bombardment, of trench warfare, and of life in the tunnels under the front lines of a battlefield like the Somme. One reviewer wrote: 'This is indeed fiction of the highest class, deeply impressive, continually moving – and not least as a meditation on the way the more terrible horrors slide away so easily from the collective human memory.' I have no hesitation in commending *Birdsong* to you this Remembrance Day – and commending it to you from a pulpit; for it will, I believe, deepen the understanding of Remembrance of any and all who read it.

Let me read you just a brief extract:

> Price was reading the roll call. Before him were standing the men from his company who had managed to return. Their faces were shifty and grey in the dark.
>
> To begin with he asked after the whereabouts of each missing man. After a time he saw that it would take too long. Those who had survived were not always sure whom they had seen dead. They hung their heads in exhaustion as though every organ of their bodies was begging for release.
>
> Price began to speed the process. He hurried from one unanswered name to the next. Byrne, Hunt, Jones, Tipper, Wood, Leslie, Barnes, Studd, Richardson, Savile, Thompson, Hodgson, Birkenshaw, Llewellyn, Francis, Arkwright, Duncan, Shea, Simons, Anderson, Blum, Fairbrother. Names came pattering into the dusk, bodying out the places of their forbears, the villages and towns where the telegram would be delivered, the houses where the blinds would be drawn, where low moans would come in the afternoon behind closed doors; and the places that had borne them, which would be like nunneries, like dead towns without their life or purpose, without the sound of fathers and their children, without young men at the factories or in the fields, with no husbands for the women, no deep sound of voices in the inns, with the children who would have been born, who would have grown and worked or painted, even governed, left ungenerated in their fathers' shattered flesh that lay in stinking shellholes in the beet-crop soil, leaving their homes to put up only granite slabs in place of living flesh, on whose inhuman surface the moss and lichen would cast their crawling green indifference.
>
> Of 800 men in the battalion who had gone over the parapet, 155 answered their names. Price told his company to dismiss, though he said it without the bark of the parade ground; he said it kindly. They attempted to turn, then moved off stiffly in new formations, next to men they had never seen before. They closed ranks.

Finally, I want to turn away from literature to another vehicle of Remembrance. This last August I was in Madagascar, and stayed a few days in Antsiranana, formerly Diego Suarez, which boasts one of the finest natural harbours in the world. Until 1973 it served as a French naval base. During the Second World War – in 1942 – it was wrested from its Vichy defenders by British soldiers (including many from British possessions) with considerable loss of life.

On Saturday, 20 August, this year, at midday, I visited the Commonwealth War Graves Commission Cemetery at Diego Suarez. All such cemeteries I find exceedingly moving. There are always names familiar and unknown. The average age is always so young, and the love of those bereaved is always so simply and so poignantly expressed.

In that cemetery at Antsiranana there were 315 graves, all beautifully kept. There was one Malagasy gardener to look after the cemetery and tend the graves. He was most helpful and courteous to us. That 'foreign field' was a graveyard not only for English but for South Africans, East Africans, Indians and others; but as I walked slowly from grave to grave I could only think of each home that had received the same terrible news.

The midday sun shone brilliantly on that cemetery, but nothing could dispel a dark cloud within me: the overwhelming sense of the waste of war. Those memorials made me pray for each person named on each of those stones and for each of their bereaved families. And there and then I resolved that on Remembrance Day this year – when it came – I would remember *by name* those members of our Inn who are *named* on our War Memorial. It is, I thought, the least we can do at Remembrance. So will you remain seated while I simply read those names now:

From the First World War:

EARDLEY APTED
WALTER DOUGLAS ASTON
ARNOLD HARDING BALL
PHILIP LEO BEARD
WILLIAM GEORGE BEAUMONT
  BEAUMONT-EDMONDS
FREDERIC ERNEST BODEL
FRANCIS MOULL STORER
  BOWEN
THOMAS BROWNRIGG
JOHN ICELY COHEN
JOHN CHARLES EDWARD
  DOUGLAS
ARTHUR DUNNAGE
GEORGE THOMAS EWEN
ERNEST ALFRED FAUNCH
HERBERT MARION FINEGAN
ALFRED HAROLD FRY
FRANK WILLIAM GEORGE
HENRY CULLEN GOULDSBURY
NORMAN ERNEST JASPER
  HARDING
HERBERT PHILIP HILTON
GODFREY HUDSON
WALTER HIRSCH
  HURSTBOURNE
FREDERIC HILLERSDON

KEELING
LAURENCE HENRY KENNY
JAMES KEOGH
NISSIM LISBONA
GEOFFREY MASTERS
MAUNG MAUNG
ALBERT BARR MONTGOMERY
SYLVESTER NORTH EAST
  O'HALLORAN
JOHN RIDLEY PRENTICE
LESLIE WILLIAM WHITWORTH
  QUIN
CYRIL WILLIAM RENTON
WILLIAM KINGSLEY REYNOLDS
COSMO GEORGE ROMILLY
CHARLES FREDERIC RORKE
REGINALD HENRY SIMPSON
DANIEL PIKE STEPHENSON
ARTHUR JOHN NEWMAN
  TREMEARNE
ELIAS TREMLETT
ALFRED COPLESTONE WALDEN-
  VINCENT
HENRY PERCY WEBER
ERIC CRAWCOUR WILSON
COLIN BASSETT WRONG
JAMES DAWBARN YOUNG

And from the Second World War:

CYRIL FLOYD BENNETT
COLIN CAMPBELL BLAIR
JAMES GORDON CAMPBELL
JOHN LESLIE CAMPBELL
PETER ALAN CARTER
BIBHATI BHUSAN CHATTERGEE
GERAINT CLEMENT-DAVIES
CAMPBELL CRICHTON-MILLER
JOHN MICHAEL DALTON
DONALD CHARLES
  FARQUHARSON
FREDERICK ANTHONY PORTER
  FAUSET
BASIL ANTHONY FLEMING
ESMOND BIRCH GRAHAM-
  LITTLE
MAURICE GROVES
JOHN CECIL ALISTER HAYES
HENRY GRAHAM HEAD
LESLIE MARTIN HERBERT
FRANCIS EVERARD HODGSON
JOHN REGINALD JONES
HENRY WILLIAM KEARNEY

GEOFFREY YALE GLYN LLOYD
RICHARD CONNELL MANNING
HOWARD NORMAN MARLOW
MICHAEL HARRINGTON
  MATTHEWS
JOHN DESMOND MULHOLLAND
HENRY NEVILLE DASHWOOD
  RUSSELL
MICHAEL CAMPBELL
  SHAWCROSS
MARTIN TRYINGHAM
  STEPHENS
HECTOR GARRICK PILLING
HENRY DEREK RIPLEY
WILLIAM FROTHINGHAM
  ROACH
GEORGE REICHER ROYDE
HOWARD BARRETT TANNER
THOMAS FRANCIS TODD
EDWARD ROGER WAKEFIELD
REGINALD GEORGE WEIGHILL
STANLEY REGINALD WELSON

20

RELIGION IN BRITAIN SINCE 1945

Westminster Abbey; 4 December 1994

Sermons can take many forms, and my sermon this evening may end up rather like a book review. But it'll be none the worse for that, because the book is so good and, in my judgement, is so appropriate for a sermon here in Westminster Abbey. You see, the book – which has just come out – is called *Religion in Britain since 1945* and is subtitled 'Believing Without Belonging'. It's published in a series of books called 'Making Contemporary Britain', and its author is Grace Davie, who lectures in sociology at the University of Exeter and received much praise for her earlier book called *Inner City God*.

You may ask, 'Why do you think such a book is appropriate for a sermon for us who gather in Westminster Abbey?' – many of whom come from outside Britain. And I'd answer by saying, 'Such a book could possibly make you compare and contrast your situation where you come from with ours here in Britain – if you come from outside Britain.' And if you ask, 'How does sociology contribute to a sermon in Westminster Abbey?' I would answer, 'I believe it can help us to map out how – and indeed where – things are. It can spell out some of the important questions which are clearly on people's minds today: questions which may not have been there for earlier generations.' So I shall not apologize if my sermon sounds – as I say – a bit like a book review. That's exactly what it is!

Grace Davie's book begins with an Introduction which spells out the purpose of the book; and on page two of the Introduction there's an important question: 'Why is it that the majority of British people – in common with many other Europeans – persist in believing, but see no need to participate with even minimal regularity in their religious institutions?' Most people in this country, the book makes clear – whatever their denominational allegiance – express their religious sentiments by staying away from, rather than going to, their places of worship. On the other hand, relatively few British people have opted out of religion altogether: out-and-out atheists are rare.

The Introduction goes on: 'Not only do the churches represent a minority of British people, but the members that they do attract remain disproportionately elderly and female, and politically Conservative in their voting habits.' But if that is so, the question is then posed: 'Why, then, has at least a section of the ecclesiastical leadership not only assumed an increasingly active role in public life, but one that has, through the 1980s at least, been critical of a Conservative government?'

A few pages later, still in the Introduction, there's this statement: 'There can be no doubt that there are considerable variations in religious behaviour (in both believing and belonging) between different social classes, between different racial groups and between men and women. Class, race and gender are – in addition to nation or region – crucial to our understanding of the religious behaviour of contemporary Britain.'

Finally, a very pointed question is thrown out which is not irrelevant to us in Britain: 'What about the disturbing evidence of fundamentalism world wide?'– people, for instance, who take the Bible literally. Behind that question is the very important question for many an enquiring mind: 'How seriously do we take the subject of truth?'

In the next chapter, I noticed a rather important aside: 'The British are more moralistic than one might expect – taking seriously those of the Ten Commandments that have a moral rather than a religious reference.' Meaning, for instance, 'Thou shalt not commit adultery' rather than 'Thou shalt love the Lord thy God with all thy heart and mind and soul'. And then there is this rather fascinating comment:

> Virtually all voluntary associations have been finding it difficult in the last few decades to attract and retain members. In other words, 'belonging' has been simultaneously losing its popularity in religion and in other fields as well. The split between believing and belonging is therefore part of a broader pattern of change which happens to affect religious organisations amongst others. It's not a problem unique to religion and does not necessarily arise from the inner dynamics of religious organisations alone.

That particular chapter is entitled 'A Rapidly Changing Context', and it refers, for instance, to the growing numbers of elderly; and the changing role of women in contemporary society – most women expecting to enter the labour force at some point in their lives – and the effects that this and other factors have on believing and belonging. The dramatic increase of divorce is, of course, another factor, so too is, of course, the arrival of significant numbers of black Christians, and Muslims, Sikhs and Hindus.

The next chapter is on the 'Sacred and the Secular'; and the period 1970 to 1990 is entitled significantly: 'The re-emergence of the sacred'; then there's another important section on 'Religion in a consumer society' – and on what characterizes it. I suggest we should be particularly sensitive – not uncritically so – to all who have in any way been helped by the charismatic movement or by what is called New Age spirituality.

I found myself stopping and thinking for quite a while over one particular paragraph of the book. It's a quote from a well-known journalist, Clifford Longley. He says:

> There is an impatience about journalism which attracts a certain sort. But Religion is often a waiting game: the only view which makes sense is the long view. Newspapers are bound to be concerned with the ripples-on-the-surface of life; religion is about the deep ocean currents which are often completely hidden and which move enormous masses of water over long distances very slowly. But we know, particularly in Britain astride the Gulf Stream, that deep ocean currents are crucial to the overall climate, while making little difference to today's weather.

The chapter I found most interesting was the one headed 'The Ordinary Gods of British Society'. I wonder what you think of this statement: 'Religious belief, when not associated with active membership of a church, tends to be associated with superstitious belief while church attendance tends to be antithetical to superstition.'

Grace Davie pays special attention to the significance of religious broadcasting and its relation to believing without belonging. The audience figures for *Songs of Praise* and *Highway* often exceed those for *Match of the Day*, and the opinion poll of *Today* listeners discovered unexpected support for the religious three minutes just before 8 o'clock every morning on Radio 4. But undoubtedly, religious broadcasting has a somewhat uneasy relationship with the institutional churches. Grace Davie calls it 'Believing without Belonging – par excellence'.

In the next chapter, the question is pressed: 'Why is it that women are more religious than men?' Though I'm glad that question is immediately revised to 'Why are women's religious sensitivities different from those of men?' because I well remember how as a parish priest in Camberwell, when I knocked on doors to do baptism visits, if the husband opened the door and saw my dog-collar, he'd invariably and immediately take fright and say something like, 'Hang on, vicar, I'll just go and get the wife.' He assumed religion was the wife's department.

Grace Davie movingly says:

> My own inclination is to favour those explanations which underline the proximity of women to birth and death. Understandably, these moments continue – even at the end of the twentieth century – to evoke echoes of the sacred, for they must, by their very nature, bring to mind questions about the reasons for existence and about the meaning of life itself. Very few women give birth without any reflection about the mysteries of creation and very few people watch someone die (especially a close relative) without any thought at all about why that person lived or what might happen to them after death. It's true that medical science has, up to a point, altered the way in which these events are perceived. It's usually the case, for example, that birth and death now take place in a medical rather than a domestic environment, and

both states will be defused in medical parlance. But the giving of birth remains, despite everything, one of the most profound experiences of a woman's life. . . .'

One of the most serious and important statements in the whole book is the simple sentence in relation to church-going: 'By far the most common group to be unrepresented were young people in general, and in particular teenagers.' There, surely, is a subject for your mission agenda which must not be evaded or treated simplistically.

There are sections of the book on both religion in schools and on religious education – which of course have something to say to the question of the absence of teenagers from congregations. There's a section on 'Church and State' and another on 'Religious Professions, Lay and Ordained'. It would be easy to dismiss the subject of 'Church and State', but in an Abbey like this, that would surely be unwise! And it's worth saying, the report *Faith in the City* – the Archbishop's Commission on Urban Priority Areas – achieved something by working with the government as well as by its criticisms of the government.

But, finally, let me read you one of the last paragraphs of the book which I think is particularly worth pondering.

We in England live in the chill religious vapours of northern Europe, where moribund religious establishments loom over populations that mostly do not enter churches for active worship even if they entertain inchoate beliefs. Yet these establishments guard and maintain thousands of 'houses of God', which are markers of space and time. Not only are they markers and anchors, but also the only repositories of all-embracing meanings pointing beyond the immediate to the ultimate. They are the only institutions that deal in tears and concern themselves with the breaking points of human existence. They provide frames and narratives and signs to live by, and offer persistent points of reference. They are repositories of signs about miraculous birth and redemptive sacrifice, shared tables and gift-giving; and they offer moral codes and exemplars for the creation of communal solidarity and the nourishment of virtue. They are places from which to launch initiatives which help sustain the kind of networks found, for example, in the inner city; they welcome schools and regiments and rotary clubs; they celebrate and commemorate; they are islands of quietness; they are places in which unique gestures occur of blessing, distribution and obeisance; they offer spaces in which solemnly to gather, to sing, to lay flowers, and light candles. They are – in Philip Larkin's phrase – serious places on serious earth.

21

THE GLORY OF
NORWAY

Westminster Abbey; 11 December 1994

'And they shall bring the glory and honour of the nations into it.'
Revelation 21.26

When, some weeks ago, I heard that there would be a Norwegian choir with us this evening, I was of course delighted, but also a little daunted. I began to wonder the best way of fitting such an offering into our evening service. But as I thought, a verse from the Book of the Revelation of St John the Divine came into my mind. In speaking of the New Jerusalem it says: 'And they shall bring the glory and honour of the nations into it.' And I thought: what more appropriate place than Westminster Abbey to think of 'the glory and honour of the nations', and suppose we were to think together this evening of 'the glory and honour' of Norway in particular, surely all of us present, wherever we come from, would be greatly profited. And so I began to think very personally of what 'the glory and honour' of Norway has meant to me in the last half century or so. And this evening I shall simply share with you the fruits of my thinking – for what they are worth.

Long before I was ordained, when I was a boy of fourteen, I went out to work at a shipping firm on the Thames which specialized in Norwegian shipping. It was 1939, the very beginning of the Second World War. One of my jobs was to take ships' captains to the Custom House. When Norway was invaded, in 1940, I remember looking after one particular captain, Einar Tvedt, who had been cut off from his family by the invasion, and was of course very greatly distressed.

It wasn't long before the King of Norway, King Haakon, nearly seventy years old, arrived in England to lead and continue Norwegian resistance in any way he could. He was a man greatly revered and respected here in England – as indeed we respected all Norway's continued costly and courageous resistance. Perhaps it was in part this war-time atmosphere which gave me a particular affection for the people of Norway, and made me grow particularly fond of the Grieg A Minor Piano Concerto. I even bought the piano score and began to try to play it.

If you say 'Norway' in England, and think of its 'glory and honour', to many it will immediately speak of Edvard Grieg, who in turn, through his music, will bring the picturesque folk heritage of Norway to mind. Perhaps it's worth saying, especially after the European vote, that Grieg studied at the Leipzig Conservatoire, and then for several years made Copenhagen his main base. But Grieg's songs, sonatas and orchestral suites undoubtedly speak eloquently of the 'glory and honour' of Norway.

It was in 1945, when I was twenty and a student, that I saw at the New Theatre, St Martin's Lane, a wonderful production of Ibsen's *Peer Gynt*. It was a new translation, and had a cast beyond compare: Dame Sybil Thorndike as Aase; Ralph Richardson as Peer Gynt; Laurence Olivier as the Button Moulder. The incidental music was the great music of Grieg.

I was simply bowled over by the performance. I can still see the young Ralph Richardson, as Peer, putting Sybil Thorndike, as Aase, on the roof of the farm-house. I can still hear Solveig singing her song. But, most of all, I can see Laurence Olivier, the Button Moulder, meeting Peer – Everyman – at the end of his journey, at the crossroads; and I can hear him saying to Peer: 'You were going to be a shining button on the world's waistcoat; but your loop gave way.' No line in a play had meant more to me up till then. And I have to say, I interpreted the remark somewhat personally!

But what that production of *Peer Gynt* did to me was to make me vow to see every Ibsen play I could, whenever I could: *A Doll's House*, which occupied three hours on television only last night, *Ghosts*, *An Enemy of the People*, *The Master Builder*, *Brand*, *Hedder Gabler*, *Little Eyolf*, and so on. Most of Ibsen's plays seemed to me to deal with a major and controversial social question: local government and corruption; marriage breakdown. They all helped me on my own Gyntian journey of discovering my own humanity, and what it means to exist in society.

But again, it interested me that Ibsen went into voluntary exile from Norway, to Europe: to Rome, Dresden and Munich, for nearly thirty years, from 1864 to 1892. The Norwegian 'glory and honour' in Ibsen seemed inseparable from Europe.

There seemed to me little doubt that Ibsen effected a revolution in the world of drama, and that great drama could be one of the most important instruments to help each one of us discover our divine humanity.

But nearly twenty years later, in 1961, Norway made its mark on my life in a quite different way: in a way which was dramatic but had nothing to do with the theatre. One of my friends and fellow theological students at university had a younger brother who became a school teacher. I was very close to the whole family. The teacher son took with him to Norway a party of schoolboys. Alas, their plane crashed on its approach to Stavanger, and all the children and all their teachers were killed. Few events in my life – in peace-time – brought home to me the precariousness of life, even of young life. It was a terrible disaster; yet the family remember to this day – and I was in touch with one of them only ten days ago – the kindness with which the people of Stavanger looked after the relatives of those involved in that tragedy. That kindness I think of thankfully this evening when I think of 'the glory and honour' of Norway.

It was in 1977 that I myself visited Norway. I had to go to a conference of Scandinavian theologians. The conference was held at a wonderful conference centre that had once been a Benedictine monastery, on an island off Stavanger: Utstein Kloster. It's an island of unbelievable beauty. I learnt there a great deal about Norway's complex religious history: one that is more ancient than any of its religious denominations.

After the conference, a young priest friend of mine flew out from England to join me, and we went to stay at one of Norway's oldest hotels, at Utne, not far from the home of Grieg. When I came back to England, I was asked to broadcast on the BBC World Service what that stay in Norway had meant to me. Here are some sentences from that broadcast:

We walked up from the quay at Utne, leaving the sound of the ferry's bell behind us, and the white church, and the red-roofed hotel, and the slate roofs of the village below us. For a while, the cars, disgorged from the ferry, raced madly by, pressing us to the edges of the mountain road; but soon there was a winding track that took us away from the road, and set us above it, high above the blue fjord, among the apple trees laden with rosy apples, and the plum and the pear and the cherry trees, with a clear view to the other side of the fjord, to the great turned-out pudding of a mountain opposite. Then fir, and birch, and red-berried rowan began to enclose us, and it was dark beneath them – though sheer below there were glimpses of the fjord, through the branches and the slender trunks of the trees. After an hour's climbing I knew the time would soon come when I could go no further, and Tom would have to go on alone. He went on, to spy out the land, but had not gone for long when he was back, bright-eyed, coaxing me to keep going a little longer, and to climb just a little higher, to see what he had seen. We went on – and I was glad of his hand at one point to help me higher than I could have climbed by myself. Then, suddenly, there was the clearing he had seen: an open meadow; and, beyond the meadow, stretching miles into the distance, and merging into distant clouds, a blazingly clear fjord. It stretched for thirty or forty miles, with, either side, fold upon fold of mountain, crowned sometimes with the snows of a glacier. We sat there, silently, gazing into the distance. Then Tom got up to climb towards the summit. He was gone for an hour, and when he returned we sat there silent again for another hour or so, just gazing at the view. Then Tom stretched himself out on the grass in the sun's fierce glare, and slept, till an old peasant woman with her dog came to gather the dried hay of the meadow, and it was time to go down the mountain and retrace our steps towards Utne.

I shall never forget that view. It filled me with wonder.

That was on holiday in Norway, and it was a particularly romantic view. But the sense of wonder can take hold of us at all sorts of times . . . when I take time to observe another person – a friend, perhaps, or a so-called delinquent; or when I look at the lights at night on a block of flats; or when I take time to think how marvellously even I myself am made – when I take time to wonder.

Wonder, I believe, lies at the very heart of religion: at the very heart of life.

On that visit to Norway I could not *stop* wondering at what surrounded me. The fjords are, of course, marvellous, but I found them also frightening. They made me wonder at the unbearable billion years that it had taken to fashion them; at the subterranean fire that made all molten with primeval violence; at the engulfing tide that froze a whole world – and then at our Ice Age ancestors. It's odd, but understandable, how we tourists from other countries scale down history and mountains to snapshots which we can cope with. We seem to have to reduce 'the glory and honour' to the size of, say, our camera!

I saw Norway in summer and mostly in sunlight, but I was aware that the sun would disappear for much of the year; and faith needs always to cope with darkness as well as light. Which leads me to my last perception of 'the glory and honour' of Norway.

An American friend, a few years ago, asked me to look after another American who was coming to live in London. She was the widow of a Norwegian ship-owner. Her name was Larson, Patricia Larson. We became great friends. Her house was both a home and a marvellous art gallery; but all the paintings she possessed were by one artist, Edvard Munch.

I don't suppose any Norwegian would want the paintings of Munch to represent all 'the glory and honour' of Norway. His best-known painting, 'The Scream', has at its centre a harrowing, terror-ridden figure. In his diary Munch wrote: 'I was walking along a path with two friends. The sun was setting. I felt a breath of melancholy. Suddenly the sky turned blood-red. I stopped, and leant against the railing, deathly tired: looking out across flaming clouds, that hung like blood and a sword over the deep blue fjord and town. My friends walked on. I stood there, trembling with anxiety, and I felt a great infinite scream pass through nature.'

Munch painted what he felt and saw and heard. The person in the picture is screaming – as well as the colours. Either as a painting, or as a print in black and white, it's not a comfortable work of art. You can't put it on the living-room or bedroom wall. In fact, in Munch's own handwriting, in the upper red area of the painting, was written: 'Can only have been painted by a madman'. That painting often comes into my mind when I hear one particular verse from the prophet Isaiah: 'The Voice said "Cry"! And he said, "What shall I cry?" All flesh is grass . . .'

There are lots of people in this world who feel at some time or other they simply must cry out loud. Sometimes, of course, they are mad. Sometimes they just cannot contain the pain and anxiety they are having to bear. Sometimes it's not their own pain that makes them cry out, but the terrible things they have to observe in the world around them: starving, or homeless, or ill-treated children, perhaps.

Although sermons sometimes seem stuffy, I've always felt that a preacher is meant to cry out – at least from time to time. The voice says 'Cry!' – and you know you have to. Sometimes you have to be a voice for those who otherwise would have no voice of their own.

And alongside Munch's picture of 'The Scream', another comes into my mind. It's of someone comfortably off – man or woman – sitting in, say, the corner of a railway carriage, reading the morning paper. It's full of tragedy, but they're simply turning the pages as though there was nothing in them worth noting.

I think there's much of 'glory and honour' in Munch's paintings. They are most of them about love and death. And again, to assess and value Munch without the influences he met in Paris, like Gauguin, would be quite impossible. Munch and Europe are inseparable.

This evening, I've tried to set before you one person's reflections on the glory and honour of one nation, in some of its music, drama, art – and kindness; and perhaps that kindness is summed up and symbolized by the Christmas tree Norway so generously gives to us for Trafalgar Square each year. Perhaps what I have said will spur you to reflect on the glory and honour of your nation – whatever it may be – and on my text: 'And they shall bring the glory and honour of the nations into it' – that is, into Jerusalem.

22

JOSEPH AND JESUS

Gray's Inn Chapel; 29 January 1995

This first Sunday of term in the New Year always presents the Preacher with problems. Christmas now seems rather a long way away, yet it's the first time we've met since Christmas.

It's still the season of Epiphany, and this year it's the fourth Sunday after Epiphany; but part of me feels it's about time the Wise Men had passed over the horizon. And although it's the first Sunday of term, and the first Sunday we've met in chapel in the New Year – and we're delighted to welcome our new Treasurer to chapel, in the Hilary term – yet twenty-nine days of a New Year is a very long while; and I have the feeling that if I were to say 'Happy New Year', some of you would have to say, 'Well, the New Year hasn't so far been very happy for me – and neither has it been, for instance, in Japan.' And this weekend is the Auschwitz Commemoration. You may remember that Eliot's Magi, on their journey, ask: 'Were we led all that way for Birth or Death?'

So what shall I preach about, this problematical Sunday? Well, first of all, let me say something about two Christmas presents I've enjoyed.

After Christmas I went away for a few days to stay with some friends of mine, at Curry Rivel, outside Taunton. They have two children under five – one of them, Ben, is my godchild; the other, Charlotte, has leukaemia and is in desperate need of a marrow transplant, and was, understandably, up and down during those days.

The children had been given a present which in fact captivated us all. It's a game called 'Buckaroo', in which you have to try and load all sorts of things on a toy metal mule (saddle, lassoo, and so on) until it eventually collapses – but it only collapses bucking and kicking. Hence 'Buckaroo'. You all shout 'Buckaroo!' when the great moment of collapse comes.

I suppose you'd expect a preacher not only to enter into the game and enjoy it, but to say, 'Sometimes life's a bit like that!' But being with young Charlotte, whom I was privileged to baptize just over four years ago, and knowing that she is fighting leukaemia – and, indeed, for her life – and that each day and each week she has to have this and that done to her through drugs and injections, and so on, I'm not surprised that *sometimes* it's all too much for her, and that *sometimes* she 'kicks' –

though most of the time she's marvellous, thanks particularly to Great Ormond Street.

When I went up to her room, late on New Year's Eve, when she was fast asleep, you can imagine my heartfelt prayer for her was 'Happy New Year'; but, as you can also imagine, the mystery of what God is up to in all this is for me – as it is for all of us, not least her parents – beyond words, and, indeed, all thought.

But, by way of comment, let me tell you of another of the presents I've enjoyed this year. It arrived in a cardboard tube, quite a while before Christmas, from a friend of mine, Ralph Deppen, who was Archdeacon of Chicago when I first met him in the 1960s, and who now lives in retirement in Los Angeles. Art and artists have always meant a great deal to him; and it was a splendid idea of his to send me, as a present, a print of a painting in the Norton Simon Foundation Gallery in Pasadena. It's by Giovanni Battista Gaulli, sometimes called Baciccio, who was a pupil of the Baroque master Bernini. I'm afraid I'd never heard of him before.

The subject of the painting is most unusual. It's Joseph, holding the Christ-child in his arms. His strong, gentle hands support the infant, and hold him tenderly close. The child reaches up to play with Joseph's flowing beard. The two brightly lit figures of Joseph and the infant are set against a dark background. But within the darkness, the columns of a building can be discerned, suggesting that the painting may be alluding to the circumcision of Christ, and his presentation in the temple, or perhaps the columns may hint symbolically at the whole House of Israel, or it may be that the darkness is the darkness of all that lies ahead for Jesus: for the child Jesus.

But, in the foreground, it's a supremely joyous painting. The brown drapery of Joseph, and the white swaddling clothes of the babe, curve and fold like joyous waves. Joseph's face radiates delight in the child, and the face of the child, looking up and into Joseph's face, is also suffused with delight.

I have to say, that painting has tremendously helped me this Christmas and New Year. I don't think I've ever thought before so much about *Joseph*. I've known, of course, that betrothal in Jewish law – indeed, the mere possibility that one party believed himself or herself to be betrothed to the other – constituted a relationship which prevented marriage to any other, and a betrothed girl became a widow if her fiancé died. After betrothal, a man was legally the husband. I've known that as a good Jew, Joseph might have shown what a zealous Jew he was if he branded Mary with public disgrace. But he rose above that. The thought – the possibility – of bringing Mary into the glare of publicity clearly passed through Joseph's mind.

The record of what happened, in the Gospel according to Matthew, will be fresh in all our minds at this time:

> Then Joseph her husband,
> being a just man, and not willing to make her a public example, was minded to put her away privily. But while he thought on these things, behold, the angel of the Lord appeared unto him in a dream, saying, Joseph, thou son of David, fear not to take unto thee Mary thy wife: for that which is conceived in her is of the Holy Ghost. . . .

St Luke has a rather different way of telling the story. Mary is 'a virgin betrothed to a man whose name was Joseph, of the house of David.' She protests to the angel Gabriel that she has, literally, no husband; and voices her incredulity at what the angel has promised. But soon she voices her submission: 'Be it unto me according to thy word.'

What struck me about that painting I've received is how wonderfully it depicts the faith of Joseph. All doubts, suspicions, conscientious scruples and struggles, regrets, anxieties, have eventually vanished. Now there is only delight: delight in the child Jesus, whom Mary has mothered and whom Joseph has agreed to father – in the sense of seeing to his upbringing, so that it wouldn't be long before people would say: 'Is not this Joseph's *son*?'

In one of his longer poems, entitled 'For the Time Being', and which he subtitles 'A Christmas Oratorio', W. H. Auden reflects on this subject of what he calls 'The Temptation of St Joseph', and he gives to the chorus, in this verbal oratorio, some pretty sharp thoughts on the situation. The chorus say:

> Joseph, you have heard
> What Mary says occurred;
> Yes, it may be so.
> Is it likely? No.

And, a little later, the chorus butts in again:

> Mary may be pure,
> But, Joseph, are you sure?
> How is one to tell?
> Suppose, for instance . . . Well . . .

And then, a third time, the chorus has its say:

> Maybe, maybe not.
> But, Joseph, you know what
> Your world, of course, will say
> About you anyway.

Joseph himself says:

> All I ask is one
> Important and elegant proof

That what my Love had done
Was really at your will
And that your will is Love.

The Angel Gabriel replies:

No, you must believe;
Be silent, and sit still.

As most of you know, I'm not myself married, and I haven't any children. But one of the greatest privileges of a priest is to conduct christenings. I've told you how I baptized Charlotte four years ago. Already twice this year here in chapel, I have gathered an infant in my arms at a baptism and sprinkled water upon it. Next Sunday I shall baptize another. I think I almost know what was in Joseph's heart and mind as he looked on the face of the infant Jesus. I almost know what Baciccio was trying to paint.

In these days since Christmas, I've finished reading the remarkable autobiography of Nelson Mandela, which he has called *Long Walk to Freedom*. In it he describes most movingly how his second youngest daughter, Zeni, who married Prince Thumbumuzi of Swaziland, came to visit him in prison on Robben Island, and brought with them their new-born child. Having been in prison so many years, Mandela hadn't in fact seen his now grown-up daughter since she was about her own baby daughter's age. Mandela's son-in-law hands him in prison his tiny granddaughter, whom Mandela says he did not let go of for the entire visit. And he writes: 'To hold a new-born baby, so vulnerable and soft, in my rough hands, hands that for too long held only picks and shovels, was a profound joy. I don't think a man was ever happier to hold a baby than I was that day.' Mandela was Joseph that day; and he named the child 'Zaziwe' – which means 'Hope'.

In fact, I well remember one of the first babies I ever baptized as a vicar in Camberwell, south London. I had taken the marriage of the father and mother, and they had been given a room over the bride's father's cobbler's shop. There was a great housing shortage at the time – 1959. I would pass the shop on the way to the bus stop from my vicarage several times a week. And one day, before the baptism, just after the baby was born, I heard someone knocking furiously on the upstairs window as I was passing; and when I looked up, there was the beaming face of David, the proud father of a baby boy. 'Come up, vicar, and see the baby!' he shouted. And I did. And we stood by the cot, just looking at the babe. 'Ain't it marvellous,' said David. He was no regular churchgoer. Indeed, he had been on probation. But nothing could suppress his delight in his son.

There is something of David's delight that day in Camberwell in the painting of Joseph and the Christ-child that I've been given. But there is something even more than delight. There is reverence and awe: awareness of the fragile, damageable creation in Joseph's hands – and a sense of mystery.

The Victorian theologian F. D. Maurice says that, 'Baptism is the proclamation by God that this child is a child of mine.' He does not say that simply of the Christ-child. He says it of *every* child. That painting of Joseph and Jesus says something, therefore, that might be painted of every father, and, indeed of Everyman – in the old sense of *Everyman*, the great sixteenth-century mystery play.

And yet what lay ahead, at thirty-three, for Jesus, in the darkness, was literally crucifixion, so that Jesus cried, 'My God, my God, WHY?'

'Were we led all that way for birth or death?'

I can't myself solve, and I do not have much insight into, one of the greatest mysteries of life: child suffering. I can say that I know that when I hold in my arms a baby – or a child like Charlotte – I know something of the glory of God. And I know that in Christ's triumphant suffering, we have the profoundest comment on suffering that this world affords, and that that too reveals the glory of God.

I can say that Auschwitz would never have happened had every Christian in Germany held on to and proclaimed the conviction that 'in every man for ever – "Heathen, Turk or Jew" – I meet the Son of God'. And we come here to chapel each week – each year – each New Year – to receive new life, new insight, new strength to maintain and proclaim that conviction.

And today I want to say a profoundly Happy New Year to you all.

23

THE MISERERE

Gray's Inn Chapel; 5 February 1995

It was the commemoration of Auschwitz last weekend which made me resolve to preach this Sunday on Psalm 51, sometimes called the 'Miserere', and to ask the Director of Music if we might have the incomparable Allegri setting of it as the anthem. It seemed to me that there was much to be said for thinking together about one of the great treasures of both Jewish and Christian spirituality. For although Psalm 51 is, of course, Hebrew in origin, the Psalter was therefore the Prayer Book of Jesus, and thus is the model for us.

Psalm 51 is unequalled in all the Psalter for its exposition of a sense of sin, and for the directness, the candour, with which it confronts what that sense of sin reveals. It begins with the true penitent's impulse to cry to God: against whom the Psalmist recognizes his sin has, in the end, been committed. He goes straight to the heart of the matter: 'Have mercy upon me, O God.'

But there, already, are two 'problems', so to speak, for many of us today: the sense of sin and the sense of God. It matters a great deal, of course, how we think of God when we approach him: not least in penitence. In fact, every Kyrie ever composed – indeed, every Kyrie ever said or ever sung – says something about what that particular person thinks of God whose mercy he, or she, is asking.

Some modern Kyries are easy-going – to the point of a kind of trivial complacency: others, like that in Verdi's *Requiem*, speak of a God of wrath, and fire, and terror, before whom we cower down. But there's also the exquisite 'Have mercy, Lord, on me', in Bach's *St Matthew Passion*, with its incredibly consoling and merciful solo violin. It matters greatly to whom we believe our Kyries are addressed: how we think of God when we say: 'Lord, have mercy; Christ, have mercy; Lord, have mercy.'

Perhaps I might confess, that when I first took on my job as your Preacher, seventeen years ago, I was somewhat intimidated by the image of a judge in scarlet and ermine. I could not then conceive of the possibility of a judge as a *friend*. I learnt quite quickly that judges can actually – sometimes – be very loving, and can sometimes even need love. Now, after seventeen years, I'm quite sure that it's of overriding importance that we should all learn to love our judge and that our judge *is* love: that justice is part of love and love of justice. And it is in that knowledge we need to approach Psalm 51. For the Psalmist tells us in the very first verse of the psalm several important things about the God in whom he believes: whom he knows to be his judge. He credits him with the capacity for mercy; with the capacity for loving kindness; with the capacity for an abundance of tender mercy. And this is all, of course, centuries before Christ: probably just after the exile of the Jews from Israel.

But let us just dwell on the marvellous picture of God the Psalmist gives us: 'Have mercy upon me, O God, after thy great goodness. According to the multitude of thy mercies . . .' (BCP). And at the end of that first verse he credits God with one more capacity: the capacity to obliterate, to erase, to blot out his sin, to make it as though it had never been.

I wonder whether Shakespeare had this psalm in mind when he made Macbeth say:

> Will all great Neptune's ocean wash this blood
> Clean from my hand? No, this my hand will rather
> The multitudinous seas incarnadine
> Making the green one red.

And Lady Macbeth – with no sense of sin – says: 'A little water clears us of this deed.'

The Psalmist knows his guilt before God, but, knowing it, knows also that his God can wash away every trace of his guilt. So he prays: 'Wash me throughly' – and the word he uses is used most often of washing garments and treading on them to get rid of every stain. So the Psalmist continues, 'and cleanse me . . .', and *that* word is used not only of washing but also of purifying metal.

The merciful, loving, tender God, the Psalmist believes, can do all this, and the Psalmist pleads with him to do it. And that pleading also says something about the Psalmist's idea of God. His God is so personal that he can be talked to – literally prayed to, beseeched. God, we can say, is the 'Ground of the Psalmist's beseeching' – to use the great phrase of St Julian of Norwich. And that beseeching – to blot out his sins – leads on to confession. His knowledge of God and his knowledge of himself go together: 'I acknowledge my transgressions.' I know them, and 'confess my sins continually' – that's perhaps a more accurate translation than 'my sin is ever before me'. And the Psalmist expresses that sin in three different words: transgression; iniquity; sin. You feel he is putting 'the lot' before the Lord, so to speak: making a clean breast of it.

As I've suggested, there's no beating about the bush with the Psalmist. He goes straight to the heart of the matter: 'Against *thee*, thee *only*, have I sinned,' he says. Whatever wrong he may have done to this person and that, he sees that his sin is primarily against God: guilty before God is the heart of his penitence.

He has sinned against God, but – and here's another addition to his picture of God – his sin, he knows, hasn't escaped God. His sin is in the very sight of God. His God is a God who is aware of him, in the deepest sense of that phrase. That is another very important part of the deeply personal view of God he has.

And then comes a verse that our Prayer Book doesn't really make clear: 'that thou mightest be justified in thy saying and clear when thou art judged'. More accurately expressed it would be: 'When you, God, speak: when you, the judge who is merciful, full of loving kindness, tender, speak – the God who is able to see all: when you, God, judge, your judgement is *just*, and the sentence you pronounce is, literally, "pure", clear, transparently right. You're that kind of a God.'

The Psalmist then goes on to say, not by way of excuse, that with him it's not just a case simply of this sin and that, or something that's only recently cropped up. He makes the profound observation that this *bias* towards sin goes back to his very beginning: he knows there's something of it at the very deepest depths of his nature: 'In iniquity I was brought to birth, and my mother conceived me in sin' (NEB). This is uttered not as a neat theological dogma of original sin, but as a simple but profound fact of the Psalmist's experience. But he goes on to say immediately: 'It's in this very depth of me: in the deep-seated interior of me, that you, God, desire truth – you require it in the inward parts.' The response to God of *faith* – for that's really the meaning of the Hebrew here of truth – and of what the Psalmist calls 'wisdom', knowledge of God, reverence for God, understanding of God – that's what God will give: he will enable him to 'understand wisdom secretly' – that's to say, deeply, profoundly, in the hidden depths. So the deep-seatedness of his sin is to be replaced by depths of faith and understanding. The Psalmist's God is that kind of a God – who can initiate and restore this union and communion where there has been God-lessness and iniquity. This God can restore a deep-seated and utter integrity.

So the Psalmist prays again: 'purge me' – un-sin me – 'with hyssop' – the wild herb whose leaves were said to be of cleansing power: 'wash me that I may be whiter than snow'. 'Fill me with joy and gladness' – where sin has brought only gloom and sadness. 'That the bones which thou hast crushed may rejoice.'

That's surely a most marvellous metaphor. The 'fragile body', of which one of our hymns sings, meant to be 'full of health and full of vigour', 'glorious and resplendent' – but look at it now: bones broken, lung-cage collapsed, legs and arms and skull crushed like the result of some terrible accident or catastrophe: the body a diseased wreck instead of the thing of glory it was meant to be. But again, the God to whom the

115

Psalmist is praying is a life-giving God: a healing God – someone who 'brings people back alive'. It's this thought that makes the Psalmist pray yet again. 'Hide your face from my sins. Turn your face from them. Blot out all my iniquities. Create in me a clean heart, and renew a right, a steadfast, spirit within me' – not just a fitful spasm of repentance.

Yet still there is an uncertainty in the Psalmist: a fear. He knows how near he has come to separating himself from God; his God has given him even that possibility: the gift of the possibility of betraying God and himself. He has therefore a fear, like that of John Donne, the great Dean of St Paul's and Preacher to Lincoln's Inn:

> I have a sin of fear, that when I've spun
> My last thread, I shall perish on the shore . . .

So he prays in imploring desperation: 'Cast me not away from thy presence, and take not thy Holy Spirit from me' (BCP). Again, remember, this is centuries before Christ and before Pentecost: 'take not thy holy spirit from me'. 'Restore the joy of your help,' he says. 'Sustain me by your generous, your willing, your free spirit.' And then, after penitence, after confession, comes a real and renewed intention to live a new life. 'Then will I teach transgressors thy ways, that sinners may turn to thee.'

There's what we call a textual problem about the next verse. The Prayer Book, and indeed most translations, have 'deliver me from blood guiltiness – from having blood on my hands – O Lord'. But, in Hebrew, the word for 'silence' is almost the same word – and it makes such sense – after saying that 'once he's forgiven he will speak to transgressors of the ways of God', to pray that he may be delivered from silence. And in the very next verse he continues that thought: 'Deliver me from silence: that my tongue may sing aloud of your righteousness.' And he goes on with the words so familiar to us: 'O Lord, open thou my lips; and my mouth shall show forth thy praise.' That, I find, can be said specially after one has made confession and received absolution.

It's worth reminding ourselves that what the Psalmist has taught us is that it's after thought of God's loving-kindness and mercy that penitence comes; and it's from penitence that confession flows; and it's from penitence and confession that prayer to him who can give new life to our crushed bodies flows; and then we begin to want to say, 'Enable me to tell out the greatness of the Lord': 'O Lord, open thou my lips'.

The psalm closes with one of the most beautiful utterances in the whole Psalter. Far in advance of much of the thought and practice of his times the Psalmist repudiates the idea of material sacrifices: animals, and so on. He says: it's not the whole burnt offering which is supposed to atone for sin which does so, in the eyes of God; it's the broken spirit, the contrite heart, which God will not despise. What an unforgettable radical that man must have been labelled by some of the regular Jewish temple goers, and by the Jewish hierarchy of his day! Fancy: getting rid of *animal* sacrifices!

The last two verses, most scholars agree, formed no part of the original psalm. They say the very opposite of what the Psalmist just said: and you can almost see one of the religious 'conservatives', one of the enthusiasts for animal sacrifice, insisting they should be put in. 'Then shall they offer young bullocks upon thine altar' (BCP).

I hope I have been able to convey my conviction that Psalm 51 is a marvellous spiritual treasure from our common Jewish–Christian heritage: a model of penitence and response to God, even for twentieth-century people. But I must also confess that it raises for me several questions, which, to end, I must briefly share with you.

First, it portrays in the Psalmist a man who has come to a picture of the forgiving God ages before Christ. This psalm, we can say, is some of the very best of Jewish spirituality. Often we Christians are tempted to write off other spiritualities, but the best of other spiritualities often reveals the Christ before Christ: the Holy Spirit at work before Pentecost; and we ignore such other spiritualities at our peril.

But there's a quite different question that this psalm raises in me. I've said that the Psalmist's sense of sin, his penitence, is directly related to God. That's one of the main glories of this psalm. And it may be a glory that church-going people, lay and ordained, can recognize, because God is real to us – at least from time to time – and therefore so is a sense of sin – from time to time. But the people with whom, in the main, you and I have to deal – and, indeed a large part of myself – start much further back than that. People with whom I have to deal, rarely get in touch with me because of their sense of God or their sense of guilt before God. They ring me up because their partnership of one sort or another has broken up and they're in hell; or because the pain of bereavement or suffering is too much; or because they can't keep their hands off the whisky bottle or the secretary. Or because the business deal they've pulled off, which should have given them a sense of purpose, has left them with a sense that everything's pointless, empty and meaningless. A direct sense of sin against God is, I find, very rare.

And it is significant that *my* sense of God this morning came, primarily, not through *reading* Psalm 51 and its words, but listening to the version of it set to music by Gregorio Allegri more than three centuries ago, and sung so marvellously by our choir: a version in which the literal meaning of the words was hardly to be discerned. Could it be that the gateway to God for us is very different from the gateway the Psalmist opened? God has given us, I believe, many gateways to him. He has given us the gateway of beauty and wonder. He doesn't mind which gateway we take. And thank God, it's for *our* own sakes he wants us to find, and know, and love him.

24

'WHO DO YOU SAY THAT I AM?'

Grendon Underwood Prison Chapel; 19 March 1995

'Who do you say that I am?' That's the question Jesus suddenly sprang on his friends. It's surely one of the most important questions we can ever ask anyone. Sometimes we ask the question in an offhand sort of manner, when we're put out: 'Who d'you think *I* am?', 'Who d'you think *you* are?' But for Jesus, at that time, it was a serious question. He really wanted to know the answer.

It would be very interesting, if we could break into small groups now, and if we were to ask the question of one another: 'Who d'*you* think that I am?' I daresay we could spend the whole morning on that. Jesus actually asked: 'Who d'you *say* that I am?' – knowing that we all get labelled by different people in different ways, and that he would be no exception.

Jesus' friends would say one thing about him. The Roman soldiers, who were the police of their day, would say another. So would the chief priests. I suspect Jesus' men friends might have described him in one way and his women friends – like Mary Magdalene – in another. Mary, his mother, would have said different words about him from Joseph.

I wonder, who would you want to describe you? Your wife or your girlfriend? A man friend? Your probation officer? Who's best at judging you? Who knows you best? Who have you allowed to get to know you? To know you best? And if you were allowed to stand up and say who you are, I wonder what you'd want to say about yourself.

These days, scientists are able to describe us in one way: so much calcium, so much water, so much this, so much that. But a scientist alone wouldn't be able to say what makes you you. Who could best do that?

Someone probably has to know us quite a long while to be able really to describe us. 'I knew Jimmy when he could hardly walk.' 'I knew Jimmy when he'd just started at school.' 'I knew Jimmy as a teenager. I could take you to his home.' 'I knew Jimmy when he'd just left school, and got into his first scrapes.'

'Who do you say that I am?'

'The other day they got Jimmy to see the therapist here. Jimmy was astonished at what *he* had to say about him, though they only had an hour together.'

If you were asked to answer for yourself as to who you are, I wonder what categories you would want to use?

'I'm not really such a bad sort of chap!'

'I'm not bad looking – though I was better once.'

'Of course, I haven't got much money.'

'I like my kids.'

'I've never had a job – any job I've ever had I've never been able to hold on to . . .'

'I'm forty, so I'm finished. I don't suppose I'll be able to get a job when I get out . . .'

People often come up to me, as soon as they see my dog-collar, and say: 'I'm afraid I'm not very religious myself.' It's as though wordlessly they feel I've asked them: 'Who do *you* say you are?' And they feel compelled to answer: 'I'm afraid I'm not very religious.'

When I was first a vicar in Camberwell, south London, I quickly had to arrange to see two people who'd been waiting to get married. I also soon had to see one of the local probation officers. I let the two whom I'd prepared for marriage out of the vicarage door as I let the probation officer in. They crossed on the doorstep. 'Why are you seeing *them*?' asked the probation officer. ''Cos I've been preparing them for marriage,' I said. 'You know who they are?' asked the probation officer. 'Well, I know that they want to get married, and I've just enjoyed seeing them for an hour. Nice couple of kids, I thought.' 'Well,' said the probation officer, 'I'd better tell you: he belongs to a gang at the Elephant and Castle.'

I took David's marriage, and they moved into one room above his father-in-law's cobbler's shop. And in due course, as I was passing the shop, on my way to the bus stop in the Walworth Road, I heard someone furiously tapping on the window upstairs. It was David. 'Vicar,' he shouted, 'Come up and see the baby!' I went upstairs. They only had that one room, and were crowded round the carry-cot. 'Ain't it marvellous!' said David.

'Who do you say that I am?' Member of a gang at the Elephant and Castle? Father of a child? A loving father? Part of a loving marriage? Part of a marriage that's struggling?

I've spent seven years now writing the biography of Bishop Trevor Huddleston. He's very different from the person I thought he was when I began writing. When I asked him who was his closest friend as a child, he said, 'My imaginary friend. I talked to him every day.' That suggested a very lonely child. His parents were mostly in India till he was a teenager.

He was called to be a monk. I've interviewed most of his fellow monks who are still alive and who were alongside him in his first years as a monk. They were unanimous that he showed no obvious gifts of leadership. When he was thirty he was sent out to South Africa: to a vast black parish which is now Soweto. Above all, I think it was the love of the children in that parish which transformed him and brought out his hidden gifts, particularly of leadership. Nelson Mandela has said recently that no British person has done more for the black people of South Africa than Trevor Huddleston.

Jesus asked his friends, the disciples, to say who *he* was. They'd watched him, day after day. They'd noticed he had a knack of spotting the outcasts of society. He called one of them down from the branches of a tree, where he'd been hiding, and watching him through the branches. Jesus astonished him by asking him to come and have a meal with him. His disciples had seen Jesus with the crowds and they'd seen him separated from his home and family and looking a bit alone. They'd seen him deal with raving lunatics. They'd watched him use what they could only call his gift of healing: laying his hands on people and praying over them.

But they hadn't yet seen him suffer on the cross. Some of them would actually see him die. They'd hear him cry out, 'Father, forgive them. They don't know what they're doing.' And while he was in agony on the cross they heard him cry out at the top of his voice, 'My God, my God, WHY . . . ?' And seeing him suffer like that told them who he was in a way they'd never otherwise have known. Not many years later, some of his friends tried to put down in writing what it all meant to them: who they said they thought Jesus was.

But I think the question as to who *we* think Jesus is is very closely related to who we think *we* are. When we start thinking who *we* are we begin to see – believe it or not – what we have in common with Jesus, and what separates us from him.

I'd want to say to anyone who asks me who I think I am that there's something of God in me. The image of my maker is still there – like a kind of trademark that I can't remove, no matter how hard I try. And I'm sure that if I were allowed time to get to know each one of *you*, one by one, I'd find the same to be true of you.

If you said to me: 'Who do *you* say that I am?' I'm quite sure in the *end* I'd want to say: 'You? You're a son of God.'

25

WHISTLE-BLOWING

Septuagesima, Gray's Inn Chapel; 12 February 1995

'Cry aloud, spare not, lift up thy voice like a trumpet . . .'
Isaiah 58.1

After our Lessons this morning from Isaiah and from the epistle general of St James, I think I need seek no further justification for taking as my subject today 'Concern for Standards in Public Life'. We all, of course, know well that a committee on that subject, under Lord Nolan, has been set up, and is giving it urgent attention.

It's clearly a very extensive, even diffuse, subject; and I try, as your Preacher, to avoid generalities; so I have to say I was gratified, but not all that surprised, to discover recently that a charity has been formed, and has needed to be formed, to look after people who have found it necessary to 'blow the whistle' in our society today. That itself is probably a sign of the times – indeed, of the standards in public life today – that there's now a recognizable phrase to cover the procedure – whistle-blowing – so frequently is it needed.

There may be some here who, thank heavens, have so far escaped familiarity with the phrase, or indeed with the procedure. It means, roughly, that in your work, or some other part of your life, you discover something's going on which ought not to be going on, and you wonder whether it's your duty to 'give the game away': to rat, to sneak, to split – or not, and whether, if you do, you can survive the hostility there may be from colleagues and others, including, of course, your employers. The charity called 'Public Concern at Work' offers support and advice to all such whistle-blowers. Whistle-blowing in the past has, of course, been reserved for trains and sportsfields; but now, alas, it's used – has had to be used – in relation to 'sleaze'; and sleaze may take many forms.

You may wonder why I should want to preach to you a sermon on this particular aspect of concern with society's standards: and the honest answer is that I didn't, until a couple, whom I will simply call Conrad Dehn and Son, asked me whether the subject interested me, and whether I had any theological comments to offer on it – indeed, whether I thought it might deserve a sermon; and, after spending some time reflecting, I came to the conclusion that it did.

It seems to me that at the very simplest, whistle-blowing could be in certain circumstances a way of delivering some people from evil. It's also clear that what is required of many a whistle-blower today is considerable spiritual strength: courage in place of fear; the recognition of the need to speak out, to 'cry aloud and spare not: to lift up the voice like a trumpet'. And there are some curious common phrases which encapsulate common attitudes that militate against whistle-blowing: 'Keep your head down'; 'Keep your nose clean'. We in England often talk despisingly of the failure of the German people to stand up to Hitler. Yet, nowadays, we almost make a god of keeping quiet ourselves.

My hero, Trevor Huddleston, in his stand against apartheid, met with a blanket of opposition in England from, for instance, the Foreign Office, and other government circles – for decade upon decade. Nelson Mandela would say that Trevor Huddleston has been a wonderful whistle-blower.

Yet the more I've thought upon the subject, the more I've found it difficult to restrict the subject simply to a series of causes a charity might serve.

Some of you, on a previous occasion, may have heard me tell of my strange dealings with the notorious Anthony Blunt, whom I first knew at Trinity College, Cambridge, when he was an Honorary Fellow of the College, and I was its chaplain. I saw him most after his exposure. We used to meet in his flat off the Edgware Road, and there he tried to convince me that the motivation for all he had done was his conscience. Spying, for him, I think he would have maintained, was a kind of whistle-blowing: a duty; and parts of his case were persuasive. He said that as an adolescent, the child of a Paddington vicarage (just round the corner from where we met), he was disgusted at Paddington's poverty, and that as an undergraduate at Cambridge in the Thirties, he was angry at the gap between rich and poor, and that only by becoming a communist, and an active communist, did he feel he could clear his conscience. Indeed, I can never forget the strength and passion with which he said one evening: 'Eric, if you had been in Cambridge when I was an undergraduate, you would have done what I did.' You'll not be surprised to hear I was not entirely convinced, but I think it's not least that experience which makes me want to look quite closely at whistle-blowing and whistle-blowers.

It's not, of course, unusual for Angels of Darkness to appear, or to attempt to appear, as Angels of Light. In *Macbeth*, Banquo tells us:

> And oftentimes, to win us to our harm,
> The instruments of darkness tell us truths,
> Win us with honest trifles, to betray's
> In deepest consequence.

It's not surprising, surely, that Angels of Darkness should appear as Angels of Light. I'm sure that if I were an Angel of Darkness I would try to find some way of getting some charity to embrace my cause, and perhaps the local vicar to have compassion on me; and, what's more, I'm quite sure it would be right for the vicar to have all the compassion he could muster on such an Angel of Darkness.

I have quoted more than once in this pulpit my favourite lines from the Irish poet 'A. E.' – which significantly were also favourite lines of Graham Greene:

In ancient shadows and twilights
Where childhood had strayed,
The world's great sorrows were born
And its heroes were made.
In the lost boyhood of Judas
Christ was betrayed.

I have learnt in forty years of ordained ministry that every Angel of Light has to be looked at very closely and carefully. There is usually some darkness somewhere in us all.

Clive Pontin was, I suppose, one of the earliest and most notorious whistle-blowers in, let us say, their most recent clutch of appearances. Were people, I wonder, so wrong to find themselves looking closely not only at Clive Pontin's cause, but at him? It seemed to some as though to be a whistle-blower was a necessity of his being: that, even though his cause was objective and substantial, it was subjective too – too subjective for his cause to be the whole story. There are born whistle-blowers; and any charity needs to be well aware of that.

I have already mentioned Judas as a possible whistle-blower: who sought opportunity to leak the Jesus story to the chief priests – for a consideration – but I can't myself believe that money was his main motive – certainly not thirty pieces of silver. Perhaps there was something of the Pontin-type hidden agenda there.

The prophets, to my mind, were almost all whistle-blowers of a kind. They were often like members of the underground resistance in Germany or Russia or South Africa.

And you could build up quite a case for Paul the whistle-blower – and Peter. For there were, and are, Jews – but not only Jews – who find the Law a very convenient cover up for quite a lot of unrighteousness or pseudo-righteousness. Law itself is often a huge protection of established respectable disorder. And it desperately needs from time to time a whistle-blower, probably from within – someone who knows the rules of the game and the ropes: 'who's in: who's out'. It's a mixed metaphor to say that you often need a mole as a whistle-blower.

Even charities can become too respectable, so that the whistle is only

123

blown for causes that will win the respect of the majority. In every crowd there are people who need whistles blown for them, because, frankly, they could never blow them for themselves: the little people, the aged, the disabled.

As an unrepentant and lifelong left-winger and the director of a charity, I've got caught up with quite a lot of righteous anger related to quite a lot of different causes: whistle-blowing of a certain kind; but that makes me very familiar with the unrighteousness of those whose righteous anger boils over; and sometimes their righteous anger is most evident in their self-righteousness. I suppose what I'm saying is that any charity for whistle-blowers will need not only to be good at sussing out the worth of the cause, but the worth and motivation of the whistle-blower. At least one section of my sermon should therefore be labelled 'The Self-righteousness and Mixed Motives of the Whistle-Blower?' – and the question mark is important.

To go back to Anthony Blunt. You may remember that Alan Bennett wrote a play about him as a spy, called *A Question of Attribution* – seemingly all about something as harmless as a suspect Titian. The heart of the matter was elsewhere. In his preface to his play *Another Country*, about a kind of Philby, Bennett also wrote:

> It suits governments to make treachery the crime of crimes, but the world is smaller than it was, and to conceal information can be as culpable as to betray it. As I write, evidence is emerging of a nuclear accident at Windscale in 1957, the full extent of which was hidden from the public. Were the politicians and civil servants responsible for this less culpable than our Cambridge villains? Because for the spies it can at least be said that they were risking their own skins, whereas the politicians were risking someone else's.

Well, I'm not so sure about that! But Bennett continues: 'Of course Blunt and Burgess and co. had the advantage of us in that they still had illusions. They had somewhere to turn. The trouble with treachery nowadays is that if one does want to betray one's country there is no one satisfactory to betray it to. If there were, more people would be doing it.'

Whistle-blowing, and a charity for whistle-blowers, are, I believe, important, because many of us now need to betray what we may have given our loyalty to - but to betray it on principle: for a higher, transcendent principle. The whistle-blowers of today may be the prophets of today.

The phrase 'Another Country' comes, of course, from Cecil Spring-Rice's hymn 'I vow to thee my country'. But, far from implying that every Christian must above all be a patriot, that hymn implies what Nurse Cavell said: that 'Patriotism is not enough'; indeed, that every Christian has a loyalty that transcends the simple loyalty of patriotism. In the end, a Christian is a cynic about every other loyalty than the

Kingdom of God. He – or she – is totally loyal only to the Kingdom of God – wherever and whenever it manifests itself: in marriage, family, friendship, country, party. Our Christian loyalty is always primarily to 'Another Country'. So every Christian is a potential whistle-blower; and the chief attributes of that other country are justice, truth and love, and the enemies of the Kingdom are greed and the lie – in high places and low – and naked power unrelated to justice, truth and love.

When I come to examine why I am a Christian, and indeed why I am a priest, I often find myself traversing muddy and murky ground. But then the clouds of complexity vanish: the sky clears, and I simply see Jesus standing before Caiaphas and Pilate, and a cross set against the skyline. It is Jesus' personification of truth which I find so often makes the coward spirit brave. In the end, it is Christ crucified who speaks to me most powerfully: the Christ of compassion – even for his betrayers – and who says, to each one of us, with our mixed motives: 'Cry aloud, spare not, lift up your voice – not only as a whistle, but as a trumpet.'

26

THE ROYAL BANNERS
FORWARD GO

*The Chapel Royal, St James's Palace; Palm Sunday
1995*

'The royal banners forward go' is one of the greatest of all the Passion-tide hymns of the Christian Church; we shall be singing it later in the service. It was written thirteen centuries ago by Venantius Fortunatus, who, Helen Waddell avers, 'got his name out of a fairy tale'. He produced eleven books of collected verse, and among them was:

> The royal banners forward go;
> The Cross shines forth in mystic glow . . .

That marvellous English translation of what, again, Helen Waddell calls 'the greatest processional of the Middle Ages' – *Vexilla regis prodeunt* – is by the Victorian hymn-writer, John Mason Neale, who also produced 'Jerusalem the golden', 'O happy band of pilgrims', and many other great English hymns.

'The royal banners forward go.' Could there be a more appropriate theme for the Chapel Royal on Palm Sunday? The cross, the royal banner of *all* royal banners. The cross is, of course, at the very centre of our own national banner: the Union Jack. Sir Cecil Spring-Rice, Ambassador to Washington in the First World War, author of 'I vow to thee my country', when he was suddenly relieved of his post, said when he reached Ottawa in January 1918:

> The world has had many ideals. Two of the most prominent are present in the minds of us all. We have seen the relics of Egypt or Assyria. We have seen the emblem of the ancient religions, the ancient monarchies – the king on his throne, the badge of sovereignty in his hand, the scourge. We have read of the ruins of a palace once decorated with pictures of burning cities, troops of captives being tortured to death. That was the banquet hall of the King of Assyria. That is one type of civilisation.

He went on:

> There is another, the sign of which is the cross. I need not tell you what that means, but I must say this: the cross is a sign of patience-under-suffering,

but not patience-under-wrong. The cross is on the banner under which we fight – the cross of St George, the cross of St Andrew, the cross of St Patrick; different in form, in colour, in history, yes, but the same in spirit, the spirit of sacrifice.

We are all subjects of the Prince of Peace, who fought the greatest fight ever fought upon this earth, who won the greatest victory, and won it by his blood. . . . That is the cross . . .'

Only a fortnight after that speech, while still in Ottawa, Cecil Spring-Rice suddenly died.

'The royal banners forward go'.

If *we* want to set forward the royal banner of Christ, each one of us needs to find ways of drawing close to Christ's cross – especially in Holy Week. Each Holy Week is an invitation to each one of us to enter more deeply into Christ's cross and Passion. Wherever we are – here, in London, or away with family or friends – we shall each find some way of entering more deeply into the cross, so that we may forward the royal banner.

It is our Christian belief that there is a cross in the heart of God before ever the wood was seen on Calvary, and that life – all life – springs from that tremendous cross hid in the heart of God's love and life. Creation itself, we believe, is God sharing himself with us. The hymn says:

> But even could I see him die,
> I could but see a little part
> Of that great love which, like a fire,
> Is always burning in his heart.

It's surely not surprising that, if that be so, at the heart of so many of our common human experiences there is the deep intuition, the knowledge, the evidence, the conviction, that life, at its heart, is about sharing and creating, and, indeed, often about restoring and redeeming – at cost. All our *altruism*, I believe, stems from the cross-like heart of God. But that conviction and experience is revealed within the three great characteristics of our world: time, place and persons. Without time – nothing. Without places – nothing. Without persons – nothing.

The cross-like, self-giving God so loved that he gave: gave us time, places and persons. But the heart of the Christian gospel is that although something of the self-giving God is revealed in *all* his world – in every moment of time; in every place; in every person – it was part of his plan and purpose to reveal himself particularly in one particular place; at one particular time; in one particular person. God so loved that he gave himself particularly in and through that particular person, at that particular time; in that particular place.

T. S. Eliot wrote:

> at a predetermined moment, a moment in
> time and of time,
> A moment not out of time, but in time, in what we call
> 'history': transecting, bisecting the world of time, a moment in
> time but not like a moment of time.
> A moment in time, but time was made through that moment: for
> without the meaning there is no time, and that moment of
> time gave the meaning.

Because that moment 'gave the meaning', thinking about the cross, the royal banner, means discovering the cross at the heart of our own everyday experience, our own common human experience, our own selves: discovering the cross-like self-giving of God at the very heart of our own existence.

We need to discover the self-giving cross-like love of God in creation. But we shall do that the more certainly if first we familiarize ourselves with the self-giving cross-like love of God in Jesus: in the goodness of Jesus; in the healing of Jesus; in Jesus searching for the outcasts of society; in Jesus looking after us prodigals and bringing us home; in the self-giving cross-like love of God in Jesus, the Good Samaritan. But, above all, in the self-giving cross-like love of God in the cross itself: alongside our sufferings; saying 'Father, forgive them'; and even wrestling with the bewildering mystery of life, and crying with us and within us 'My God, my God, WHY?'

To maintain that the 'royal banner', the self-giving and redeeming love of God, is, so to speak, behind and above and within the whole world, raises many questions. But in the darkness of this world, which is sometimes black beyond words, the light of God's self-giving love often breaks through and lightens our darkness, and the darkness cannot overcome it.

There is, first of all, the odd fact to consider that though this world contains so much misery for so many, the numbers of those who commit suicide are not all that many, and many of those who do are no longer of sound mind when they do. On the whole, we most of us seem to find something to approve of in this world, in spite of all. And if you look at photographs of, say, the homeless, in one of the great cities of the Third World, and if you read accounts even of the most desperate situations in, for instance, the prison camps of the world, you will often be surprised, indeed, astonished, by joy: in children's faces and between one person and another. This week, a commentator on the *Today* programme reported his astonishment at seeing children smiling, and even laughing, in their most terrible circumstances in Burundi. From the cross in the heart of God a natural grace seems to be given to most of us to bear our burdens: a remarkable resilience; a Lear-like power to endure, and to do more than endure: to discover something for which it is worth enduring.

And there's another simple fact to consider. To those whom God has given greatest capacity for life and love he has also given the greatest capacity for suffering. It's the instruments of greatest sensitivity that are the more easily damaged. With our human sensitivity to warmth we are also the more easily burnt. Water, which gives us life and health and joy, can as easily drown us. God has made us so finely that our breakdown and our destruction are never far away. Yet it's not only Christians who recognize that rarely do we learn more, receive more, than from suffering. This is not, of course, true of all; and some suffering is literally intolerable; but I have known, and know now of many, who conceive of suffering itself as the best gift they have received from life. They have received it from the cross. They have received it under the royal banner.

But I find myself often asking: what kind of a God would it be who left no sign anywhere in the world, anywhere in history – no sign of light in the darkness – to the thousands and thousands in misery? God would not have been good; God could not have been God, had he not come at some time to this world to share the misery of humanity. This alone, I believe, is sufficient reason for God becoming man, and suffering and dying as he did: to share, in love, the lot of man; literally having compassion, sympathy: suffering with and alongside us. The cross is – to use the important title of a recent book – *The Justification of God*.

It helps me to call to mind the man Christ, who could not have been man but for the whole evolutionary process, like other men. It helps me to consider the man born not in Western civilization, but in a Palestine village, where poverty and misery will have been among some of the unalterable facts of life. It helps me to consider Jesus growing up, not as an infant prodigy, but learning, like other boys – which means ignorant like other boys; subject to want; subject to misunderstanding. It helps me to consider Jesus as a creature of his time: enmeshed in the power structures of his time. It was within that web that Jesus was bound – and free; suffered, and was triumphant in suffering.

It helps me to consider Jesus hungering, feeling, loving, weeping, bereaved, terrified of death: at the mercy of the disciples' fecklessness, and the treachery of his betrayers; dying, a young man of thirty-three; innocent, yet nailed to a cross – like a rat to a barn door. It helps me to consider Christ praying in the midst of all this; bewildered in the midst of all this; asking to be delivered from all this: 'Let this cup pass from me.'

The accounts of Gethsemane in the Gospels, of course, differ, yet they each add something worth adding. Consider Christ's prayer 'Let this cup pass from me'; but then consider him praying: 'If this cup may not pass from me' – the cup of his own suffering: the cup of the world's suffering – the sharing of it all – 'if this cup may not pass from me except I drink it: Thy will be done.'

And consider him saying at the last: 'The cup which my Father has given me, has shared with me, shall I not drink it?' Eventually he sees it all as the 'gift of my Father'. He sees through it all to the tremendous cross hid in the heart of God's love and life. He both sees the royal banner and is himself the royal banner.

There's no *answer* to the world's suffering: no solution to the problem of pain and evil. There was no *answer* to Christ's suffering; there's only some light upon it sometimes in the darkness. The light shines in the darkness and the darkness does not overcome it – in the end. It sometimes takes a very long while; we have sometimes to wrestle all night, until the break of day, before, looking at the royal banner, we can cry: 'O ye light *and* darkness, bless ye the Lord.'

God *is* love: self-giving love. He is the royal banner; and he invites us to contemplate this Holy Week – for our own sake and for the sake of his world – the ikon, the banner, of self-giving love that lies at the heart of himself and at the heart of his world.

There I might end what I want to say today on 'the royal banner'. But I want to add a single paragraph to what I have already said, for today is the fiftieth anniversary of the death of one of the best and bravest Christians of our time: Dietrich Bonhoeffer.

How he set forward the royal banner of the cross in Nazi Germany! When he died, in Flossenburg concentration camp, his great book of *Ethics* was unfinished. But there is one passage in it which can serve today both as his memorial and as our entrance into Holy Week. Bonhoeffer wrote: 'In a world where success is the measure and justification of all things, the figure of Him who was sentenced and crucified remains a stranger and is at best the object of pity. The world will allow itself to be subdued only by success.' Then Bonhoeffer added: 'The figure of the Crucified invalidates all thought which takes success as its standard.'

'The royal banners forward go' – but by ways which are strange. Jesus himself invites us this week to follow him along the way of the royal banner: the cross.

27

SHAKESPEARE'S BIRTHDAY

Eton College Chapel; 23 April 1995

Shakespeare's birthday – which is, of course, today – always brings back to me some rather special memories.

One Sunday, in 1967, I was preaching at Christ Church, Chelsea, and decided to take *King Lear* as my subject. I'd noticed, when I went into the pulpit, that in the pews, just in front of it, was an old lady, bent over, and swathed in black. She was unrecognizable as anyone in particular.

After the service, the vicar said to me: 'The old lady in front of the pulpit would like to have a word with you.' She turned out to be the eighty-five-year-old Dame Sybil Thorndike: undoubtedly, in her time, one of England's greatest actresses – particularly in Shakespeare, and notably as Lady Macbeth and Portia. Sybil Thorndike wanted me to write an oration for her, which she was due to deliver at a service of commemoration in honour of Shakespeare, on his birthday, in Southwark Cathedral, a stone's throw from London Bridge and from the site of the Globe Theatre. She wanted me first to come and have tea with her – where she lived, at Swan Court, in Chelsea – to discuss what might be appropriate to include in such an oration.

The tea, to my delight, turned into a kind of private performance of Dame Sybil's favourite passages from Shakespeare. She had a great sense of humour, and strong likes and dislikes.

She was aware that her audience would include young people who were still at school, as well as people of her own age. She said, 'Our *first* object must be to stop those at school thinking of Shakespeare simply as "set books". Somehow,' she continued, 'let's get them to think of their problems and the problems of today, and to ask: "What did Shakespeare have to say about *this* problem and *that*? He is sure to have said *something* – something worth saying, and would have said it beautifully."'

We singled out one or two major subjects. 'Authority', she said 'will always be a problem. Can't I do that passage from *Lear* you quoted in your sermon?' It was when the banished Kent, disguised, comes to Lear, who has been shorn of all his royal power.

The King asks Kent: 'What art thou?'

'A very honest-hearted fellow, and as poor as the king.'

'If thou be as poor for a subject as he is for a king, thou art poor enough. What wouldst thou?'

'Service.'

'Whom wouldst thou serve?'

'You.'

'Dost thou know me, fellow?'

'No, sir; but you have that in your countenance which I would fain call master.'

'What's that?'

'Authority.'

Sybil Thorndike was a remarkable combination of femininity and masculinity – which made her wonderful as St Joan, which Shaw wrote for her in the 1920s. We talked of Cordelia, and how, in *Lear*, Cordelia combines most marvellously passion and order, innocence and maturity, defencelessness and strength. Sybil Thorndike wanted somehow to include the sentence of Cordelia's attendant, who is full of wonder at Cordelia's control over her passions, and likens it to the successful conquest of a rebellion: 'It seemed she was a Queen over her passion, who, most rebel-like, sought to be king o'er her.'

Dame Sybil was politically left-wing – which is why she got on so well with Shaw, and played Candida, as well as St Joan, supremely well. I put this passage into her script because of her social concern: 'Homelessness. There are many homeless here in London tonight. [It was 1967.] Did Shakespeare say something about *homelessness*? Well, listen to this from *Lear*:

> Poor naked wretches, wheresoe'er you are,
> That bide the pelting of this pitiless storm,
> How shall your houseless heads and unfed sides,
> Your loopt and window'd raggedness defend you
> From seasons such as these? O, I have ta'en
> Too little care of this: Take physic, pomp;
> Expose thyself to feel what wretches feel,
> That thou mayst shake the superflux to them,
> And show the heavens more just.'

The Sixties were a time of rebellion: a time for the outsider. 'Edmund in *Lear*', said Sybil. 'He's *my* sort of fellow.' 'Why should I stand in the plague of custom?' Edmund cries.

It was difficult to see how to include all that Dame Sybil wanted to include. I managed to include for her just a few lines from *Richard II*:

> Cover your heads, and mock not flesh and blood
> With solemn reverence: throw away respect,

Tradition, form, and ceremonious duty,
For you have but mistook me all this while:
I live with bread like you, feel want,
Taste grief, need friends: subjected thus,
How can you say I am a king?

And then, suddenly, Sybil exclaimed: 'The *Sonnets!* We *must* include a sonnet or two!' It was then that her actor-husband, Sir Lewis Casson, entered the room. He looked to me as old as she – and proved to be older: over ninety, and very frail. It was seeing him *with her* – the two of them so aged – that made me insert Sonnet LXIV – on 'Time' – which ends:

Ruin hath taught me thus to ruminate–
That Time will come and take my love away.
This thought is as a death, which cannot choose
But weep to have that which it fears to lose.

But, on the day, the way Dame Sybil *spoke* those words was quite unforgettable. Lewis, her husband, was sitting in the front row of the cathedral, just below the pulpit, and looking even more frail and near to death than he had looked when we first met. Sybil looked directly at him, from the pulpit, and put her script down and said, as though she were addressing him alone:

Time will come and take *my love* away.
This thought is as a Death, which cannot choose
But *weep* to *have* that which it fears to lose.

Let me end what I have to say, this Shakespeare's birthday, with the end paragraph of that script I was so honoured and privileged to prepare for Dame Sybil: 'That Sonnet alone could be Shakespeare's epitaph, his commemoration. But if you wanted just a line, a phrase, of Shakespeare's to commemorate him, what about these words of Lear to Cordelia, which comment on the supreme concern of every one of us: why we are here at all. Lear invites Cordelia – and the people of London gathered in the Globe Theatre 400 years ago – and you and me today, to

take upon's the mystery of things
As if we were God's spies.'

28

PSALM 90

Gray's Inn Chapel; 14 May 1995

In February of this year, I preached to you what used to be called an 'expository' sermon on Psalm 51, sometimes called the 'Miserere'. This morning, I want to preach a similar sermon, on Psalm 90, which was of course our psalm this morning. It is one of the two psalms appointed in the Burial Service of the 1662 Prayer Book. It's another great treasure of Jewish and Christian spirituality.

In its English version, the Prayer Book Psalter is also a marvellous compendium of poems. And I choose Psalm 90 today because it was the psalm on which the seventeenth-century hymn writer, Isaac Watts, based his great hymn 'O God, our help in ages past' – which seems to me so appropriate for our thoughts as we meet at the end of a week which has seen the commemoration and celebration of Victory in Europe – and for another, more personal, reason: the tenth verse of that psalm baldly states that 'the days of our age are three score years and ten'; and some of you will know that that fact has particular significance for me, for since Good Friday this year: '. . . Of my three score years and ten, seventy will not come again!' And you have marked that fact with singular kindness and generosity.

It's in fact very difficult to date most of the psalms more precisely than between the eleventh and the sixth centuries BC. But that in itself is surely remarkable: that, for instance, this psalm, this poem, is at least 2,500 years old.

This particular psalm is a *cri du coeur*. In some ways it's a hymn; in some, it's a prayer; in other ways, much of it is a kind of dirge on the futility of all human effort and existence: on the evanescence of all human achievement. In immortal words, it speaks of our mortality.

As we begin to look at the first verse of the psalm – which you will have heard in those wonderful last moments of Elgar's – and Newman's – 'Dream of Gerontius' we have just had sung for us – perhaps it may be profitable to compare the Authorized Version, based on a text that is often uncertain; the Prayer Book version, based on Coverdale; and, lastly, the New English Bible version.

The Authorized Version has: 'Lord, thou hast been our *dwelling place in all generations*.' The Prayer Book has: 'Lord, thou has been our *refuge*:

from one generation to another.' The New English Bible has: 'Lord, thou
hast been our *refuge, from generation to generation.*'

Psalm 90 starts with a declaration of the Psalmist's faith. He speaks
of the eternal nature of God and of the dependence of man. In all
generations man has found God a dwelling, a home, a refuge, a
stronghold: 'Before the mountains were brought forth, or ever the earth
and the world were made: thou art God from everlasting, and world
without end' (BCP).

To the Israelites, the mountains were regarded as the most ancient
part of the earth; and God is portrayed as, literally, in travail, to bring
forth the earth. 'Thou art God.' 'Thou *art.*' That is the Psalmist's faith.
Yes, but 'Thou turnest man to destruction' (BCP) – literally, 'You turn
man back into dust.' God gives, and God withdraws, the life-force. He
returns man to the dust whence he was taken.

'For a thousand years in thy sight are but as yesterday: seeing that is
past as a watch in the night.' (BCP). God is above time and change, the
Psalmist says. A thousand years to him are like a four-hour watch. We're
like a dream that vanishes at daybreak; like grass that springs up in the
morning, but, after only a day, is dried up and withered. So we are
'brought to an end by thy anger and silenced by thy wrath'.

The Psalmist's picture of human transitoriness is echoed by
Shakespeare's:

We are such stuff as dreams are made on
And our little life is rounded with a sleep.

Psalm 90 is clearly written Before Christ. As yet, there is no experience of resurrection or of joy. It's almost stoical. But after that beginning to the psalm – which is about the brevity and uncertainty of life –
the Psalmist moves on to *Israel's* life: spent under the cloud of God's
wrath because of Israel's sins.

Again there's a contrast. This time it's the purity of God and the
iniquity of man: 'Thou hast set our misdeeds before thee: and our secret
sins in the light of thy countenance' (BCP). What we hide from ourselves
is open to the full light of God's presence.

The Prayer Book continues: 'For when thou art angry all our days
are gone: we bring our years to an end as a tale that is told' – it's a
marvellous simile the Prayer Book uses for the Hebrew, '*as a tale that is
told*', which the New English Bible translates 'like a murmur': like a
whisper that fades away from human hearing. Then comes that
memorable verse: 'The days of our age are threescore years and ten'
(BCP). In fact, for the Israelite, seventy years was not a normal or average life span. It was the span of a very fortunate man. And, in Israel, it
was unusual to live for seventy years, and very exceptional to live for
eighty.

So the Psalmist emphasizes again the brevity of life. In the Prayer Book version there are nine words which are more poignant and powerful than whole paragraphs and pages. It simply says of life: 'So soon passeth it away, and we are *gone*.' I think those are some of the most dramatic, yet realistic and truthful, words in the whole of the Bible – indeed, in the whole of literature. Life: 'So soon passeth it away, and we are gone.'

And then the Psalmist, speaking for the devout Israelite, asks: 'Who feels the power of thy anger? Who feels the power of thy wrath like those who *fear thee*?': like those who are aware of who you are. And this question leads to a prayer: 'So teach us to number our days: that we may apply our hearts unto wisdom.' Grant us that wisdom which begins with reverence, with awe, with a proper fear and awareness of who you are, so that we use our short life to best effect. The New English Bible reads: 'Teach us to order our days rightly, that we enter the gate of wisdom.'

The last four verses of the psalm are really a prayer for relief; and although the Psalmist does not specify or make clear the particular suffering from which he seeks relief, the prayer that he utters is one of readiness to continue as a faithful servant of God, even if no relief comes. Again, it's a most beautiful fragment of Hebrew poetry:

Turn thee again, O Lord at the last: and be gracious
unto thy servants.
O satisfy us with thy mercy, and that soon: so shall we
rejoice and be glad all the days of our life.
Comfort us again now after the time that thou has plagued
us: and for the years wherein we have suffered
adversity.
Shew thy servants thy work: and their children thy glory.
And the glorious majesty of the Lord our God be upon us:
prosper thou the work of our hands upon us, O prosper
thou our handy work (BCP).

So, in the compass of seventeen verses, the Psalmist has taken us from that first vista of God the creator, in travail to bring the earth into existence:

Lord, thou hast been our refuge: from one generation
to another.
Before the mountains were brought forth, or ever the
earth and the world were made: thou art God . . .

– and has taken us to another sight: of the brevity of our human existence:

The days of our age are threescore years and ten; and
though men be so strong that they come to fourscore years
. . . so soon passeth it away, and we are gone . . .

But then he returns to trustful faith in God, who has him, and all of us, in his hands:

> Shew thy servants thy work: and their children thy glory.
> And the glorious Majesty of the Lord our God be upon us . . .

No wonder that psalm inspired Isaac Watts to write:

> O God, our help in ages past,
> Our hope for years to come,
> Be thou our guard while troubles last
> And our eternal home.

By the last line of his hymn – 'And our eternal *home*' – Watts takes us back to the first line of the psalm: 'Lord, thou hast been our refuge'. 'Home' is Watts's word for 'refuge'. It's a powerful way of thinking of God. I wonder: do you ever think of God as your *home*? It's, for instance, a helpful thought for most of us when we begin our prayers. 'Man goeth to his long home' was a thought we had read to us this morning from the Book of Ecclesiastes.

When Bishop Mervyn Stockwood went to visit the dying Earl Attlee, in the Westminster Hospital, in October 1967, he simply said to the Bishop: 'I want to go home.' Mervyn was quite clear that the agnostic Attlee was not talking of his home at Great Missenden. 'Home' is one of the simplest words for who and what lies beyond.

Shakespeare, in *Cymbeline*, for instance, giving virtually a funeral oration and benediction, says:

> Fear no more the heat o' the sun,
>   Nor the furious winter's rages;
> Thou thy worldly task hast done,
>   *Home* art gone and ta'en thy wages . . .

Wordsworth, in reminding us of the 'Intimations of Immortality', which he assumes we will all have had, writes:

> Our birth is but a sleep and a forgetting:
>   The Soul that rises with us, our life's Star,
> Hath had elsewhere its setting,
>   And cometh from afar:
> Not in entire forgetfulness,
> And not in utter nakedness,
> But trailing clouds of glory do we come
>   From God, who is our home . . .

Or if we prefer something literally more 'homely', there's the Negro spiritual:

> Swing low, sweet chariot –
> Comin' for to carry me home;
> I looked over Jordan and what did I see?

A band of angels comin' after me –
Comin' for to carry me home.

That 'spiritual' echoes Psalm 90. But our 'home' isn't situated only in the Beyond:

O God, our help in ages past
Our hope for years to come
Be thou our guard *while troubles last*
And our eternal home.

29

JO'S BOOK

Gray's Inn Chapel; 21 May 1995

A book has been published this week which is rather special, and today I'd just like to share some thoughts on it with you. In fact, I had something to do with its publishing. Andrew Daynes, the author, brought the manuscript with him one day when he came to see me, and asked me whether I thought it should be published. I had no doubt whatever that it should.

The book is simply called *Jo's Book*[1], and Jo was Andrew's firstborn son. I knew Andrew when he was ordained in St Albans Diocese in 1973, and part of my job then was to take care of the younger clergy. Andrew was first a curate at Radlett, then came to St Albans Abbey as chaplain to the Abbey and the school. Jo was born in 1975.

I only knew him in his first five years; then he went off, with his father and mother and two sisters, to Dorset, to Bryanston School, where Andrew is still the chaplain. My clear memory of Jo is of a sunny, smiling cherubic face, red as an apple, with a head of lovely white curly hair. I remember him then, as a three-year-old, eagerly pulling at his reins, when he was out with his mother for his afternoon walk around the Abbey.

I remember his sister Katie being born just about then, and, two and a half years later, another sister, Rachel, who alas had Down's Syndrome. I can remember the night of her birth, and how Andrew, and Hil, his wife, had to struggle to come to terms with the fact that, from that day forward, they had a severely handicapped child to care for.

As I say, I didn't see anything of Jo all the time he was at Bryanston. So why do I want to preach to you about him today? Partly because, as I say, the book about him has come out this week – *Jo's Book* – and the former Archbishop of Canterbury, Lord Runcie, has written a compelling foreword for it.

NOTE
[1]Copies of *Jo's Book* are available, price £5.75 (inclusive of postage and packing), from The Jo Daynes Fund, Bryanston School, Blandford Forum, Dorset DT11 OPX. Cheques should be made payable to Bryanston Conference Centre Ltd.

I suppose I also want to talk about Jo today because the first week of June would have been his twentieth birthday; but last Wednesday was the first anniversary of his death. Jo was due to go up to Jesus College, Cambridge, this September to read English, but in between Bryanston and Cambridge he met what we call 'an untimely death'. Nothing romantic. He was doing a part-time job in his year out, with another Bryanstonian, teaching in a black African school in Zimbabwe, near Peterhouse. They were returning to Peterhouse in the back of a car. A tyre burst. The car overturned. All the occupants of the car were thrown out. Jo died in the ambulance from 'diffuse cerebral injuries'.

His father's book is an 'astonishingly robust' book – to use Lord Runcie's words – for someone who is telling the tale of an appalling personal tragedy, and its effects on a family, and on a circle of lively and talented young contemporaries.

Jo's father has written a book that I'm sure will be compared with *A Grief Observed* by C. S. Lewis; but although it has some similarities, it's very different. It's not least about the support the 'Squad' of half-a-dozen contemporaries of Jo, at Bryanston, gave to Andrew and Hil in their grief, and how the 'Squad' themselves coped with their grief. It's about the poetry and music that was eventually chosen for Jo's funeral. It's really about a grief shared as much as a grief observed.

Andrew Daynes manages to set down what he continues to believe. He doesn't trumpet it; he records it. He sets down, for instance, the sermon he gave on Speech Day 1993, when Jo was leaving Bryanston; and neither Jo nor he knew, of course, what lay ahead. Much of it comes from a Dutch monastic rule: an unpromising source, one might have thought, for a public school Speech Day sermon. Let me share with you just a paragraph or two:

> Following Jesus does not mean slavishly copying His life. It means making His choice of life your own, starting from your own potential and in the place where you find yourself. It means living for the values for which Jesus lived and died. It means following the path He took and seeing things as He saw them. If there is anything in which this life, this way, can be expressed, in which God has revealed Himself most clearly, it is the reality of love. You are someone only in as far as you are love, and only what has turned to love in your life will be preserved.
>
> What love is you can learn from Jesus. He is the one who has loved most. He will teach you to put the centre of yourself outside. For no man has greater love than he who lays down his life for his friends. He will also teach you to be unlimited space for others, invitation and openness. . . . This is the mystery of the gospel and there is no purpose in endless talk about it. Be silent – for it will be true and genuine only if you practise it.
>
> So keep Jesus Christ before your eyes. Don't hesitate to go anywhere He leads you; don't stay where you are and don't look back, but look forward with eagerness to what lies ahead.

'What can I say to you all', Andrew said, as his last words in chapel to his son, and to the others who were about to leave the school, 'except "Go with God, for he most surely will go with you".'

In *Jo's Book* there are some marvellous extracts from Jo's travelogues sent back from Zimbabwe, including the account of an evening trespass into war-torn Mozambique, only a few days before the accident that killed him:

> The landscape here is striking, mostly granite rock, pitted, gnarled and worn by the elements, so it looks like moon rock. The silence up here is immensely calming; it's easy to lose yourself in thought. The sunsets are also staggering, staining the sky with intermingling shades that rise to meet the night sky. The peaks and ridges are thrown into sharp silhouettes, black against the multicoloured backdrop. It's as if you're suddenly given a new lucidity of vision, viewing the same scene, but appreciating the contours so much more . . .

I think I owe it to Andrew to read you a few paragraphs of what he himself has to say about his own belief:

> There is no doubt that the great tragedies in life force you to evaluate your fundamental beliefs, your own understanding of the shape behind it all. Jo's death has clarified my perspective without seriously changing my faith.
>
> Behind the facade of this life is mystery, and the mystery is purposeful and loving. In the sheer overflowing of his love, the mystery called the world into being and achieved the glorious creation of humanity, free creatures destined to share in the life of love.
>
> We encounter the mystery in moments of depth; when we discover that we are in love, when we feel our love wounded, when beauty in nature or art stops our breath, when in our loneliness a hand reaches out to hold us, when death is all too real. My closest encounters with the mystery were undoubtedly at the births of my children. After helplessly watching the pains of labour, to hold in one's arms seven shrivelled pounds of new life is to come very close indeed to the heart of God.
>
> There are very few answers to the great human questions. All we can do is to point men and women towards the great mystery of God, because only there do the questions themselves begin to make any kind of sense. We point, not from any position of strength or assurance, but rather, as these last months have so clearly shown, from absolute impotence and vulnerability. To us, exposed and fragile, wounded beyond description, the words of power have been spoken, and we have been drawn, uncomprehending, down into the mystery of suffering love . . .
>
> It was not until Father Paul brought Jo's body into church and led us in prayer that a new particularity hit me with such force that it made me cry. God understood what it meant to lose a son. God had been precisely where I was. He knew the wrenching pain of the death of a beloved only son. The mystery drew very close.

I said that there's quite a lot about music and poetry in *Jo's Book*. The music I must leave unplayed. The poetry? I had myself sent Andrew

three lines from Edith Sitwell he had not known, but which he said had
helped them. In her poem 'Eurydice', Edith Sitwell wrote:

> Love is not changed by Death
> And nothing is lost and all in the end is harvest.

Andrew includes a sentence from a letter of Wordsworth on which
I've not been able to cease reflecting: 'I loved the Boy with the utmost
love of which my soul is capable, and he is taken from me – yet in the
agony of my spirit in surrendering such a treasure I feel a thousand
times richer than if I had never possessed it.' I hope you understand
why I have chosen to preach on Jo and on *Jo's Book* this morning.

Andrew speaks of the 'golden line' from Henry Vaughan, 'They are
all gone into the light'.

To my mind, it makes all the difference *in the world* to what you do in
the world and the way you do it, if you believe – to use Wordsworth's
words, read at Jo's funeral – that 'trailing clouds of glory do we come,
from God, who is our home'. I used those words in my sermon last
Sunday. And, in fact, I see my sermon today as the complement and
completion of the one I preached to some of you last week on Psalm
90. I know that some of you found Psalm 90, last week, a little gloomy.
I find the faith of Andrew and Hil Daynes strengthening and encourag-
ing. It's the kind of Easter faith of which a sermon on the fifth Sunday
after Easter, Rogation Sunday, should rightly speak. Rogation Sunday
– 'Asking' Sunday – Praying Sunday. *Jo's Book* teaches us all the kind
of Easter faith we need to ask for, to pray for.

30

PENTECOST

Evensong, Gray's Inn Chapel; Whit Tuesday, 6 June 1995

It was about seven weeks after the first Good Friday; once again, Jerusalem was thronged with pilgrims. There was a sudden sound like a tornado. What looked like tongues of fire came to rest on those who were there; and some of those who came surging together at the sound were astonished to hear the proclamation in their own languages and dialects of what God had done. That is what it says in the Acts of the Apostles.

On reading that story today, I imagine most of us are somewhat cynical. But so, too, were many of the people there that first Pentecost. They said straight out: 'They've been at the bottle!' It is, of course, quite impossible now to be certain what precisely happened, but no one would be claiming too much who said it was a time of great spiritual conviction and enthusiasm: conviction that the Spirit of God was at work.

At other times of such spiritual intensity in the history of the Church, similar experiences have been described. In 1647, George Fox, for instance, the founder of the Quakers, wrote: 'After this, a pure fire appeared in me; then I saw how he sat as a refiner's fire . . . I was moved to pray; and the Lord's power was so great, that the house seemed to be shaken.'

But St Luke, in the Acts of the Apostles, saw in the manifestations of the Spirit at the first Pentecost something more definite than the general spiritual experience of *individuals*. What he describes is more social, connected with human fellowship, belonging and membership one of another. *Individual* spiritual experience has often been known to lead people to be rather thoughtless about other people. Not seldom they become difficult to live with; alas, self-interest and self-concern all too often lurk behind religion and worship. But what St Luke describes is something which was first and foremost concerned with the *corporate* life of the *whole* of society. It was God's power reversing the *curse* of Babel: re-creating fellowship where the sin of man had brought only division and separation. It's immediately clear, when the story of the Tower of Babel in Greek is compared with the Greek of this passage in the Acts of the Apostles, that the writer had the babble of Babel very much in mind. Pentecost, to the author of the Acts of the Apostles, was, as I say, the reversal of the curse of Babel. Where there is obedience to the will of God, where the Holy Spirit is at work, the writer of the Acts is underlining, there is once more unity and mutual understanding. The scattered nations, races and tribes are brought together.

Is there a word from the Lord here, for us, as we gather for Evensong in the chapel of this Inn of Court on Whit Tuesday evening 1995?

In fact, I read that story from Acts a few days ago just after I had been reading the latest *Bulletin* of the Runnymede Trust – which is, I suppose, the most reliable charity concerned with issues of racial justice and equality. I read:

> Ethnic minorities remain under-represented as employees of criminal justice agencies. For example 1.5 of all police officers and 5.3 of probation officers are of ethnic minority origin. Four circuit judges out of 510 and 11 recorders out of 866 are from ethnic minority backgrounds. There are no ethnic minority members among the 95 judges, 29 Lords Justice or 10 Lords of Appeal.

As, last year, the Policy Studies Institute's report, *Ethnic Minorities and Higher Education*, made clear, changing the racial pattern of our criminal justice system to one that's more representative is not least a matter of education, and that's rarely short term. The sudden descent of the Holy Spirit doesn't miraculously make up for what has been systematically denied. And if we are concerned with the Spirit bringing together the scattered races, education is, of course, crucial; not least of white people, like ourselves.

Maybe there *is* a word from the Lord. But in my heart and mind, this Evensong is coupled with another thought.

Stanford in G is one of the most beautiful settings of the Magnificat there could be. I often used to think of Charles Villiers Stanford seated at the organ of Trinity, Cambridge – first as organist, then as Professor of Music. The gifts of the Spirit were so manifest in the beauty of what he wrote, that it was right that at his end he should be buried next to Henry Purcell in Westminster Abbey.

But I have often wondered what picture of the Virgin Mary was in his mind when he composed his Magnificat in G. Some think he had in mind an Old Master: Mary, the Virgin, sitting at her spinning wheel, singing sweetly as she spun. Perhaps, but by itself *that* picture of the Virgin Mary and the Magnificat simply will not do. (My mentor Eric Abbott – Dean of King's College London and, later, Dean of Westminster – used to say: 'Never ask "Will it *do*?" but "*What* will it do?"'!)

Mary was the wife of a working carpenter. Her song is one of revolution, in which she prophesies her son will cast down those in power, send the rich empty away, and fill the hungry with good things. Any setting of the Magnificat which induces slumber and acquiescence is to be questioned. Thomas Hancock, one of the outstanding clergy of the nineteenth century, wrote: 'The Magnificat is the inspired summary of the tendency and direction of the future social history of humankind.'

So from the picture of the Church that the first Pentecost gives us, and from the Magnificat, the message we receive from the Lord this Whit Tuesday is not one that can leave us complacent. If Evensong has been to us what it should have been, the Spirit of the Lord will have left us as it left his first disciples – disturbed.

31

VARIETIES OF GIFTS

The 'First Mass' of the Reverend Philip Hesketh; Holy Cross, Bearsted, Kent; 2 July 1995

'There are varieties of gifts . . .' (REB)
1 Corinthians 12.4

It's a great privilege for me to be invited to preach for you this evening at Phil's first celebration of the Eucharist. The readings – 'For the Guidance of the Holy Spirit' – have been chosen, I know, with great care. The Epistle began with that memorable phrase: 'There are varieties of gifts . . .'

In fact, it's not a particularly good translation into English, but it's difficult to find a better one. It should probably read, 'There are *allotments* of gifts . . .' because that's what it literally means. But I wonder if there are any allotments these days in Bearsted – or are they a thing of the past? In my childhood, you used to be able to get an allotment from the council which you could cultivate for yourself – and some would thus escape the wife for hours! But the *Oxford Dictionary* defines an allotment as 'a small plot of land to be held for cultivation by the poorer classes at a small rent', so I can see why even unemployed people, who'd be far better off with an allotment, are rather reluctant to have one.

Well, as I say, St Paul tells the Christians at Corinth that there are 'allotments' of gifts; and they are gifts of God's love, which was pre-eminently active in Christ, but is now operative in Christians, like you and me. We *all* have these gifts, says St Paul.

It is of course tempting after an ordination to concentrate on one person – the person ordained – and one sort of gift. But St Paul is saying that *every one* of us is given gifts of God's grace. Ordination is, of course, an occasion for gratitude to God for the gift he has given to the person and persons ordained, and today we're thankful to God for Phil's ordination. But I'm quite sure that St Paul, were he here – and Phil who *is* here – would want to say to us all this evening: 'Do you, each one of you, see *yourself* as spiritually gifted? – Because you *are*. God has given *you* your spiritual allotment.'

I said that I preferred to use that word 'allotment'. But I'll tell you why I'm not entirely happy with it, and that's because my childhood

memory of allotments is that most often people worked at their allotment for *themselves*. They might give the odd cabbage or cucumber
away, or keep it to show off at the local Garden Fête; but St Paul thinks
of all the gifts God has given us as *God's* gifts, not ours.

Continuous thanksgiving and gratitude to God for the gifts we have
received is one of the secrets of the Christian life: gratitude, and
acknowledgement of whose gifts they are. But the gifts God has given
us need to be recognized and developed. Perhaps one of the chief obliga-
tions of the *ordained* ministry is to try to talk with each member of the
congregation, and say: 'What d'you think is your particular gift in the
Body of Christ; and how d'you think it can best be developed?'

The pastoral gifts of those ordained need to be used these days not
least in perceiving the gifts of the congregation, and in helping them to
perceive how best those gifts can be developed and used. So I see this
evening not least as a Eucharist in which we pray for the recognition
and development of the gifts of us *all*. Those gifts are manifest in the
whole Body of Christ. So this is bound to be an ecumenical occasion;
for, manifestly, God works not only through the Church of England.

It's the centenary this year of Westminster Cathedral, in London.
That Roman Catholic cathedral was in the Church of England parish
where I said *my* 'first Mass', so I saw a lot of it. My bedroom overlooked
its grounds, and I knew well various of the priests on its staff. And I
feel bound now to work with Roman Catholics wherever I can. We have
someone at the moment working in the office of Christian Action who
is a member of a Catholic religious order. Catherine Shelley is doing a
marvellous job building bridges between the organization Church Action
on Poverty and Members of Parliament. She undoubtedly has her *allotment* of gifts.

But both Phil and I began our Christian life in the Methodist Church;
I owe a huge amount to my Methodist Sunday School teachers. I can
still remember Mrs Hasler telling me to close my peepers when I had
them open during prayers at Sunday School; and I can still see Miss
Womack lifting her hands off the piano keys and bringing them down
again while we sang 'Hear the pennies dropping' and 'Jesus loves me,
this I know'. I am bound to be ecumenical, out of my debt of gratitude
for my Methodist upbringing; and I'm sure Phil feels the same. But I
must say something this evening about the gift of the priesthood, which
has now been given to Phil, and which was given to me forty-three years
ago.

It's terribly tempting, after an ordination, to say, 'He's a priest. He's
not.' Or even, now: 'She's a priest. She's not.' But to think that way is,
I'm sure, an abuse of what St Paul had in mind when he asked the
Christians at Corinth to think of the Christian ministry in all its variety.
It's good for us, at Phil's 'first Mass', to remember, I think, some other

words of St Paul: 'The bread which *we* break' – all of us; 'The cup of blessing which *we* bless.'

Phil, tonight, will be a priest for us all and to us all by summing up and representing, and focusing what we *all* do. The whole Body of Christ is priestly. Phil represents us all at the altar this evening; he gathers up the priesthood of us all. Every human being, if we're to discover the meaning of our humanity, needs to discover the priest within us; to discover what it is to be a priest. And that's true, of course, as much of women as it is of men.

One of the greatest sayings of that great theologian of the Church, St Augustine, in his great book *The City of God*, was: 'It is the mystery of yourselves which is upon the altar.' It's one of the profoundest sayings ever uttered by a Christian; and it would be foolish of me this evening to do more than quote it, reiterate it, and leave you to ponder it. But there could be no more appropriate time to reiterate it than at a 'first Mass': 'It is the mystery of yourselves which is upon the altar.'

Finally, I want to speak to you as someone who has just passed his seventieth birthday, and who was therefore ordained in a very different Church and a very different world. It is, as I've said, a great joy and privilege to be the preacher at Phil's 'first Mass'. I think very thankfully – as many of you will do – on every remembrance of Phil and Sugina. But as a man who has been ordained priest, as I say, forty-three years at Michaelmas, I want to say a sentence or two. People sometimes ask me: 'If you had your time again, would you be a priest?' I never have the slightest hesitation in answering 'Yes'. I couldn't be myself without responding to my vocation.

But one danger of ordination, I believe, is that people have a static idea of it, in a very changing world, and say: 'Now I'm ordained' or 'Now *he's* ordained'. But this *is* a very changing world, more so now than ever; and we are very changing people. We are always discovering more of ourselves and of our world, and should be.

Each year we have to relate the gifts of God in their variety to the different person we have become and the different world we now inhabit. And that is true of all our vocations, all the varieties of ministry. Each day, each month, each year, requires from us a fresh consecration, if our ordination and vocation is to remain fresh. That may require new theological understanding, new psychological understanding, new spiritual perception. So, just as we consecrate afresh bread and wine, we need to consecrate afresh ourselves and the mystery of ourselves which is upon the altar.

We are present – thank God – at Phil's '*first* Eucharist'. It will not be the last. Each day, each week, each year will require a fresh consecration – not only of bread and wine. As T. S. Eliot wrote:

We must be still and still moving
Into another intensity
For a further union, a deeper communion.

And that is true of us all, no matter what our vocation, no matter what our gifts are in the variety of gifts God has given to us all.

32

'REMEMBER YOUR LEADERS'

The epistle to the Hebrews, chapter 13, verse 7, Gray's Inn Chapel; 9 July 1995

During this last week, much of our time and attention has been focused on the leadership of one of our political parties. It has, indeed, been all but impossible to *forget* our leaders. At the end of this week, let me make a very simple statement. To my mind, there are few stronger reasons for belief in God than the existence of our human capacity for leadership.

That thought has been borne in upon me over the years in a variety of ways. I have always been fascinated by the subject of leadership. It seems to me undeniable that there are many styles of leadership, and different styles are appropriate on different occasions. Some situations do not allow of or require discussion: they need direct and immediate action and directive leadership. There's not time for discussion when, for instance, there's a fire. Most other situations require the leadership of persuasion, and persuasion involves respect, not least, for the freedom of others. It demands the perception and evocation of the gifts of others, which may as yet be concealed. Leadership often requires a perception of the possible options, and an education concerning the choices which are valid and available. We call only one type of leadership 'charismatic': the kind that is obvious and evident and manifest in a moment; but the point of my statement – that there are few stronger reasons for belief in God than the existence of our human capacity for leadership – is that, in the end, *all* our gifts of leadership are God-given: all are to some extent charismatic.

I have a whole section of my library at home devoted to biographies, and at least half of them are of leaders, different sorts of leader: Montgomery – military leader; Churchill – political leader; Livingstone; King George VI; Bertrand Russell; Archbishop William Temple; Lord Birkett; Malcolm Sargent; St Francis of Assisi, and so on. But there are other shelves which treat of leadership through, say, drama: Shakespeare; Shaw; Ibsen. And then there's fiction: *The Good Soldier*, for instance, of Ford Maddox Ford.

This week, while all the kerfuffle has been going on about the Conservative Party leadership, I've been occupying myself with an enthralling book: the memoirs of a German officer from 1932 to 1945. He's called it *Bounden Duty*. It's the very personal account of Alexander Stahlberg's experiences of thirteen crucial years. His account includes fascinating glimpses of Hitler and his entourage, and of Field Marshals von Manstein and Rommel, and of the Duke and Duchess of York – later, King George VI and the Queen Mother. I've never read a better description of the conflict between duty and conscience. Stahlberg is pulled in opposite directions by his military oath of obedience to the established government and by a growing realization of an intolerable situation at which his personal honour and sense of humanity recoiled. I would, in fact, be happy just to take that one book as an illustration of my claim that there are few stronger reasons for belief in God than the existence of our human capacity for leadership.

'Remember your leaders' says the epistoler to the Hebrews. Yes – reflect upon them, whoever they may be, good and bad. Their capacities for leadership, fulfilled or ignored, are witness to the Giver of all gifts.

I most often find it best to begin any search for faith – for reasons for belief in God – simply with our common humanity. I don't myself like rushing to overtly ecclesiastical sources. But on the subject of leadership it would be silly for a Christian priest to remember all sorts of other human beings but to fail to remember Jesus Christ, our Lord; for in him I believe we have an example of leadership second to none. I could preach a score of sermons – indeed, a hundred sermons – on the subject, and it's difficult to know where to begin.

Let me now simply suggest a kind of scaffolding for a study of what Jesus has to say to us about leadership. I would want to start with St John's Gospel: chapter 13 – the Passover and the Betrayal. Jesus, we're told, 'riseth from supper, and laid aside his garments; and took a towel, and girded himself. After that he poureth water into a basin, and began to wash the disciples' feet, and to wipe them with the towel wherewith he was girded.' Peter, you'll remember, wants to refuse. Jesus says: 'Ye call me Master and Lord: and ye say well; for so I am. If I then, your Lord and Master, have washed your feet; ye also ought to wash one another's feet. For I have given you an example, that ye should do as I have done to you.' There's a sermon, surely, there – on leadership.

Or turn to St Luke's Gospel, chapter 6: 'And it came to pass in those days, that he went out into a mountain to pray, and continued all night in prayer to God. And when it was day, he called unto him his disciples: and of them he chose twelve, whom also he named apostles.' There is a strange *comparison* there, and also a stranger *contrast* with the events of this week. Delegated leadership. That's a very important subject.

151

In that same sixth chapter of St Luke, there's more on leadership: 'And he lifted up his eyes on his disciples, and said, Blessed be ye poor; for yours is the kingdom of God. Blessed are ye that hunger now: for ye shall be filled . . .' The Beatitudes are Jesus' teaching on values: on *leading* values. The *leader* must always be to some extent a *teacher*, not least, maybe, by silent example.

Return to St John's Gospel: to chapter 10. The parable of the Good Shepherd is one of the most profound passages in all literature on leadership. 'I am the good shepherd, and know my sheep, and am known of mine.' 'The good shepherd giveth his life for the sheep.' How different that is from all leadership that is ultimately self-regarding.

Sometimes it's the effects of leadership – of Jesus' leadership – that are noted in the Gospels, maybe in only a few words. When, in St John's Gospel, Judas comes to the Garden of Gethsemane, we read: 'Jesus, knowing all things that should come upon him, went forth, and said unto them, Whom seek ye? They answered him, Jesus of Nazareth. Jesus said unto them, I am he. As soon as he had said unto them, I am he, they *went backward*, and *fell to the ground.*' There's charismatic leadership for you.

Sometimes the leadership of Jesus is dramatic and powerful: witness his Cleansing the Temple; or witness his words to the Pharisees concerning Herod. St Luke records the Pharisees coming to Jesus and saying: 'Get thee out, and depart hence: for Herod will kill thee. And he said unto them, Go ye, and *tell that fox* . . .' And he gives them a piece of his mind.

It is to the Pharisees and the Herodians, who come to him with a trick question, to 'entangle' him, the Gospel says, asking: 'Is it lawful to give tribute to Caesar, or not?' Jesus answers with the skill of parliamentary question time, but with great profundity too. Similarly, 'The scribes and Pharisees brought unto him a woman – taken in adultery; and when they had set her in the midst, they say unto him, Master, this woman was taken in adultery, in the very act.' It's like a contemporary arrest on Sunset Boulevard. Jesus' dialogue with the woman is one of the great human encounters. The Pharisees rehearse the Law: the law of stoning. In that sexist law, only the woman was guilty. Jesus writes on the ground 'as though he heard them not'. And then he says, 'He that is without sin among you, let him cast a stone at her.' And when Jesus and the woman are left alone he says, 'Woman, where are those thine accusers? hath no man condemned thee?' And he says to the woman: 'Neither do I condemn thee; go, and sin no more.' There, surely, is moral leadership and authority. It's that *authority* that enables him to say: 'Come unto me, all ye that labour and are heavy laden, and I will give you rest.' There, too, is leadership; but it would not be if his promises proved empty.

I have said to you I could preach a score of sermons – indeed, a hundred – on this subject of Jesus and leadership. There are a hundred sayings of Jesus which illustrate different aspects of leadership, but there is only one place to end such a sermon and, indeed, such a series of sermons: at the cross itself. It we want to 'see Jesus', the Leader, there is no doubt where we must go and where we must stay for quite a while: Calvary, the paradoxical place of his weakness and his strength. 'Now when the centurion, and they that were with him, watching Jesus, saw the earthquake, and those things that were done, they feared greatly, saying, Truly this was the Son of God.'

The moral and spiritual authority of Christ crucified has continued to speak powerfully to the world for 2,000 years. But let us be conscious that all this theory of leadership, albeit the leadership of Christ, has to be transferred to our practice; this example of leadership has to be followed in human lives like ours. Any sermon on leadership has to 'take flesh' in the situations that surround us now. The touchstone and test of Christ's leadership has to be brought to bear upon, for instance, our new political scene. And upon our social scene.

Marsh Farm, Luton, is a housing estate I have known very intimately for over twenty years, but it's not significantly different from many another housing estate I know – on Merseyside, and in Manchester, in Birmingham and Bristol, and here in London. 'Law and order' in our land still needs to be informed by the insights of Christ's leadership. But let no one pretend that the application of Christ's example of leadership to our human scene is ever achieved simply. At the moment I am in close touch with a young man, a bishop's son, in Sarajevo, who is one of the United Nations' senior staff. It would be näive to suggest there is one single simple Christian answer to that tragic human scene.

And at this time I am in the middle of reading another book – *Confusions in Christian Social Ethics: Problems for Geneva and Rome* – by Ronald Preston, Professor Emeritus of Social and Pastoral Theology in the University of Manchester. I would not be unhappy if I were told that any sermon of mine must be submitted to Professor Preston; for though a preacher's rhetoric has its place, in the end words must be translated into the compromising and complex realities of our human social scene: including, of course, words like mine this morning, on Jesus and leadership: 'Remember your leaders.' Remember Jesus Christ.

33

A TIME TO SPEAK

Winchester Cathedral; 24 September 1995

I take for my text this morning two familiar verses from the third chapter of the Book of Ecclesiastes: 'To every thing there is a season, and a time to every purpose under the heaven . . . a time to keep silence, and a time to speak . . .' Those words have become very well known via modern folk singers. But I need not remind you that Ecclesiastes is what we call 'Wisdom literature', which has a Greek background, but was probably written in Palestine two centuries before Christ. It is ancient and tested wisdom; but it is ancient and modern.

There's a story in Eberhard Bethge's great biography of Dietrich Bonhoeffer which is remarkably relevant to this theme. Bonhoeffer and Bethge, in 1940, were in Memel, in East Prussia. They were sitting in the garden of a café when the news of the Fall of France came over the loudspeakers with a fanfare of trumpets. Immediately, people jumped up and began singing the Horst Wessel song and the German national anthem. Bethge remained rooted to his chair; but he was astonished to see Bonhoeffer not only standing, but raising his arm in the Nazi salute, and lustily joining in the song. Bonhoeffer whispered to Bethge: 'Are you crazy? Put up your arm!'

There were German Christians who never spoke; there were others who spoke when Bonhoeffer believed it right to be silent. But the last decade of Bonhoeffer's life is to me one of the clearest testimonies to the truth that 'there is a time to keep silence and a time to speak'.

More than fifty years ago, on 26 October 1944, Archbishop William Temple died, and George Bell, Bishop of Chichester, stood out as supremely well qualified to succeed him as primate of England. 'There is no doubt' – I'm quoting Ronald Jasper, Bell's very sober biographer – 'that his speeches on the War had destroyed his chances of succeeding to the primacy.'

Dr Alan Don, Dean of Westminster, wrote in his diary: 'The Prime Minister [Winston Churchill] admires courage and deplores indiscretion; and George has been both courageous and indiscreet in his speeches about the War' – mainly, of course, concerning the blanket bombing of German cities.

On 9 February 1944, Bell spoke in the House of Lords, having checked his arguments first with Captain Liddell Hart. His friend, Lord Woolton, wrote:

> I remember seeing him sitting on the bishops' bench, and I went to him and said, 'George, I believe you are going to make a speech.' He replied, 'Yes, I am.' I said, 'George, there isn't a soul in this House who doesn't wish you wouldn't make the speech you are going to make.' He looked a little downcast at that, and I said, 'You must know that. But I also want to tell you that there isn't a soul who doesn't know that the only reason why you make it, is because you believe it is your duty to make it as a Christian priest.' That was true: the House held him in the greatest respect, in complete disagreement.

I have never ceased to feel ashamed that the Church of England never had George Bell as Archbishop.

I shall never forget as a young chaplain of Trinity College, Cambridge, sitting next to Otto Frisch, the Jacksonian Professor of Physics, a Fellow of the College, at dinner one evening. Frisch was a refugee from Nazi Germany. When Hitler was making speeches, Frisch said he kept silent: 'I'm a physicist,' he said to himself. 'I must get on with my science.' But Frisch's father was a Polish Jew, so eventually Frisch came to England. It was while working in Birmingham that he did the work which proved that an atomic bomb was possible. It was in 1943 that he was shipped with a few dozen scientists to Los Alamos to work on the first bomb. After the explosion of that bomb, Frisch said there was a lot of discussion about how to use the weapon. Should it be used at all? Should it be demonstrated on an uninhabited island? Quite a lot of people said: 'Scientists should stick to matters of their own competence.' Frisch was convinced that that was an ostrich-like attitude. But, he said to me at table, that he was filled with shock and dismay when he heard General Groves, the United States General in overall charge of the atomic bomb project, say to the British scientist, Sir James Chadwick, who had discovered the neutron: 'You realize, of course, that the whole purpose of our working on this project is to subdue the Russians' – a remark which was made when the Russians were supposed to be our allies. Frisch agonized over whether he should keep silent at what he had heard or whether he should speak out.

Bonhoeffer, Bell and Frisch. But there's another person I want to cite in relation to 'a time to keep silence and a time to speak': Bishop John Robinson. I should remind you that Bishop Robinson literally had the mantle of Bishop Bell fall on him – he inherited much of Bell's episcopal robes; indeed, he was buried in Bell's cassock.

It was in September 1960 that I found myself having to respond to the request of Bishop Robinson – who was as much my friend as my suffragan bishop – to tell him whether I thought he should appear in court to defend the publication of the unexpurgated edition of *Lady Chatterley's Lover*. The request raised new questions: not simply whether

155

some human being or other should speak out on the subject, not simply whether a literary expert should speak out, but whether a bishop of the Church, albeit a suffragan bishop, should speak out. A suffragan bishop is a man under authority, but he is also a man in authority, with authority.

I had no doubt that John should appear in court and speak in defence of the publication. There were a score of others, far more qualified than I, to advise him, and who were willing to speak and were willing *him* to speak: the Master of the Temple, T. R. Milford; Canon Edward Carpenter, later Dean of Westminster; Fr Martin Jarrett-Kerr CR, an expert on D. H. Lawrence; T. S. Eliot; E. M. Forster; and so on.

But Archbishop Fisher did not at all approve. He said to the Canterbury Diocesan Conference on 5 November 1960:

> The Bishop had full right to appear as a witness on the point of law involved. But to do so would obviously cause confusion in many people's minds between his individual right of judgement and the discharge of his pastoral duties. . . . In my judgement, the Bishop was mistaken to think that he could take part in this trial without becoming a stumbling block and a cause of offence to many ordinary Christians . . .

One of the most telling references which John Robinson made in his own defence was a quotation from Archbishop Cosmo Gordon Lang. The Archbishop, in addressing the London Diocesan Council for Rescue Work on 4 April 1930, had said:

> I would rather have all the risks which come from free discussion of sex than the great risks we run by a conspiracy of silence . . . I notice how silence has given place to complete and free discussion. In my judgement this is a great improvement. In the old days silence drove one of the necessary natural instincts within. Nowadays people recognize sex as one of the great fundamental questions of human society, and all thoughtful Christians and citizens ought to take their part in discussing the great problems with which it deals. . . . We want to liberate the sex impulse from the impression that it is always to be surrounded by negative warnings and restraints, and to place it in its rightful place among the great creative and formative things.

Most people would agree that it was because he was a bishop that John Robinson's evidence made the impression it did – and was remembered. The trial was undoubtedly significant, though it was only the beginning of the trial of the Bishop of Woolwich.

When John Robinson decided it was 'time to speak' on *Lady Chatterley's Lover*, he had no idea that the furore he was causing then was as nothing compared with the avalanche he would cause two and a half years later, in March 1963, when his bestseller, *Honest to God*, was published.

I do not need to remind you, but it is important that I should underline that it was again not only what John said, it was who he was that said it. It was a *bishop* who had written *Honest to God* and it was a particular bishop, someone now known as 'The Lady Chatterley Bishop'. There was a cumulative notoriety to him, that is to say: a cumulative opportunity and responsibility. One piece of speaking led to another.

But it did mean that however responsibly John Robinson believed he was dealing with what was on his heart and mind – and the record is that he consulted very widely as to whether he should publish *Honest to God*, and that he had attempted to consult the Archbishop of Canterbury himself – the reception by the Archbishop of Canterbury, Michael Ramsey, hurt him greatly. The Archbishop spoke on television, without in any way getting in touch with John in the twelve days since publication, and had some very negative things to say about *Honest to God* and its author. Ten years later, in 1974, Michael Ramsey confessed his 'initial error in reaction'. 'I was soon to grasp', he said, 'how many were the contemporary gropings and questions which lay behind *Honest to God*.' But for a number of years Bishop John had to bear the second censure of an archbishop, and Michael Ramsey was someone for whom John had a great affection and respect. It took Michael Ramsey years fundamentally to revise his judgement. It takes time to speak; it takes time to apologize. It needed years; it needed not only time to speak, but time to consume, and to consider, and to reflect, before a more adequate judgement was reached.

Time itself is one of the most important words in our text. It is one of the most important elements in our existence. There is an appropriate patience and an appropriate impatience in all Christian action. We need a sense of history. We need, not least, a sense of the time when it is utterly impossible to keep silence.

Recently I've been reading a book called *The Model Occupation: The Channel Islands Under German Rule 1940–45*. It's by Madeleine Bunting, a Cambridge historian who held a fellowship and taught at Harvard. Madeleine Bunting interviewed over a hundred people – islanders, forced labourers on the islands, German soldiers – who lived through the five-year Occupation. She tells the riveting human story of the only part of Britain – the only part of the Church of England, the only part of this diocese – to fall under Nazi rule. It was inescapably 'a time to speak' and 'a time to keep silence'.

There were love affairs between island women and German soldiers; betrayals and black marketeering; individual acts of resistance; feats of courage and endurance. Every islander – every church-goer – was faced with uncomfortable choices. Where did patriotism end and self-preservation begin? What was collaboration and what was legitimate pragmatism? And what moral obligation did they have to the thousands of emaciated and ill-treated slave labourers the Nazis brought to the islands to build an impregnable ring of defences around them?

There are still survivors of the biggest mass murder ever to take place on British soil – 2,000 died of starvation and disease. Madeleine Bunting has penetrated the web of lies and apathy, not least of British citizens, which allowed the German officers responsible to escape justice. Britain often prides itself on 'standing alone' in those dark days. But perhaps 'standing alone' saved us from crucifying dilemmas of when to speak and when to keep silence – which the Channel Islanders could not escape.

There is one subject on which it is peculiarly difficult to speak *in public*, and often to do so is what we nowadays call 'inappropriate'. That subject is 'sex and sexuality'; I've already quoted Archbishop Lang on the 'conspiracy of silence' that used to surround sexuality.

Five years ago, I decided it was time for me to speak personally and publicly on the subject of homosexuality, because so much human damage is, I believe, still done by the 'conspiracy of silence'. I decided it was my duty to let those in authority in Gray's Inn – where I'm privileged to be 'the Preacher' – know that I would be 'coming out', as they say, as a homosexual, in a TV programme, and to say that if they wanted me to resign, I would of course do so. Had I told Gray's Inn the nature of my sexuality when I was offered the appointment, seventeen years ago, I have little doubt I would not have been appointed – for reasons of homophobia, prejudice, and so on; but after a dozen years of getting to know one another, the Treasurer of the Inn – the boss man that year – simply said to me, with a kindly smile; when I told him my intent: 'Well, Eric, what's new?'!

It seemed to me, not least from that experience, that there is a time to come out: a time when you can communicate as persons. It would have been wrong, I believe, for me not to have come out. I do not myself believe in what is called 'Outing', because I believe it's right to reverence people's own right to, and responsibility for, judging the 'time to speak and the time to keep silence'.

I think it's my duty in this particular pulpit this morning to speak: to say that I'm somewhat dismayed that so little guidance seems to have been given by the hierarchy of this diocese, to the clergy and people of their deaneries and parishes, to encourage them to think together, and then maybe speak out, on this complex subject of sexuality. It has, in my judgement, been a serious evasion of responsibility. The General Synod of the Church of England commended the Report *Issues in Human Sexuality* to be studied by the dioceses. That commendation has been greeted by a deafening silence in this diocese, but, of course, not in this diocese alone.

To end, let me simply remind you of that figure of Dietrich Bonhoeffer giving the Nazi salute. That incident, that picture, that ikon, is still with me, and will be to my dying day. Put it another way: I passionately believe that every Christian has to walk the way that Reinhold Niebuhr called 'The Ethics of Compromise' – of 'Moral Ambiguity': which means that on many subjects we have the inescapable Christian duty to wrestle with the question of 'the time to speak' and 'the time to keep silence'.

34

THE ANNIVERSARY OF THE ORDINATION OF BILL KIRKPATRICK

*St Cuthbert's, Philbeach Gardens, Earls Court;
29 September 1995*

It's a very great privilege, Bill, to be asked to preach at the twenty-fifth anniversary of your ordination to the priesthood, which happens also to be the forty-third anniversary of mine.

It seems to me providential for both of us – indeed, for many of us – that the Gospel appointed for Michaelmas is about children: children and the Kingdom:

> He called *a child*, and set him in front of them . . .
> Unless you turn round and *become like children* . . .
> Whoever humbles himself and *becomes like this child* . . .
> Whoever receives *one such child* . . .
> If anyone causes the downfall of *one of these children* . . .

It didn't occur to me, when I thought what should be my subject this evening, to look further than this concentration of the Gospel on children. I found it unavoidable. Nor, Bill, do I imagine you will query or quarrel with my selection of subject.

I remember when, way back in the Sixties, when I was vicar of St George's, Camberwell, you first told me, in the garden of Worcester College, Oxford, something of yourself; how you said you were born in Calgary, Canada, but that you didn't know your parents for quite a while; that a Mrs Florence Kirkpatrick, hitherto owner of a private orphanage in Vancouver, had eventually picked two babies out of fifty, of which you were one; that you were unofficially fostered by a Mr and Mrs Kirkpatrick, but that 'Kirkpatrick' isn't your real name; that in due course, you discovered who your father was, but you've never met your mother; and that there's still some uncertainty surrounding your birth.

When the Kirkpatricks eventually told you you weren't theirs, I know it was no surprise to you. You'd have been more surprised if you had been. I remember you saying that, as a child, you felt neglected; that you were dyslexic; that the first real friend you had was when you were eighteen; and that you never felt you belonged.

In view of all that, no one will be surprised that I couldn't get past the Gospel's concentration on children. But, truth to tell, I don't think I've ever been able to think of your childhood, Bill, without at the same time thinking, and thinking thankfully, of your eventual ministry.

St Julian of Norwich, whom I know you have come to love, tells us that 'our wounds are seen afore God, not as wounds but as worships'. And, thank God, by the time you and I met, already your wounds were being turned into worships. By the time I began to get to know you, you had already begun your ministry as a nurse, a psychiatric nurse, and, indeed, as a principal nursing officer.

Bill, I can't believe that, in your training as a psychiatric nurse, no one ever told you of Dr Winnicott; and I can't believe that, as you came to grips with Winnicott, you did not refer what he has to say not only to those to whom you were called to minister, but to yourself. Let me quote a sentence or two from that great man:

> The very start of ego-development, the very origin of self-hood, depends entirely on the baby's mother providing him at first with a near-perfect, secure, supportive human relationship. Only as the baby's own strength grows can the mother withdraw, by graduated stages, the completeness of her supportive presence, so as to allow her child to develop his own individuality. . . . The baby begins by being actually a part of the mother physically, and in a state of complete emotional identification with her mentally. Out of this state of physical and psychological embeddedness in the mother, the baby has to be helped to achieve not only a physical, but also a psychological birth. The second is a longer process.

Your psychiatric training, Bill, it seems to me, was one of God's ways of turning your wounds into worships. But, for one reason and another, being a psychiatric nurse didn't completely satisfy your inner quest, your inner desire, your inner drive to be the person you believed you were meant to be.

Recently, I went up to Glasgow, to see the new leader of the Iona Community, Norman Shanks. That visit brought back to me many a memory of the time I spent on Iona just before I was ordained. Before I went to Iona itself, I spent some time with George MacLeod and a group of young delinquents, camping in salmon fishing huts on Mull, just opposite Iona. George told us many a story during those days together, but there's one which has returned to me since my visit to the new leader of the Iona Community.

George MacLeod told us that when he was a young officer in the First World War, one of his duties was to look after a young man who had been severely wounded: gassed, blinded and shell-shocked. George had to take him behind the lines to a rest camp, where, as part of their programme of recreation, the soldiers had set up a boxing ring. Between the bouts of boxing, George had to lead the young man into the ring, and to tell the crowd that the young man had completely lost his memory, and that if anyone recognized him they were to shout out. George led the man round the ring, but there was only silence. Then suddenly the man himself screamed out: 'Can nobody tell me who I am?' George said that throughout his ministry the agonized cry of that young man had haunted him, yet he'd heard that cry in and from so many other wounded people.

We all want to discover who we are, but that so often means an anxious struggle for survival as a person amongst persons, on the part of basically unloved and injured individuals, who have never been able to feel sure of ourselves, and who are haunted by feelings of timidity, unworthiness, inferiority, shyness and loneliness. Our sexual aberrations often arise out of a desperate hunger for love and a fear of isolation. And this, of course, goes far beyond what we usually think of as our 'childhood'.

There's only one thing I don't like about the Gospel for today, and its concentration on children: it can so easily make people think that children are, let's say, only those under ten. But the child in all of us is always there. And, in many of us, that's through little fault of our own; so that when we read the Gospel's words it would be misleading to think that 'children' only refers to 'little ones', 'young ones'. The child in me is still there at seventy: for better, for worse. But as with you, Bill, so with me – and, no doubt, most of us: the Lord has gone on dealing with the child in us from year to year.

Some people, as they look at your CV, will simply say – and rightly: 'What a marvellous ministry!' You will know that at Centrepoint, and in Reaching Out, and in Streetwise Youth, and in Body Positive, and in all your ministry in Earls Court, just as it was in your psychiatric nursing, you were learning all the time to minister to the child in yourself, and to let the child in you be ministered to. And all your years, he who is love has been turning your wounds into worships – in you and through you, and your friends.

Winnicott once made the intriguing suggestion that the very first symbol for human beings is the cuddly teddy bear, or some similar object, that represents for the tiny baby the mother who gave it to him. It enables us to grasp mentally the fact of our mother's environing and supporting presence, even when, or especially when, we cannot see her.

I can remember, through the arches of the years, Eric Abbott saying to me when I was a student at King's, in about 1950, that he divided the woes of undergraduates into two: there were those who had never had a teddy bear and spent all their life compensating for that fact; and there were the others who had had a teddy bear and spent all their life trying to throw it away.

As the teddy bear is the first and simplest symbol of relationship, that relationship on which our very existence as persons depends, so for the adult and more mature mind, the word God – undefinable, indescribable, itself a symbol, and only to be talked about with lesser symbols – the term God represents the human experience of the personal relating to the ultimate and transcendent reality that brought us to birth as persons, and made us capable of what we call spiritual experience.

Bill, what I think many of us thank God for, is that you have never stopped 'embracing the mystery', to use a phrase that is all too familiar to you: the mystery of your creation; the mystery of your childhood, with all its wounds; the mystery of friendship; the mystery of iniquity; the mystery of relationship, not only with other human beings but with the Divine; the mystery of redemption. Your priesthood has meant embracing the mystery of the Divine in the child, in your friendships and in all your relating and beyond all human relating.

You have ministered from the heights and the depths of your own experience – your own wounds turned into worships – and you have been enabled to minister to those who have been similarly wounded. I think, of course, not least of those wounded, and maybe fatally wounded, by AIDS. (And you will, I'm sure, be particularly aware of and will be including in your intercession this evening, many whom you have loved but, alas, see no longer.)

But on this evening, this anniversary evening, I'm sure you will be seeing your ordination itself within, as it were, God's economy: God's strategy of turning your wounds into worships and dealing with the child in you.

You have often spoken, Bill, of how the actual act of ordination, by Bishop Trevor Huddleston, just because for so much of your life you had seemed to yourself to be a rejected person, was for you the actual act through which you knew yourself to be 'accepted in the Beloved': accepted by God. Through the act of ordination, the child in you – which was in grave danger of being rejected yet again by the Church – was finally accepted. Sometimes I think God saves a person, claims a person, by ordination, because, humanly speaking, he cannot do it any other way!

At the end of the day, at the end of *this* day, I'm sure you would want to say to us, to all your friends so gladly gathered together, and say in the words of her whom I will now, of set purpose, call the *Mother* Julian: 'Wouldst thou learn thy Lord's meaning in this thing? Learn it well: Love was his meaning. Who showed it thee? Love. What showed he thee? Love. Wherefore showed it he? For Love. Hold thou therein and thou shalt learn and know more in the same. But thou shall never know nor learn therein other thing without end.'

35

'THE PREACHER OF
THE YEAR AWARD'

Gray's Inn Chapel; 5 November 1995

Many of you will know that *The Times*, and something called 'The College of Preachers', which is supported by the present Archbishop of Canterbury and the former Archbishop, Lord Coggan, have been running a competition for what they had chosen to call the 'Preacher of the Year Award', with a First Prize of £1,000 plus a specially commissioned piece of sculpture, and with five runner-up prizes of £200 per person (or should I say 'per parson'?).

The final of the competition was held at St Pancras Church on the Euston Road on All Saints' Day, last Wednesday. I had another engagement at the time, but had I been free, nothing would have induced me to attend such a competition, though the prize sermon by the Reverend Barry Overend, of St Chad's, Headingly, Leeds, published yesterday in *The Times*, was, in my judgement – for what it's worth – an excellent sermon: given the reservations I shall later share with you about such an event and occasion.

Some members of the Inn had expressed the hope that I would take part in the competition, and made it clear that their desire was intended to be kind and complimentary; but I have to say that never, for a split second, have I been able to entertain the idea. Nevertheless, the fact that I have been so *certain* I should *not* take part has provided me, paradoxically, with, I think, a fruitful subject for a sermon; for it has involved me in thinking afresh, and putting into words, just what I believe a sermon is; and I have little doubt there could be considerable value in my asking you also to think upon the subject today.

Where shall we begin? Well, a sermon, surely, involves reflecting on what God may want said about a particular subject, to particular people, in a particular place, at a particular time; and involves wrestling with the most appropriate way of expressing and communicating the result. Here, in Gray's Inn, that could well be *one* sort of sermon; but the same subject, at some other time, in, say, the church where I was once vicar, in Camberwell, in inner south London, in the 1960s, would necessitate a quite different script. Indeed, a particular subject might be appropriate here, but inappropriate in Camberwell – and vice versa.

The suggestion that sermons can be judged *apart from the situations that provoke them, that call them forth,* is, to my mind, untenable; and that some judges can be judges for every situation as well as every sermon is even more misleading. A preacher needs to know his situation before he can preach to it. As, frequently, a visiting preacher, I know just how demanding that can be. The judge of a sermon cannot qualify as a judge without entering into the situation that provoked the sermon at least as profoundly as the preacher – and, hopefully, even more so.

Put it another way, when the word of the Lord comes to a prophet – and here Jesus himself should be thought of as one of the prophets – the prophet will almost invariably have had to immerse himself in the local scene and situation. And to set someone up, or to set oneself up as a man, or woman, to judge the message of the prophet is a very dangerous, and often a very arrogant thing indeed. Jesus himself said: 'A prophet is not without honour, save in his own country and in his own house.' He also said: 'Woe unto you when all men shall speak well of you', when they tell you you're a *prize* this or that.

Now I hasten to say that I'm not suggesting that the preacher or the prophet is above criticism: 'We have this treasure in earthen vessels.' But I can say in this place, better perhaps than in many another, that not only are preachers earthen vessels, so too are judges.

Talking of arrogance, there is of course a danger of arrogance in thinking that what you have to say is 'the Word of the Lord', but it can be even more arrogant to get up in a pulpit and simply give your own ideas, without any sense of the obligation to strive to do more than that: without wrestling, as I've said, with what God might want said on this particular subject, to this particular people, in this particular place, at this particular time. It seems to me of fundamental importance that a preacher should at least seek to say what God wants said. And that doesn't sort well with submitting the result to some group of judges, like the avowed atheist Sir Ludovic Kennedy, and John Selwyn Gummer, who have £2,000 or so of prize money to distribute.

Not seldom, what the preacher has to say will be disturbing, because it will be God's judgement on a situation. 'Go ye and tell that fox,' said Jesus of Herod, to certain Pharisees. He spoke with authority, and that authority was beyond those who sought to sit in judgement upon him and his words. Sometimes a sermon is a message of judgement; sometimes, of mercy; sometimes, of hope; sometimes, of wisdom. Most often it should have an authority which comes from beyond those who seek to sit in judgement upon it.

I am not suggesting that what a preacher has to say is alone the 'Word of the Lord'. Indeed, I sometimes shudder when, after, say, the reading of a passage from Paul – or even *some* passages of the Gospels – the reader proclaims, 'This is the Word of the Lord' – which manifestly it is not. I like George Herbert's words: 'Judge not the preacher; for he is thy judge.' And I like the picture of the aged Gladstone, with his hand cupped to his ear, drawing a stool close to the pulpit so that he could catch all that the newly ordained curate of Hawarden had to say. When I kneel down before preaching or before preparing a sermon, I have always found the simplest prayer the best: 'Speak, Lord, thy servant heareth.' It's the voice of the Lord the preacher needs to hear; so, too, he must remind himself, does the congregation.

Certainly, the idea of a sermon that can, in the end, be judged like an essay is offensive. A sermon is not something which is mine, to be handed over to some committee, whether of ecclesiastics, or scholars, or literati, or whatever. Any sermon lacks its distinctive element if it is not stamped with its relationship to God. Again, this does not contradict the fact that the good sermon involves a dialogue with the congregation, and that the congregation will have its own insights. The preacher as, so to speak, the 'servant of the Word', must always be thinking, formulating, doubting, questioning, questing, interpreting and wrestling as the congregation's representative. He has to wear and bear the congregation on his heart and mind. He has, indeed, to be open to scholarship and criticism, and not to biblical and theological scholarship and criticism alone. But in the end, every sermon lives on the hope of somehow enabling contact to be made, or re-made, or maintained, between God and the congregation gathered together. Without this hope a sermon is but random talk. I never feel I have the right to enter the secret recesses of people's hearts, yet I would be failing in my duty were I to think a sermon to be a talk by me, and no more.

True, an aura of holiness, which no longer exists, used to surround the preacher and the pulpit; and I am myself sceptical about attempts to restore it. There is a relaxation now about worship, and indeed about styles of preaching, which there wasn't at one time. Yet I still believe we are handling holy things in worship, and in sermons; and the two are inseparable; and I just can't entertain the idea of sermons being entered in a common competition.

It is highly significant, surely, that a sermon comes within worship, within a liturgy: Holy Communion, Mattins, Evening Prayer. The sermon is, so to speak, hedged about with prayer, and embedded within it. It is thus explicitly more than just a talk, and certainly more than a lecture. It is, in a sense, prayer continued: extended. With our Lancelot Andrewes window, you will know I quote him whenever I can. Andrewes shared the conviction of Fulgentius, the sixth-century North African bishop, that the preacher must realize he may do his work 'better by the piety of his prayers than by the fluency of his speech'. He must 'lift up to God', he said, 'a thirsty soul, that so he may give out what from Him he hath drunk in, and empty out what he hath first replenished.'

My erstwhile eccentric Cambridge friend, that preacher without parallel, F. A. Simpson, used to say: 'The way they kill the prophets these days is not by stoning but by consecrating them.' Were he alive today, I dare say he would have said: 'The way they kill the prophets these days is by nominating them "Preacher of the Year".'

Jeremiah – Preacher of the Year!
John the Baptist – Preacher of the Year!
Jesus – Preacher of the Year!
And, for his pains, let us give him a thousand pounds!

The very idea is excruciating – literally. Indeed, it borders on blasphemy. And let us recall that on one occasion 'there arose a reasoning among the disciples which of them should be greatest'. It is hardly stretching a point to call a competition a 'reasoning which should be greatest'; but a competition with a monetary reward clearly comes more from an age and ethos of the market than of the years of our Lord.

Some of you will know that I tried to deal with this subject lightly in a letter to *The Times* a few weeks ago. To tell you the truth, a 'Preacher of the Year Award' seems to me a sort of echo of P. G. Wodehouse's *The Great Sermon Handicap* – with Lord Coggan as a most improbable substitute for Bertie Wooster. But, for the reasons I have given, I believe the subject should be treated with the utmost seriousness. I cannot conceal from you my deep dismay and misgiving at all that has surrounded, and has been involved in, this competition.

'Put your preacher forward,' pleaded *The Times*. Yes, I agree. Put him – or her – forward: in your prayers; and put all preachers forward in them; and pray for yourselves – that the words of our lips and the thoughts of all our hearts shall now and always be acceptable in thy sight: O Lord, our strength and our Redeemer.

36

CHARLES WILLIAMS

Gray's Inn Chapel; 19 November 1995

'. . . what hast thou that thou didst not receive?'
1 Corinthians 4.7

It's fifty years this year since the sudden death of the author and scholar Charles Williams, from whom I feel I have received a very great deal – though not many people these days read his thirty volumes of poetry, plays, literary criticism, fiction and theological argument. I have received so much from him, that I'd like to preach a sermon this morning in his memory.

I was fourteen, in 1939, when a soldier who was stationed at our vicarage first recommended the writings of Williams to me. That soldier, John Rowe, a sergeant at our local gun site, had left theological college and joined up – he had been reading Classics at Leeds University. (Later, he would be Vicar of St Mary's, Bathwick.) What Williams wrote, I found to be just what I needed at that time.

In 1939, Williams had written a book called *The Descent of the Dove*, subtitled 'A short history of the Holy Spirit in the Church'. In 1940, in *The St Martin's Review* – the rather upmarket magazine of St Martin-in-the-Fields – he wrote an article entitled 'The Church Looks Forward'. That year he also wrote an article in *The Dublin Review* on 'The Image of the City in English Verse', and in 1941 he wrote another article in that journal on 'The Redeemed City'. His book *The Forgiveness of Sins* was published in 1942.

I read those writings when the bombs were falling on the city of London, and friends of mine were being killed by them, and in the RAF and the Fleet Air Arm; and I needed to hear about a city which would rise from the ashes of our earthly cities. I was finding life complex and confusing at the time, and Williams seemed to address that complexity and confusion. At the beginning of the war it was easy to simplify: to turn Hitler, for instance, derisively into *Schicklgrüber* and all Germans into unmitigated evil. That was, perhaps, the only way you could bomb them.

There was a passage in *The Descent of the Dove* which I found particularly helpful. Quoting what people sometimes say, Williams wrote:

'If I cannot be *certain*, then what is the use of thinking or believing anything?' – which is an evasive way of saying, 'Since I cannot be God, I refuse to be man.' Others, desperate for the security of a rock to stand upon, resort to unreasonable but comforting dicta such as 'This is self-evident . . . this was revealed . . . this can be proved.' The assurance thus acquired, however, is illusory. It is the old trouble which the wise Greek had seen so long ago: 'Give me an inch of earth to stand on and I will move the world.' But there is no inch of earth; there never has been; there never . . . can be.

The war also confronted one with naked evil. It was impossible – I found – to evade thinking about the problem of evil, and therefore thinking out the cross afresh – which Charles Williams had done – and forgiveness, which he had also done. He wrote:

> There is no split second of the unutterable horror and misery of the world that the Omnipotence did not foresee (to use the uselessness of that language) when he created; no torment of children, no obstinacy of social wickedness, no starvation of the innocent, no prolonged and deliberate cruelty, which he did not know. It is impossible for the mind of man to contemplate an infinitesimal fraction of the persistent cruelty of mankind, and beyond mankind of the animals, through innumerable years, and yet remain sane. . . . The Omnipotence contemplated that pain and created; that is, he brought its possibility – and its actuality – into existence. Without him it could not have been; and calling it his permission instead of his will may be intellectually accurate, but does not seem to get over the fact that if the First Cause has power, intelligence, and will to cause a universe to exist, then he is the First Cause of it. The First Cause cannot escape being the First Cause. All the metaphors about fathers giving their children opportunities to be themselves fail, as all metaphors fail. Fathers are not the First Cause. God only is God. The pious have been – as they always are – too anxious to excuse him; the prophet was wiser: 'I form the light and create darkness: I make peace and create evil: I the Lord do all these things.'

In his book *He Came Down From Heaven*, first published in 1938, Williams wrote, with reference to those who say:

> in love or in laziness, 'Our little minds were never meant . . .' Fortunately there is the book of Job to make it clear that our little minds were meant. A great curiosity ought to exist concerning divine things. Man was intended to argue with God. . . . The pretence that we must not ask God what he thinks he is doing (and is therefore doing) is swept away. The Lord demands that his people shall demand an explanation from him. Whether they understand it or like it when they get it is another matter, but demand it they must and shall. . . . Such a philosophical curiosity is carried on into the New Testament. It accompanies the Annunciation. The Blessed Virgin answered the angelic proclamation with a question: 'How shall these things be?'

What I received from Charles Williams was, not least, the sense that there is an underlying and profound rationality to things, in spite of all appearances to the contrary. He had an ability to keep one eye on the city of London and the other on the city of God. Working as a publisher, in the shade of St Paul's, in the offices of the Oxford University Press in Warwick Square, he saw the cross on the dome of St Paul's as a saving sign during the war – and through and beyond the cross he spied heaven itself.

It was when I left working on the riverside to begin training for ordination, at King's College in the Strand, and met the dean, Eric Abbott, who became my friend and mentor, that he introduced me to more of Charles Williams, not least through the two marvellous anthologies that Williams assembled: *The Passion of Christ*, in 1939, and *The New Christian Year*, in 1941.

In *The Passion of Christ* there is a remarkable passage from a Lancelot Andrewes Passiontide sermon, in which he describes Gethsemane:

> Christ began to be troubled in soul, says St John; to be in agony, says St Luke; to be in anguish of mind and deep distress, says St Mark. To have His soul round about on every side environed with sorrow, and that sorrow to the death. Here is trouble, anguish, agony, sorrow, and deadly sorrow; but it must be such, as never the like, so it was too.
>
> The estimate whereof we may take from His sweat in the garden; strange, and the like whereof was never heard or seen.
>
> No manner violence offered Him in body, no man touching Him or being near Him; in a cold night, for they were fain to have a fire within doors, lying abroad in the air and upon the cold earth, to be all of a sweat, and that sweat to be blood; and not as they call it *diaphoreticus*, a thin faint sweat, but *grumosus*, of great drops; and those so many, so plenteous, as they went through His apparel and all; and through all streamed to the ground, and that in great abundance; read, enquire, and consider, if ever there were sweat like this sweat of His. Never the like sweat certainly, and therefore never the like sorrow . . .

I do not think any single passage has more influenced my own preaching and preaching style than this passage. I've always felt that, however ignorant and unskilled a child of Andrewes I am, I look to him as a kind of father-figure in preaching. And with his tomb in Southwark Cathedral and his being an erstwhile Bencher of Gray's Inn, I feel I have good reason to do so.

At the end of my training at King's, I went to my first international ecumenical conference, in Holland, under the auspices of the World Council of Churches. The very first night I came into collision with some French Protestant and German Strict Lutheran students. To my astonishment they labelled me – and the label was not a compliment – 'typically English'. No one had ever called me that before. They did so because I had been arguing the merits of compromise, whereas they had been arguing that a Christian had to hold to 'Either/Or', 'Yes/No' positions, not 'Both/And', on the particular point we had been discussing. It was a real shock to me to be told that my viewpoint had its origins in the country of my birth.

I sat down and wrote to Eric Abbott that night, an urgent letter begging for his help; and, in answer, Eric immediately sent me a strange – but strangely helpful – reply. It was an extract from a lecture on 'Byron and Byronism', which Charles Williams had delivered at the Sorbonne in 1938, and which was subsequently published in the *Bulletin* of the British Institute of the University of Paris, April 1938. Let me read to you from that lecture:

Considering Byron and considering this whole business of English verse, it occurred to me the other day that the great difference (I submit this to you; it may be perfect nonsense, but I thought I would just like to offer it to you), between English verse – literature if you like – and French literature, French poetry, is, on the whole, that you have tended to say one thing and we have tended to say another, and the difference between these two attitudes is this. On the whole, in France, I think it is true to say, you have tended to say Yes *or* No. Now, in *English* literature – I think about the English mind – the opposite is true and I think it would perhaps be useful if we did not blame each other, if I may put it so, for a thing which is profoundly natural. The English have on the whole tended to say Yes *and* No. It does obviously sound ridiculous to you. I beg you not to be quite so sure that it is all that ridiculous. I do think that if you read, for instance, some of the English poets, if you feel the English attitude, the English scepticism and the English belief, there is a union of opposites, or at least there is an effort towards that union of opposites which does want passionately to unite apparently irreconcilable things. It may be quite useless, it may be quite silly, but I say it exists, and I say it is not our fault, as it were: it is in our blood, when we try and do things which have this effort towards uniting a 'yes' and a 'no'. It is not enough that we should say yes, it is not enough that we should say no; it is not merely because we are not good logicians – that doesn't matter at the moment – it was born and bred in our blood and in our bones. Why, of the greatest of our poets, is it quite impossible to know really what philosophy he held? Precisely because of this; because we get to the end of Shakespeare's work only to find that he has included everything, he has included every tendency. You continually see this sort of habit, of hesitation. Why, when we die for things we do not believe, why, when we are martyrs for the things of which we are sceptical, a thing you would never do because the greatness of your genius is different; why do we go into battle with a cry which sounds half a derision of the things for which we are about to die? I will not say it, but I do suggest that when you are martyred, you are martyred for the things you support, for causes which you profoundly and passionately believe; and I say when we are martyrs, we perish for things in which we believe and yet do not believe, and I say, if I may, that it will be a very great thing if the two minds, if the two cultures, if the two passions of poetry and art, if our two very great traditions could for a little while sometimes be tender to each other and pardon each other. No doubt you can forgive us, that is comparatively simple; but could you possibly bear us to forgive you? That is the real difficulty. It is quite easy to be tolerant of others, but it is difficult to be tolerated by other people. If we could bring together those two lobes of the mind, those two sides of human existence, if we could begin to appreciate those cultures profoundly on that basis, I am not sure that anything, anyhow so far known to man, could be greater than the union of the interchanged knowledge of those two states of mind.

It was in 1973 that I came very close to Charles Williams – in a rather odd sort of way. That year, Robert Runcie, then Bishop of St Albans, invited me to be Canon Missioner of St Albans. We had been friends for twenty years. It was time for a change from Southwark, and I gladly accepted the invitation.

But as soon as I got to St Albans, I was confined to bed with disc trouble. So it was that Robert Runcie first came to see me in St Albans when I was in bed. He did not waste much time in consolations, but said: 'Well, there's something you can do while you're in bed. You can write this year's leaflet for the Week of Prayer and Almsgiving we have each year at St Albanstide.' 'Couldn't I do that next year'? I asked. 'I know nothing about St Alban; nothing about St Albans; nothing about St Albans Diocese.' 'Yes,' said my bishop, 'I see the force of your argument. But the thing ought to have gone to press a week ago; and you're the only one with the time to do it.' You know when you're on a loser with Robert Runcie, so I caved in quickly; but I said: 'Well, I refuse simply to write "hagiolatry" about St Alban. Could you bring round all the "evidence" you can for the *historical* St Alban?' I ought to have been warned by the smile on the face of the Bishop as he left my bedroom. He returned within the hour, to dump on the end of my bed an armful of tomes, pamphlets, etc.

The more I read about St Alban, the more I was fascinated by the story of someone who gave shelter to an unnamed priest, who in company with other Christians was being pursued by the Roman Emperor, Severus; and the fact that Alban put on the clothes of the priest, and was killed instead of the priest. I was fascinated, not least, because the story seemed to me 'pure Charles Williams', so many of whose stories were of what he called 'substitution' – except that the story of St Alban was history, not fiction. But the story was a 'substitutionary story' *par excellence.*

My next visitor was a young priest at the Abbey, Keith Jones, appointed this year Dean of Exeter; I had known Keith as a curate in Southwark. He was an intelligent young man. I judged he would know about Charles Williams, so I asked him directly: 'Tell me what you know about Charles

Williams.' 'Well,' he said, 'I'm taking Holy Communion to his sister tomorrow morning.' It turned out that Williams's parents had moved out to St Albans from Holloway in 1894, when Charles was eight, and his sister, Edith, five. They'd bought a shop in Victoria Street, St Albans, near the Art School and began to sell artists' materials. Charles had begun his school days at St Albans Abbey School in 1894 and gained a scholarship there in 1898. He went on to Univeristy College in Gower Street in 1901.

But to me one of the most important facts is that Charles loved the Abbey and its ritual, and in particular the historical pageants – not least about the life of St Alban – which were regularly performed at St Albans: the Abbey and the school working together. That the sensitive Charles Williams, in his youth, was immersed in the life of St Alban, there can be little doubt; immersed in the life of Alban's extraordinary example of sacrificial substitution.

To conclude what I have to say today on how Charles Williams has inflenced me, I simply want to read what Charles Williams calls his 'Apologue on the Parable of the Wedding Garment', which appeared first in *Time and Tide* in those dark days of December 1940. It was my soldier friend, John Rowe, who first introduced me to it; but it was Eric Abbott whom I first heard read it, when I was a student – in the chapel of King's College Theological Hostel, in Vincent Square, Westminster. He read it during a Devotional Address on 'The Borrowed Garment'. Eric Abbott's address was on the need of grace of each one of us, and of our need to receive that grace from others.

For fifty years Charles Williams's poem has spoken to me of the very heart of the gospel:

The Prince Immanuel gave a ball:
cards, adequately sent to all
who by the smallest kind of claim
were known to royalty by name,
held, red on white, the neat express
instruction printed: *Fancy Dress*.

Within Earth's town there chanced to be
a gentleman of quality,
whose table, delicately decked,
centred at times the Court's elect;
there Under-Secretaries dined,
Gold Sticks in Waiting spoke their mind,
or through the smoke of their cigars
discussed the taxes and the wars,
and ran administrations down,
but always blessed the Triune Crown.

The ball drew near; the evening came.
Our lordling, conscious of his name,
retained particular distaste
for dressing-up, and half-effaced,
by a subjective sleight of eye
objectionable objectivity –
the card's direction. 'I long since
have been familiar with the Prince
at public meetings and bazaars,
and even ridden in his cars,'
he thought; 'his Highness will excuse
a freedom, knowing that I use
always my motto to obey:
Egomet semper: I alway.'

Neatly and shiningly achievèd
in evening dress, his car received
his figure but otherwise
completely in his usual guise.
Behold, the Palace; and the guest
approached the Door among the rest.

The Great Hall opened: at his side
a voice breathed: 'Pardon, sir.' He spied,
half turned, a footman. 'Sir, your card –
dare I request? This Door is barred
to all if not in fancy dress.'
'Nonsense.' 'Your card, sir!' 'I confess
I have not strictly . . . an old friend . . .
his Highness . . . come, let me ascend.

'My family has always been
in its own exquisite habit seen.
What, argue?' Dropping rays of light
the footman uttered: 'Sir, tonight
is strictly kept as strictly given;
the fair equivalents of heaven
exhibit at our lord's desire
their other selves, and all require
virtues and beauties not their own
ere genuflecting at the Throne.
Sir, by your leave.' 'But – ' 'Look and see.'
The footman's blazing livery
in half-withdrawal left the throng
clear to his eyes. He saw along
the Great Hall and the Heavenly Stair
one blaze of glorious changes there.
Cloaks, brooches, decorations, swords,

jewels – every virtue that affords
(by dispensation of the Throne)
beauty to wearers not their own.
This guest his brother's courage wore;
that, his wife's zeal; while, just before,
she in his steady patience shone;
there a young lover had put on
the fine integrity of sense
his mistress used; magnificence
a father borrowed of his son,
who was not there ashamed to don
his father's wise economy.
No he or she was he or she
merely: no single being dared,
except the Angels of the Guard,
come without other kind of dress
than his poor life had to profess,
and yet those very robes were shown,
when from preserval as his own
into another's glory given,
bright ambiguities of heaven.

Below each change was manifest;
above, the Prince received each guest,
smiling. Our lordling gazed; in vain
he at the footman glanced again.
He had his own; his own was all
but that permitted at the Ball.
The darkness creeping down the street
received his virtuous shining feet;
and, courteous as such beings arc,
the Angels bowed him to his car.

37

GEORGE MACDONALD
AND CHRISTMAS

Westminster Abbey; 26 November 1995

Shadowlands – the play or the film – will have refreshed the acquaint-ance of many of us with C. S. Lewis, the Oxbridge Professor of English, and writer of children's tales, and, of course, theology. Few probably know that C. S. Lewis regarded George MacDonald as his 'master'. He calls him that in the anthology he assembled of MacDonald's writings. MacDonald was a Scottish poet and novelist. He briefly became a Con-gregationalist minister. He not only influenced C. S. Lewis, but also G. K. Chesterton and Auden.

This Sunday evening, which is almost exactly a month before Christmas, by way of preparation for Christmas – and I suspect some of you may have done a bit of Christmas shopping this weekend – I simply want to read you a poem of MacDonald's and share with you a few thoughts on it. Here's the poem – MacDonald called it 'That Holy Thing':

> They all were looking for a king
>   To slay their foes, and lift them high:
> Thou cam'st, a little baby thing
>   That made a woman cry.
>
> O Son of Man, to right my lot
>   Naught but Thy presence can avail;
> Yet on the road Thy wheels are not,
>   Nor on the sea Thy sail!
>
> My fancied ways why shoud'st thou heed?
>   Thou com'st down Thine own secret stair,
> Com'st down to answer all my need –
>   Yea, every bygone prayer.

I don't want to make a meticulous analysis of the whole of that poem, but I think you'll agree the beginning is particularly striking:

> They all were looking for a king
>   To slay their foes and lift them high . . .

It refers, of course, to the Jewish people. But it raises the question for *all* of us, as to what we are looking for at Christmas, and indeed in the incarnation of our Lord, not least *this* Christmas. '*They* all were looking for a king . . .' What are *we* looking for? What lies behind all this massive output of Christmas shopping, decorations, Christmas cards and carol services?

MacDonald continues:

> Thou cam'st, a little baby thing
> That made a woman cry.

Well, one more baby to add to all the babies of the world wouldn't, of course, make any significant difference. So there's a huge weight upon that word 'Thou': '*Thou* cam'st, a little baby thing'. What we Christians believe, what we proclaim, is almost all in that one word 'Thou': in that one *word*: 'the Word' made flesh.

But I say again: one more baby to add to all the babies of the world wouldn't have made any significant difference. There's no answer to what the world is looking for simply in a baby: in the Word made merely a baby. Yet Christmas starts there. It must. There's no answer in a person that doesn't begin in a baby; and a baby is manifestly weak, helpless and vulnerable.

'They all were looking for a king . . .' I said that the poem refers to the Jewish people; but at the end of this particular week, and in this particular place, the scene of the Coronation itself, we can't quite so easily pass over that first line, and that first phrase, 'They all were looking for a king . . .', without saying that it surely does have some reference to most of us. What were a thousand million people doing, the world over, when in 1981 they were glued to their television sets to watch the Royal Wedding? What was going on last Monday evening, when so many millions of us watched Princess Diana on TV? Someone phoned me – an American, from Los Angeles – at eight o'clock Tuesday morning, to say *they'd* watched the programme. The royalty subject must surely have a profound symbolic power that touches some of our own depths, our own needs: our need, for instance, of cherished symbols, not just of abstract symbols, but of living persons – people like us; yet not like us: our need of symbols of transcendence: of glory, of what is royal and regal about our humanity – in down-to-earth terms. And, of course, that, not least, is what Christmas is – in part – about. 'And glory shone around.'

'They all were looking for a king . . .' I suggest that our regard for royalty, for earthly royalty, may in fact surprise in us deep, unfulfilled needs and desires, which in the end can only be met through 'God in man made manifest'. 'They *all* were looking for a king . . .' is perhaps more profoundly true than sometimes we're willing to admit.

I want to break off from looking at that poem for a few moments, to look at one or two people I'm in touch with, who will be looking for *something* this Christmas.

First, let me tell you of Hugo and Gina. I baptized their first-born, Alice, in Hammersmith Hospital, in the Neo-Natal Unit, in August. I'd married them in Gray's Inn Chapel, where I'm what's called 'The Preacher', the year before. Alice was actually born in another hospital on a Sunday evening. Something went wrong during the birth, and, alas, serious brain damage occurred. As yet the area and extent of the damage has not been precisely defined. The extraordinary but undoubted thing is that the brain-damaged Alice has transformed the lives of Hugo and Gina. She's been the greatest gift they've ever had.

I might couple with Alice, Charlotte, the seven-year-old daughter of my friends Tim and Ellen. Charlotte has leukaemia, and desperately needs the right sort of bone marrow match; but after ransacking the world, so far no match has been found. Tim is an academic and an antique dealer. Ellen works for a merchant bank. But their number one priority is undoubtedly Charlotte.

Another person I'm in touch with, Adrian, comes from a totally different world. He happened to pick me up from St Chad's College, Durham, when I preached there last year, to drive me by taxi to Seaham vicarage, 6 miles south of Sunderland in the North East. Chatting to him, as one does to taxi-drivers, I asked him whether he was looking forward to Christmas. 'No,' he said, rather sullenly. 'Why not?' I asked. 'I can't afford to give any presents to my kids,' he replied. He then explained he was an unemployed miner who only did taxi-driving because it was a way of getting a bit extra. I've kept in touch with him during the year. In fact, I saw him again three weeks ago when I was again in the North East – at a day called a 'Poverty Hearing', in Gateshead. I preached the next morning in Newcastle Cathedral, and I'd arranged for Adrian to come and collect me and drive me over to Seaham again. He's now on a computer course. But, as he said, 'It's difficult to do a computer course when you can't afford a computer.'

At that 'Poverty Hearing', in the hall of St Joseph's Roman Catholic Church, Gateshead, were pasted up statements of what unemployed people of the area had said, one by one, was their experience of unemployment: what its characteristics were. They were there to speak with us about what they had experienced: lack of self-respect; feeling like a second-class citizen; lack of control over one's life; loss of a sense of identity and belonging; isolation; a life shapeless and without order; strained relationships in the home; long-term decline in the quality of life; loss of hope; the struggle to manage, week after week; the inability to replace ordinary household necessities; not being able to support the family; conflict over money.

I found it deeply moving to talk one to one with those who often had been unemployed for several years. As I said, on the Sunday morning I preached in Newcastle Cathedral. On the Sunday afternoon Adrian came and drove me to Seaham, County Durham. We discussed the 'Poverty Hearing' en route for Seaham. Adrian agreed with what people had said about their experience of unemployment.

Now let's return to our poem: 'They all were looking for a king . . .' Well, not all of us are doing that.

Hugo and Gina will be quite content if there is progress for Alice on the way of healing. If, for instance, it turns out that she can speak. What a Christmas present *that* would be! A kind of Christmas bonus.

Tim and Ellen are desperate for a matching bone marrow for Charlotte: nothing could compare with *that* as a Christmas gift.

Adrian needs a computer – and cash for presents for his kids; but clearly he's desperate for significance: the significance which an appropriate job would give him, as a job has given most of us significance. But he's only one of 3 million or so jobless in Britain today.

They all were looking for *something* – to lift them high, permanently. Many, of course, think they can get that nowadays with drugs: '. . . on a high'. Who was it who said, 'Marx said, "Religion is the opium of the people"; but now the opiates of the people have become their religion'? I said earlier that there's no answer to what the world is looking for simply in a baby: in the Word made merely a baby. 'The baby Jesus' can itself be romantic avoidance.

The gospel is more than the story of a birth. It's the story of the growth of Jesus from the cradle to the grave – and beyond.

> Thou cam'st, a little baby thing
>   That made a woman cry.

But the tears of that woman were shed, most of all, at the foot of the cross. *Stabat Mater Dolorosa.*

Thou cam'st not only as a baby thing, but as a growing thing. The Word could not be revealed only in a cradle. As the carol says: 'Soon comes the cross, the nails, the piercing . . .' That's what the holly and the ivy are all about: painful growth. I wonder whether we think enough and speak enough and proclaim enough about growth.

> In stature grows the heavenly Child
>   With death before his eyes . . .

There is a good deal of the gospel in growth. Hugo and Gina have visibly grown through the gift of Alice, through the gift of the brain-damaged Alice – though her birth has made both a man and a woman cry. '. . . With death before their eyes . . .'

I think it's because of the growth of the Christ-child from a little baby – a 'little baby thing' – to a full-grown man, that MacDonald can say in the second verse of his poem, 'O Son of Man . . .' And thus our development, to use St Paul's phrase, 'unto a full grown man' – a full-grown person – becomes for clergy and laity a kind of obligation that is laid upon us all in what we call Christian spirituality. And spirituality includes, of course, our sexuality.

Even Prince Charles and Princess Diana have had to do some growing up, and still have more to do, it seems to me. We *all* have.

In the last verse of George MacDonald's poem, he uses a wonderful phrase. He says that God will come to each one of us by his 'own secret stair'. It's a marvellous thought, isn't it, that whoever we are, prince or pauper, whatever our age, baby or grown-up, youthful or aged, he will come

> down Thine own secret stair,
> Com'st down to answer all my need –
> Yea, every bygone prayer.

38

IN MEMORIAM: RONALD FARROW

St Mary-le-Strand; 27 November 1995

Most of you, I'm sure, will be familiar with Eliot's *Murder in the Cathedral*, and will remember how the knights, having completed the killing of Thomas of Canterbury, advance to the front of the stage and address the audience, explaining – or attempting to explain – what happened. No one, they say, regrets what happened more than they do. They each in turn address the question, 'Who killed the Archbishop?', as coolly and rationally as possible. Finally, the first knight says: 'I think there is no more to be said, and I suggest you disperse quietly to your homes. Please be careful not to loiter in groups at street corners, and do nothing that might provoke any public outbreak.'

Dr Pauline Webb preached a memorable and marvellous sermon at Ron's requiem and funeral. Now, today, I have been asked to give this address; and I can't quite rid myself of the feeling that I am here like one, or all, of those Eliot knights. And I suspect that's because all of us, or almost all of us, feel a bit guilty at Ronald's death. Certainly *I* do.

You see, I was what Ron would insist on calling his 'spiritual director' – though I dislike the term. Clearly, *I* failed – and it's not the first time I've failed with a priest who has had an alcohol problem. If they don't turn up to see you – and, more and more, Ron didn't – do you ignore it? Or do you put the pressure on? And if they pretend there's 'no problem', do you somehow make it plain that you don't believe them? Do you play the role of spiritual director, so called, as though you had the right to be at their wheel, so to speak? Or do you leave them in charge?

It is, of course, one of the fundamental problems of spiritual counselling. But if you leave people with their freedom, as I'm quite sure you should, you'll not escape a sense of guilt when they use their freedom to do themselves damage: perhaps irreparable damage. And, of course, that's not the experience only of spiritual directors: it's the experience of any friend. And the more you love, and the more you've got close to your friend, the more you will feel you have failed.

Not many weeks ago – since Ron's death – I was talking with another person for whom alcohol is an immense problem. 'Could you tell me', I asked, 'just what alcohol means to you?' He was silent for a long time, and then, through tears, cried: 'Only when I've drowned myself in drink have I brought my unutterable loneliness to an end.' No one, surely, is to be blamed for trying to bring that feeling to an end. But it does leave those around them feeling guilty: that whatever they *have* done, they have not been able to end the other's 'unutterable loneliness', and thus their need of alcohol. And 'unutterable loneliness' may not be the heart of the matter. 'Unutterable insignificance' may be more accurate.

Most of us will know that Ron was devastated by the ending of his contract with the BBC. Whether that end was right, and handled rightly, I have no idea; and it's not for me to speculate. What I *do* know is that his work at the BBC meant everything to Ron. He could not pretend that it didn't, and he could not handle his redundancy.

I don't myself find that surprising. A friend of mine, in County Durham, who in 1989 went from Southwark to be vicar of Seaham, where three mines were closed just after he got there, told me recently that *since* he went to Seaham he has buried more suicides than in all the previous twenty-five years of his ministry. They were almost all miners who couldn't handle their redundancy. 'You are redundant' is one of the cruellest, most murderous phrases in our vocabulary, but we haven't yet woken up to that fact – in spite of 3 million or so unemployed.

My Durham friend tells me that, although those who'd committed suicide had received large redundancy payments, they felt unwanted, and had lost the only social standing they had in the community. Many drank themselves to death. Others took their lives by more instant methods: the deep waters of the sea, the rope and the overdose.

George MacDonald said we each come to God by our 'own secret stair'. Yes, but there's a dark and tragic side to us, too. We most of us have our own 'well of loneliness' which may involve secret habits and compulsions: secret stairs that lead us downward into our private hell of self-rejection, and make us deaf to every sign of acceptance, human and divine.

It was my privilege, from time to time, to talk with Ron about his path of self-rejection. There were odd coincidences which had brought us together. We were both born in Dagenham; we were both attracted to the world of broadcasting. For Ron it was a passion, and he was of course a very gifted exponent of it. We both knew ourselves called to be priests, and were both enthusiasts for the pioneer Southwark Ordination Course, I from its very first days. But we both knew that the road from Dagenham to, say, the BBC is rarely straight and smooth.

When I was first ordained, my vicar, George Reindorp, later Bishop of Guildford and then of Salisbury, himself a popular broadcaster, took me aside and told me, as gently as possible, and as professionally, that my Cockney Dagenham accent had to go; and that the parish would pay for me to go to the Abbey School of Speakers to have it removed. There were signs in Ron that something within him had told him that his Dagenham accent had to go. It wasn't an unreal inferiority. When I went to Trinity College, Cambridge, to be chaplain, I was terrified. No other word will do. With people like John Drummond, Jack Thompson and John Tusa as undergraduates there, you'll probably sympathize. In those days the effortless superiority of a largely public school world dominated Trinity, and – irrational as it may seem to some – my terror was real enough. And I observed something like that terror in Ron, not least in his anxiety to conceal it.

I've said that it's not for me to speculate whether Ron's redundancy was right – and I mean that; but for over fifty years now I've had the opportunity to observe the power structure of our land and its major institutions, like the BBC. It may well be that Ron had reached the level in his profession he had it in him to reach. It wouldn't surprise me if it had been concluded that he was not a number one person in departmental terms: that he would always do his best work at a slightly lower level. But I've watched men of no great intelligence from Cambridge get elected as, for instance, now notorious MPs. And often I've seen little men make shift to fill big places. There is still small justice and skill in much of the appointments system. So we, most of us, have to learn how to handle betrayal and disappointment, though it took *me* many excruciating years to do so. It's never easy to drain the chalice of betrayal as though it were a gift, as Jesus did.

Many people, not least in the world of the media, have nowadays to live in a highly competitive and indeed ratings-dominated world. That is not the way most of us clergy have to live, and it's no use our pretending we do. Many of us have freeholds, or have had. But perhaps the clergy can say to those who live in an admittedly different world: 'Never let your estimate of your worth depend on your ratings: they may go up and go down. The value God puts on you is what matters.' Clergy, I believe, must say such things, even if we are ourselves poor examples of believing them. And I'm not pretending it's easy to do what I say when the fall in your ratings has made you redundant, and your income has virtually collapsed and, therefore, maybe your mortgage.

None of us here is, of course, in a position to judge Ronald. We are not here to do that. We are here to give thanks for him, and for all that we found valuable in him. I am myself only here because Ron was a unique friend to me, as he was to many. And of course, we are also here to pray for him. We are also here to remind ourselves that the Lord alone knows the history of Ronald's inability to value himself as we believe the Lord himself valued and values him: having loved him into existence and never discarded him.

There's one aspect of Ron that I mustn't avoid. Ron was 'gay' (Surprise, Surprise!), and glad to be gay, and enjoyed a partnership with Ian which was the joy of many of their friends, like me. I'm sometimes told that the BBC is a bit better than the Church at respecting and valuing the private lives of its employees, not least its gay employees. But I cannot believe that the Church's failure to value the homosexual as much as the heterosexual made *no* contribution to the difficulty Ron had in valuing himself.

A few weeks ago, I was privileged to attend the inaugural lecture of Richard Burridge, the new Dean of King's College, London, just on the opposite side of the road here. I myself owe a very great deal to King's – as does, for instance, Pauline Webb. The Dean's lecture was on 'Consumer Culture and Higher Education' – not a subject wholly irrelevant to the BBC. Richard began by reminding us that the Academy at Athens was placed at the edge of the *Agora* so that its deliberations about truth, beauty and value might inform public debate in the market place. Now, he said, the *Agora* has taken over the Academy. We are all at the mercy of the market. The 'golden rule', he said, is now: 'the man who has the gold makes the rules'. He quoted from something R. H. Tawney wrote in 1917: 'The fundamental obstacle in the way of education in England is simple. It is that education is a spiritual activity much of which is not commercially profitable, and that the prevailing temper of Englishmen is to regard as most important that which is commercially profitable and as of only inferior importance that which is not.' Ron, maybe in spite of himself, passionately believed that.

In memory of Ron, and in thanksgiving for him, I think I should at least ask the question: 'How does an institution like the BBC somehow remain at the *edge* of the market as well as *within* it? Indeed, how does it *transcend* the market?'

The Dean of King's quoted Archbishop William Temple, who wrote in 1942: 'The dignity of man is that he is a child of God. His true value is not what he is worth in himself or his earthly state, but what he is worth to God; and that worth is bestowed on him by the utterly gratuitous love of God.'

Many in the BBC will, of course, not be able to share in that overtly Christian belief, yet most will, none the less, want to align themselves with that tradition in its valuing of human beings. Dietrich Bonhoeffer suggested that even Christians in the modern world need to live *etsi Deus non daretur* – 'as though God were not a given'. Christians or non-Christians, we have to work away and wrestle with not only this philosophical question, 'What makes human beings valuable?', we also have to work at the valuing and cherishing of actual individuals as the crown of creation, and to do it not least through the care, pay, employment and deployment of staff, in institutions like the Church and the BBC.

I met a man in Liverpool not long ago who was unemployed; he'd worked in Tate & Lyle all his life. I asked him how he went about getting another job. 'Oh,' he said, 'it's not like that. They've told me I'm forty, so I'm finished.'

Was Temple right? Or is it a get-out to say, 'The dignity of man is that he is a child of God. His true value is what he is worth to God'?

Ronald Farrow, alive, forced many of us to ask that question. Ronald Farrow, whom we love but see no longer, still presses that question upon us today.

39

THE TENTH ANNIVERSARY OF *FAITH IN THE CITY*

Southwark Cathedral; 2 December 1995

'Turn you to the strong hold, ye prisoners of hope . . .'
Zechariah 9.12

It's a great privilege for me to preach to you on this particular occasion from this particular pulpit. Some of you will know that I first became acquainted with inner-city Southwark, and this cathedral, when I worked for seven years, from the age of fourteen to twenty-one, at a bustling riverside wharf on Bankside, five minutes from here, on the very site where the new Globe Theatre has recently arisen. I learnt the organ here in this cathedral in those seven strange war-time years; and the relation between work at that riverside wharf and this cathedral has been at the heart of my faith for all these more than fifty years: a faith forged in the city.

For four of those years, when I was vicar of St George's, Camberwell, I would of course come here to the cathedral with some of the congregation on just such occasions as this. And for seven more years, this cathedral was my home base, when I was a residentiary canon living close by, off Long Lane, with a brief from the then Bishop, Mervyn Stockwood, to get to know, and do all I could to help, the inner-city parishes of the diocese to confront their problems, and to help the rest of the diocese to understand the particular problems of the inner city.

It was undoubtedly those years, rich in experience, that made me press Archbishop Runcie to set up his Commission on Urban Priority Areas; and I've now been back in Southwark, living in Kennington, for nearly twelve years, since 1983 when I began to work, for several years virtually full time, first with the Archbishop's Commission and then with the follow-up to *Faith in the City*.

So I preach to you today out of those fifty years' experience of Southwark. Yet I cannot claim that I know Southwark now as well as I once did; and I'm not going to presume to preach to you *about*

186

Southwark. There are impressive publications – the 'Ideas Pack' and 'Southwark Focus' – to help you celebrate Southwark's response to *Faith in the City*. I shall preach, rather, from my experience of going from inner city to inner city, all over Britain, in these last twelve years.

When I utter that inspiring and visionary verse: 'Turn you to the strong hold, ye prisoners of hope', various people and situations – including Southwark – come immediately to mind. I think initially of the very first visit that the Archbishop's Commission made – to Liverpool, and of two incidents on that visit.

Some of the Commission were in Kirkby, Liverpool – meeting the people. It was question time, after our introductory speeches. David Sheppard, the Bishop of Liverpool, was in the chair. Shortly after questions began, a very angry man got up and asked: 'Are you going to tell Maggie?' – and there was no doubt whom he meant! – 'Are you going to tell Maggie to invest in Liverpool? Yes or No?' There was a horrible hush. Then one of the Commission stood up. He was a top businessman. He quietly explained that before he'd journeyed to Liverpool that day, he'd consulted his board as to whether there was any special message he could bring with him to Liverpool. And there was. BICC, his firm, was going to increase its investment in Liverpool by several million pounds – in hi-tech fibre-optic cable. 'That's the good news,' he said. But the result of the re-equipment of the plant with the most up-to-date technology would be the redundancy of several hundred workers. 'If that's so,' he asked, 'do you still want us to invest in Liverpool – yes or no?'

It was a 'moment of truth' – the first of many that would confront the Commission; and, when I muse on my text, I still think of that questioner as one of the 'prisoners of hope'. That he was a man of hope – desperate hope, understandably: hope for a job – there was no doubt. We had no easy answers for him. We had to ask ourselves: 'Does *Faith in the City* promise such a "prisoner of hope" faith that would sustain him in unemployment, but have nothing to say to the employers and others who have power in the market – not least shareholders, politicians, and indeed members of government?'

Over tea that same evening, after the questions, I went up to a man I'd never set eyes on before, another Liverpudlian. 'Are you in work or out of work?' I asked him. 'Out of work,' he replied disconsolately. 'I've worked in Tate & Lyle's all my life, till I was made redundant.' 'How d'you go about getting another job?' I asked him. 'Oh, it's not like that,' he replied. 'I'm forty, so I'm finished. They've told me I needn't register more than once every six weeks.' He was another 'prisoner of hope'.

Now let me take you to the very end of the two years' work of the Commission – ten years ago. The BBC had asked me to present the TV film that would be shown on the Sunday night two days before *Faith in the City* was launched. The producer of the film was Angela Tilby, a Reader of the Church of England, and a very gifted television producer. The film we'd made was confined to one city in the North East, Middlesbrough, on Teesside.

We'd been filming for several days, and the end was in sight; but I had to return to London to preach at the memorial service to Neil Wates, of Wates Build, who'd lived in Dulwich, but who sadly had died an untimely death. Angela Tilby suddenly said she would drive me to Middlesbrough Station. On the way, she said: 'Eric: I've got something I simply must ask you. When you make a film, you usually discover while you're making it how to end it. But I'm desperate, because our last day's filming is Monday' – (It was then Friday) – 'and I don't yet know how to end this film. You see, there's no hope here in Middlesbrough. And you can't end a film saying "There's no hope". In the train,' she went on, 'could you possibly think how *you* think it should end, and phone me from King's Cross?' 'Angela,' I said. 'I just can't. I've got my sermon to write in the train.' Angela looked crestfallen. But then I said: 'There's a phrase of T. S. Eliot's that has kept me going in many a hopeless situation in these last years: "Take no thought of the harvest but only of proper sowing".' 'That's it!' Angela exclaimed. 'Go and catch your train.'

At the time I was rather puzzled, but when I got back to Middlesbrough on the Monday, Angela met me at the station and drove me straight to the riverside, to a place where all the wharves and warehouses had recently been bulldozed and then covered with soil. It was by then a sort of man-made mound by the very side of the Tees. It had been sown with grass, and the first green blades were rising and beginning to show through the soil. Angela said: 'I want you to walk slowly up that mound, and look out over the Tees, to the ICI building in the distance, across the river – where they've just laid off several thousand workers. The cameras will follow your gaze. Then, slowly turn round and look at the Transporter Bridge over the Tees. Then turn round further and look at the old town in the distance, with the church at its centre – again, the cameras will follow you and zoom in on the distant scene. Pause for quite a while. The cameras will then come back and concentrate on that mound and on those first blades of grass. I want you to walk slowly down the mound and off into the distance, saying: "Take no thought of the harvest, but only of proper sowing".'

I have to say that most of the letters *after* that programme mentioned that Eliot quotation, and wanted to know where it came from. Poets and prophets have much in common. 'Turn you to the strong hold, you prisoners of hope,' said the prophet Zechariah. 'Take no thought of the harvest, but only of proper sowing,' said the poet T. S. Eliot. That text and that quotation have often been in my mind as these ten years since *Faith in the City* have gone by.

One evening, a year or so later, in Gray's Inn, where, part time, I'm what's called 'the Preacher', we had Mrs Thatcher, then Prime Minister, to dine. At the end of the meal, the judge in charge decided, rather to my surprise, that I should be one of the people he would bring the Prime Minister to sit next to for a while. She immediately said: 'This can't be your full-time job.' 'No,' I said. 'I spend much of my time following up the report *Faith in the City*.' 'That is a very bad report,' she said vehemently, and did not draw breath for several minutes, so that my neighbours – most of whom were barristers and judges – were somewhat embarrassed. I was not myself embarrassed, for I have had no reason to think that what *Faith in the City* said on housing, poverty, work, unemployment, race, urban policy, social care, community work, health, education and so on was seriously wrong. Indeed, I would go further, and say that in each of the ten years since *Faith in the City* was published, it's my experience that the situation in most urban priority areas has got even worse in almost every respect. In the last ten years, for instance, I've seen Youth Work virtually collapse in very many situations, and youth unemployment escalate.

A month ago, I had to go for a weekend to Gateshead, Newcastle and parts of County Durham. The whole of the Saturday, apart from going round the poverty-stricken Meadowell Estate in Newcastle, where in 1991, you may remember, there were riots, I spent all day with the Roman Catholic Bishop of Hexham and the Anglican Bishop of Newcastle, under the auspices of that remarkable organization, 'Church Action on Poverty', wrestling with some of the questions that massive unemployment has brought to the North East. On the walls of the hall of St Joseph's Roman Catholic Church, Gateshead, where we met, was pasted a list of what unemployed people of the area had said, one by one, was their personal experience of unemployment. They were there to speak to us about what they'd experienced: lack of self-respect; feeling like a second-class citizen; lack of control over one's life; loss of a sense of identity and belonging; isolation; a life shapeless and without order; strained relationships in the home; long-term decline in the quality of life; loss of hope; the struggle to manage, week after week; the inability to replace ordinary household necessities; not being able to support the family; conflict over money.

I found it deeply moving to talk one to one with those who had often been unemployed for several years. On the Sunday morning I preached in Newcastle Cathedral. On the Sunday afternoon I went to Seaham, County Durham, on the south coast of Sunderland, to see the vicar, Paul Jobson, whom many of you will remember here in Southwark. The previous month, he had written in his Vicar's Letter:

When I came to Seaham, in 1989, the three collieries of the town were still working full shifts and flat out. Within five years, all three had closed down, and their winding shafts and surface buildings wiped from the face of the earth. However, even in 1989, men were being retired early, at the age of fifty. Although they received large *redundancy* payments (and the vicar asked us to note that word) they felt unwanted, and had lost the only social standing they had in the community. 'He's a miner at Dawdon,' people would say, or 'at Vane Tempest', or 'at *the* Colliery, Seaham'. People were proud to be miners, and the loss of this status was too much for some to live with. Some drank themselves to death; others took their lives by more instant means: the deep waters of the sea, the rope, and the overdose. In three years I had conducted the funerals of more suicides than in the previous twenty-five years of my ministry. But others adapted well to leisure and retirement, and the three churches of my parish could not survive without the voluntary help of such men.

'Redundant', said the vicar, was the cruellest word he knew to describe a human being. Yet it applies to 3 million, and probably more, in Britain today. Very clearly, many, if not most, of those unemployed are '*prisoners* of hope': in the sense that they've every right to hope for a job, a home, and sufficient food and clothing. And it isn't enough simply to say, in a pietistic way: 'Turn you to the strong hold.' That won't get them the job, the home, and the food and clothing that they and their children need.

But when we turn to the 'strong hold', we find he is the strong source of justice, as the first requirement of love; and that he sends us back in his strength to challenge the whole set-up of our world: not least the whole economic set-up, and the distribution of work and income, and the whole political set-up. He sends us back to build in his strength a more caring, fairer and more just society.

I'm not myself sure that *Faith in the City* spoke strongly enough – in the power of the 'strong hold' – to the secular powers. I'm not sure we saw, then, clearly enough that there's a new industrial revolution upon us, through microelectronics; that much work as we have known it may be largely coming to an end; and that in this crisis we desperately need the wisdom of the 'strong hold' to guide and save us.

Yet to end what I have to say, I must tell you that in these last ten years I have been privileged to see people coping with amazing amounts of stress in literally hope-less situations – in the power of the 'strong hold'. I have seen groups of Christians – but not only Christians – often unemployed: supporting one another; in the power of the 'strong hold'; I have seen local churches in downtrodden areas, living lives in the power of the 'strong hold' – and being the 'strong hold' to a neighbourhood or to an estate. I have admired the honesty and realism which has delivered them from pessimism, and even imparted to them joy. I have met them in projects, though projects are never enough. I have met them mostly in small-scale operations – and the small scale, in the end, is never enough: we have to think as big as our world is, with its international and world-wide dimension in, for instance, economics.

In the middle of September, for instance, I was privileged to spend an evening in the deanery of Newham, in the Diocese of Chelmsford. (I said I wouldn't talk today about Southwark!) All the projects of that area which had been funded by the Church Urban Fund were represented at the Eucharist that evening: the East London Churches Housing and Homelessness Alliance; the Faith in the Community Project of the Area of St Barnabas, Manor Park; the Helping Hands Project in Plaistow; the Newham Conflict and Change Project; the AIDS Project of the Mansfield Centre – and a dozen other projects.

I had little doubt that all the people at that deanery Eucharist and gathering of people associated with the projects had turned to the 'strong hold'. Their hopes – I could tell, not least from their singing – were no longer their prison.

I've said that 'projects are not enough'; their funding, for instance, is only short term. In a sense, only the 'strong hold' in the end, the 'strong hold' himself, is enough: the 'strong hold' who made himself known in Jesus Christ, crucified and risen, and who makes himself known to the two or three gathered in his name.

So, on this tenth anniversary of *Faith in the City*, with the experience of what I've seen with my own eyes in these last ten years, in very different parts of our land and our Church, I say to you, with both humility and proud thanksgiving: 'Turn you to the strong hold, ye prisoners of hope.'

40

THE SEVENTH ANNIVERSARY OF THE LOCKERBIE DISASTER

Heathrow Airport Chapel; 21 December 1995

I feel very privileged to be allowed to join those of you who have gathered here, on this seventh anniversary of the disaster at Lockerbie. I understand relatives of other, not dissimilar, disasters are also here. They too are here, of course, to remember those they love but see no longer.

We who gather here may be of different religions, or indeed of none, but we are of one humanity; and it is on the mystery of our humanity – as particularly revealed through Lockerbie and other tragedies – that I'm going to ask you to reflect for a while this evening.

But perhaps I should first say that I am myself here tonight only because, in the late 1950s, I was chaplain of Trinity College, Cambridge, where Jim Swire was then an undergraduate. Just over ten years later I helped at his marriage to Jane. The years passed, and they had three children; and at Christmas, Jane would always write me a letter with the family news. Seven years ago, the letter arrived after Christmas, but had been written on 21 December. It said that Flora, the oldest of the children, having read medicine at Nottingham, had come to London to specialize in neurology. She had recently, Jane said, acquired an American boyfriend, who was engaged in similar work to her. He'd already returned to Boston for Christmas. 'Flora', wrote Jane, 'flies to Boston at 6.00 p.m. this evening, so she will not be with us at Christmas.' Jane added the particularly poignant phrase, 'You can't really hang on to them . . .' By the time that letter arrived, I knew that Flora had lost her life at Lockerbie.

I said I would ask you to reflect this evening on the mystery of our humanity. Already, it seems to me, I have hinted at several important ingredients of our mysterious humanity. Our capacity as human beings to relate to one another is a marvellous part of that mystery. Friendship, I would have to say, is probably the most important part of life to me. We could be here all this evening simply reflecting on the mystery of friendship.

But there's a randomness to our encounters in this life, which is an inescapable part of the mystery. Jim Swire and I happened to be at Cambridge at the same time. But of course that randomness of life relates to the very heart of the tragedy we are here to commemorate. People could probably have caught another plane at another time. The fact is, alas, for one reason and another, they caught that particular plane: Flight PA 103.

Sometimes people couple coincidence with randomness. Others call it 'synchronicity', others 'serendipity' – though usually when they use that word they are talking of happy coincidences, happy accidents. When we reflect on randomness, we are very soon brought face to face with another aspect of the human mystery: the mystery of Time. It's easy, of course, to take Time for granted. It's so inescapably part of the very raw material of our existence, but it's surely one of the most important aspects of our human mystery.

We are here to remember those we love, because of what happened seven years ago. Memory – remembrance – seven years – and the nature of Time – all go together. Some speak of 'Time, the great Healer'; but few of us, I imagine, would say that healing is inevitable. What we might all agree is that Time soon brings us face to face with our mortality, with our inevitable and inescapable end – as well as the mortality of those we love but see no longer. Bereavement is, not least, to be robbed of all the dimensions which are so familiar to us now: Time and space. Those we love but see no longer have moved beyond Time as we know it. Every great religion has something of importance to say about Time, and about mortality. Every great religion recognizes that we human beings, however marvellous we are, are fragile, precarious, vulnerable beings. That, too, is part of our mystery.

When I think on the human mystery, on this particular anniversary, I find myself soon thinking of our human gifts. I remember thinking seven years ago of the waste of gifts in the disaster – and, of course, it was the gifts of Flora Swire that first came to mind. But you will all be able to recall the gifts of the person – or persons – you are here to recall and commemorate.

But, let us also remind ourselves, we would not be here tonight but for the scientific skill that now enables air travel beyond human imagining when I myself was born – in 1925. And here, surely, and now, we should pay tribute to the continuous exercise of skill which maintains aircraft at such a place as this and keeps them what we call 'air-worthy'.

When we think of human gifts, there is one conclusion which is unavoidable: there is no such thing as a human 'clone': each of us is an unique human mystery, however much we have in common with others, and there's mystery in our very uniqueness.

There are, of course, gifts which are positive and gifts which are negative. The urge towards achieving justice, which has for instance manifested itself since Lockerbie, is surely, complex as it is, a manifestation of a very positive human gift. It's an image which has to be sustained, and requires other gifts to go with it: courage, patience, integrity, endurance.

But, of course, the disaster at Lockerbie is also the result of our human capacity to destroy. No one reflecting upon the human mystery can avoid reflecting upon our human corruptibility – and not only the corruption of other people. In some form or other we experience the corruption of ourselves. Every realist becomes aware of corruption in the country to which he or she belongs, in the churches, in religious organizations, and in institutions.

Again, each of the great religions has something to say on the mystery of evil as it contributes to the human mystery – and not just as a sort of abstract principle. Evil is, of course, the cause of a great deal of human suffering. You have all had some experience – probably some bitter experience – of the mystery of suffering.

All the great religions have something to say about what we should do with our suffering. I've recently read a very good book called *Pain: the Gift Nobody Wants*. It's by a doctor, and it's about the way people who suffer from leprosy lose the gift of feeling, and therefore the gift of pain, and therefore often the gift of participating in important parts of life.

The mystery of our humanity and the mystery of suffering can never be separated. I have spoken of gifts which are positive and gifts which are negative. But I think I should add that even the words 'positive' and 'negative' ought not to be treated as entirely distinct and opposed entities. The evil of Lockerbie caused, for instance, a great wave of sympathy and compassion to flow round the world. The grief of those who were bereaved was undoubtedly deeply shared by human beings in widely separated and distant lands.

The tragedy of Lockerbie was heightened for many by the very season in which it occurred. To many it was, of course, Christmastime; and never now can Christmas come – and go – without reminding them – and us – of Lockerbie. Christmas, which is predominantly about peace on earth to men and women of good will, had its peace, seven years ago, shattered.

Yet the conjunction of Christmas and the disaster at Lockerbie means, surely, that another subject has to be tackled that is deeply related to the human mystery: the subject of forgiveness. I have known many people for whom a tragic event had a second tragedy added to it: the tragedy of a hatred which eats away at its victims' humanity. How to be delivered from the canker of continuing hatred is not a subject on which someone who has not experienced bereavement, as many of you have experienced it, should speak easily. But I believe we do the terrorists' work for them when we are simply consumed by hatred and the desire for revenge.

All our human responses in this life are, of course, complex. But mystery isn't merely complexity: it's something far more profound. Our responses to events great and small, to the good events of our life and the tragedies, are as complex as our own biographies. We bring to the great bereavements of our life, for instance, the experience of our childhood. There are hidden and buried agendas in what may seem on the surface our simple responses to what has happened to us. Tragedies expose the strengths and weaknesses of our own psyches. That's why most of us need a good deal of help if, and when, we lose one of the great loves of our life.

The mystery of humanity – of my humanity, as much as other people's – was in fact brought home to me not long ago by a curiously simple event. A friend of mine, who's a doctor, told me that his six-year-old daughter said to him one evening: 'Daddy, can you explain to me how the heart works?' He was overjoyed at her question, and took it very seriously. He sat her down beside him and drew what he thought was a tolerably good drawing of the arteries of the human body, and quite a good diagram of the heart itself. But, when he turned to his daughter, she was looking very puzzled indeed. 'What is it you don't understand, darling?' he asked. 'Daddy,' she said, 'you haven't explained where all the love comes from.'

In the end, I would have to say, as a Christian, that for me Christmas – coupled with the crucifixion – is God's way of explaining to us all 'where the Love comes from': that in spite of all appearances – and all realities, like Lockerbie – the Divine Love and Compassion is at the heart of the world: and at the heart of the human mystery. I believe that all the heartache which was experienced through Lockerbie was experienced in the very heart of God himself.

I believe, in fact, that whatever else the most terrible events of our life are, they are also an invitation to journey further into the mystery of our humanity: that is to say, the mystery of life itself. It is seven years tonight since the terrible disaster at Lockerbie. I suspect that it has caused many of you to ponder the mystery and the meaning of life more than you would ever have done had that tragedy never happened to you. Whatever your religion may be, whoever God is to you and for you, may you be led further into the mystery of your humanity, and thus into the mystery of life itself.